FLORIDA STATE
UNIVERSITY LIBRARIES

OCT 28 1996

TALLAHASSEE, FLORIDA

A TWENTIETH-CENTURY HISTORY OF UNITED STATES POPULATION

Russell O. Wright

The Scarecrow Press, Inc.
Lanham, Md., & London
1996

HB
3505
W75
1996

SCARECROW PRESS, INC.

Published in the United States of America
by Scarecrow Press, Inc.
4720 Boston Way
Lanham, Maryland 20706

4 Pleydell Gardens, Folkestone
Kent CT20 2DN, England

Copyright © 1996 by Russell O. Wright

British Cataloguing-in-Publication Information Available

Library of Congress Cataloging-in-Publication Data

Wright, Russell O.
A twentieth-century history of United States population /
Russell O. Wright.
p.   cm.
Includes bibliographical references.
1. United States—Population—History—20th century.
I. Title.
HB3505.W75   1996   304.6'0973'0904—dc20   96–11410

ISBN 0–8108–3182–1 (cloth : alk. paper)

∞™ The paper used in this publication meets the minimum requirements of American National Standard for Information Sciences—Permanence of Paper for Printed Library Materials, ANSI Z39.48–1984.
Manufactured in the United States of America.

Dedicated
to
Brian, Dan, Dorota, Sandy, and Terry

Contents

List of Figures	vii
List of Tables	xi
Preface	xiii
Acknowledgments	xv
Introduction	xvii
Part I: The Nation	**1**
National Profile	2
The Sunbelt	4
Part II: The Regions	**7**
Regions Profile	8
Regions vs. Nation	18
Part III: The States	**27**
States Profile	28
States vs. Nation	30
States Summary	132
Part IV: The Cities	**139**
Cities Profile	140
Cities vs. Nation	142
Cities Summary	190
Part V: The Future	**197**
Population Projections	198
Political Implications	202
About the Author	204

List of Figures

Part I: The Nation
1-1	United States Population	3
1-2	United States Sunbelt States	5

Part II: The Regions
2-1	Population Regions	9
2-2	Combined Regions, Percent of Population	11
2-3	Percent of Population by Region	13
2-4	Combined Regions Population	15
2-5	Population by Region	17
2-6	Northeast Population	19
2-7	Central Population	21
2-8	South Population	23
2-9	West Population	25

Part III: The States
3-1	Alabama	31
3-2	Alaska	33
3-3	Arizona	35
3-4	Arkansas	37
3-5	California	39
3-6	Colorado	41
3-7	Connecticut	43
3-8	Delaware	45
3-9	District of Columbia	47
3-10	Florida	49
3-11	Georgia	51
3-12	Hawaii	53
3-13	Idaho	55
3-14	Illinois	57
3-15	Indiana	59
3-16	Iowa	61
3-17	Kansas	63

3-18	Kentucky	65
3-19	Louisiana	67
3-20	Maine	69
3-21	Maryland	71
3-22	Massachusetts	73
3-23	Michigan	75
3-24	Minnesota	77
3-25	Mississippi	79
3-26	Missouri	81
3-27	Montana	83
3-28	Nebraska	85
3-29	Nevada	87
3-30	New Hampshire	89
3-31	New Jersey	91
3-32	New Mexico	93
3-33	New York	95
3-34	North Carolina	97
3-35	North Dakota	99
3-36	Ohio	101
3-37	Oklahoma	103
3-38	Oregon	105
3-39	Pennsylvania	107
3-40	Rhode Island	109
3-41	South Carolina	111
3-42	South Dakota	113
3-43	Tennessee	115
3-44	Texas	117
3-45	Utah	119
3-46	Vermont	121
3-47	Virginia	123
3-48	Washington	125
3-49	West Virginia	127
3-50	Wisconsin	129
3-51	Wyoming	131

Part IV: The Cities

4-1	Baltimore	143
4-2	Boston	145
4-3	Buffalo	147
4-4	Chicago	149

List of Figures

4-5	Cincinnati	151
4-6	Cleveland	153
4-7	Dallas	155
4-8	Detroit	157
4-9	Houston	159
4-10	Indianapolis	161
4-11	Jacksonville	163
4-12	Los Angeles	165
4-13	Milwaukee	167
4-14	New Orleans	169
4-15	New York City	171
4-16	Philadelphia	173
4-17	Phoenix	175
4-18	Pittsburgh	177
4-19	Saint Louis	179
4-20	San Antonio	181
4-21	San Diego	183
4-22	San Francisco	185
4-23	San Jose	187
4-24	Washington, D.C.	189
4-25	California Cities	191
4-26	Texas Cities	193

List of Tables

Part III: The States

3-1	States Population Profile (1900 Census)	29
3-2	States Population Rankings 1900-2000	133
3-3	States Growth Ratio Rankings 1900-2000	135
3-4	States Population Ranking Changes	137

Part IV: The Cities

4-1	Cities Population Profile (1990 Census)	141
4-2	Cities Population/Growth Ratio Rankings 1900-1990	195

Part V: The Future

5-1	States Future Population Projections	199
5-2	States Population Rankings 1950-2050	201
5-3	Sunbelt States Electoral Vote 1900-2050	203

Preface

I started writing when I took a leave of absence from the executive suite in aerospace electronics to write a book on management (following the time-honored advice to write what you know). When that book was published in 1990, I began a new career. I wrote two statistical histories of baseball, then turned to politics to write about presidential elections. It was also a statistical history, only this time the topic was presidential elections rather than baseball.

But the books were similar in approach and theme. I learn most about a subject when I can see visually what has happened over time and then project what is likely to happen in the future. These books showed changes over time in graphs and tables containing data and comparisons never published before. It was a format that drew on my experience in the aerospace electronics industry, where I developed the ability to reduce reams of computer data to concise summaries showing what was really happening in a way everyone could understand.

A key point in my book about presidential elections is that there are fifty-one separate elections (fifty states and the District of Columbia). A candidate has to win the proper combination of these fifty-one elections to gain an electoral victory. To understand presidential elections it is necessary to understand what happens in each state. The electoral vote is based on the population of the state, and thus it is necessary to learn how the population of the state has changed and is changing over time to understand the role the state will play in present and future elections.

As a result of developing such population trends, I found I had a much better understanding of the growth of the United States during the twentieth century. I had the beginnings of a statistical history of the United States in terms of the population growth of the individual states and their major cities. It was a new way of looking at United States history, and, like most new ways of looking at things, it led to a new understanding. I also learned that to understand well the growth of the United States in terms of its population growth, it was necessary to understand population changes in both the states and the cities, because the cities grew (and declined) in a very different way from the states.

For example, twelve of the fifteen most populous states in 1900 were in the top fifteen in 1950, and thirteen of the top fifteen in 1950 remained in 1990. The percentage of the population living in the top fifteen was 64.3 percent in 1900, 65.0 percent in 1950, and 66.3 percent in 1990. Thirteen of the fifteen biggest cities in 1900 were on the top fifteen list in 1950, and the percentage of the population living in the top fifteen cities grew from 14.3 percent in 1900 to 16.5 percent in 1950. Then came a dramatic change. Seven of the top fifteen cities in 1950 were gone from the list in 1990, and the percentage of the population living in the fifteen biggest cities fell to 10.3 percent, a 38 percent decrease from 1950.

I decided to study population changes in the United States from 1900 through 1990 and then to project what would happen by 2000 and by 2050. I wanted to compare the growth of the states and the largest cities to the overall growth of the nation, to see which cities and states grew faster than the nation and which grew slower, and by how much. This book is the result of that study. It is a statistical history that has data never before published about the growth of the nation.

I discovered that a new phenomenon in world history has evolved in the United States since 1950. Although fourth in the world in size and third in population, the United States has such good distribution and communication systems and transportation infrastructure that one can live almost anywhere in the country and still be in the national mainstream. This achievement permits easy movement to preferred climatic, cultural, and tax environments with jobs and population movement leading and following each other in an iterative fashion. The result is substantial changes in population distribution.

A related phenomenon is the heavy immigration (legal and illegal) into the United States from Latin America and Asia. This drives the population of states such as California, Texas, and Florida well beyond the impacts of internal migration and natural growth. It also places the most populous states among the national leaders in the rate of growth. When the biggest states also grow the fastest, they dominate the rest of the nation in population (and electoral votes).

This book shows how the population changes happened from 1900 through 1990 and what the implications are for the future. I believe you will find that understanding the statistical history of the population growth of the United States will result in a much better understanding of how the country has developed and what future changes to expect. The Introduction that follows discusses key reasons for the population changes in the nation and also explains the book's methodology.

Acknowledgments

I want to thank the Library Department of the Bureau of the Census office in Van Nuys, California, for providing the data from their Current Population Reports series that were so useful in projecting population data beyond 1990.

I also want to thank Sandra Carroll, Arnel Floria, and Brian Wright for continuing to provide the hardware, software, and moral support necessary to keep my computer and laser printer systems doing what I want them to do.

Introduction

This book is divided into five parts: The Nation, The Regions, The States, The Cities, and The Future. Population data through 1990 are from the official census as reported by *The World Almanac*. Data for 2000 and after are based on projections by the Bureau of the Census. The population growth rate for the United States in the 1980s was 9.8 percent, the lowest rate since the 1930s. The Bureau of the Census projects a rate of 11.1 percent for the 1990s, with rates falling below 9 percent after 2000. National growth rates can be expected to slow as total population increases, but these projections may be low because the method of taking the census may change in a way that increases the count. The future is discussed in detail in Part V.

Part I, The Nation, begins with a graph showing population growth in the United States from 1900 to 2000. The actual population in the graph is compared to a normalized value representing the population that would exist if the nation grew at a fixed average rate in every decade. Thus the graph shows at a glance when the country was growing more rapidly or more slowly than the average rate. A similar technique is used throughout the book. The population growth of each state and city is compared to the rate at which the nation grew as a whole. Each graph shows clearly when the state or city grew more rapidly or more slowly than the nation, and the data beneath each graph shows the exact ratio of the growth of the state or city compared to that of the nation. This shows by how much the state or city exceeded or trailed the nation's growth in each decade. These ratios are summarized and ranked after Parts II and III.

The last graph in Part I shows the states in the nation where the average temperature is above forty degrees Fahrenheit in January. This area is defined as the "Sunbelt." The movement of population to some of these Sunbelt states, especially since 1950, is one of the key stories of the history of the United States in the twentieth century. Eight of the sixteen states in the Sunbelt had growth rates just barely above or well below the national average during the twentieth century. But the eight remaining states were among the ten fastest growing states in the nation from 1950 through 2000. This is where the story of the Sunbelt lies.

The rest of the book explains state by state and city by city how the population shifted to the Sunbelt from 1900 through 2000. This shift was due to several key changes in the nation. First, a revolution in farming productivity drove over a third of the nation's farm workers off the farms from 1948 through 1960 alone. Changes in farm labor demands also were an initial cause of black migration from the South to the major cities of the North (and West) that began in earnest around 1940 and continued through the time of the riots that took place in those cities in the 1960s. Once started, this migration was sustained by the demand for factory labor during World War II production and the heavy manufacturing boom in the following two decades. One result of this migration was a reverse migration out of the cities that started not long after 1950, a migration that still continues today.

World War II contributed to the shift toward the Sunbelt as many members of the armed forces got their first taste of life in the South and on the West Coast. They returned (or stayed) after the war because of the favorable climate and the availability of jobs and housing. The Interstate Highway Act of 1956 had the unintended consequence of greatly facilitating a national march to the suburbs and beyond, a march begun by the Supreme Court decision of 1954 outlawing segregated schools. The resulting "white flight" from major cities dropped the percentage of white students in school districts well below 50 percent by the 1960s, and it fell to nominal minimums through the 1980s.

Overlaying these cultural shifts was a change in national job creation. Heavy manufacturing contributed an ever smaller percentage starting in the 1960s, and the shift was accelerated by the car industry crash of the late 1970s and early 1980s. An initial move toward light manufacturing such as the electronics industry became a flood with the growth of the service and information industries. These industries grew rapidly in states with favorable tax or climatic environments (or both), most of which were located in a belt running from Florida through Texas and Arizona and on to California (the Sunbelt).

The constantly growing interstate highway system and the national use of computer networks supported the location of companies outside the previous northeastern/central base of industry and its suppliers. A related change that was both a result and a reinforcing cause of this shift was the relocation of baseball franchises that had been unchanged since 1903. The Boston Braves moved to Milwaukee in 1953 (and on to the Sunbelt in Atlanta in 1966), and the Philadelphia Athletics moved to Kansas City in 1954 (and on to the Sunbelt in Oakland in 1968). The

Introduction

move of the Brooklyn Dodgers to Los Angeles and the New York Giants to San Francisco in 1958 confirmed that the nation's population distribution was changing permanently. Sports franchises bloomed in response in every subsequent decade, and it became possible to find jobs and new housing in states with good weather, while still being able to attend one's favorite professional sport events.

A new unexpected consequence came from the Immigration Act of 1965 that reinforced the population shifts under way in the nation. The Act produced a wave of immigrants from the Caribbean nations and Asia who settled where jobs and/or prior immigrants existed as a support system. One result was an acceleration of the flight from large cities due to the local costs of supporting the new immigrants. Another result was that states such as California, Florida, and Texas grew at very high rates, especially considering their already large populations.

Part II, The Regions, shows the impact of the changes discussed so far on population growth in the four regions of the nation as defined in the first figure of Part II. The regions were nearly equal in population in 1990, but they were going in different directions. Graphs show how the regions grew compared to each other, and the huge shift from the Northeast and Central regions to the South and West regions, especially after 1950, is clearly evident. Graphs also show growth in each region compared to the growth rate for the nation, and these graphs show that growth has slowed dramatically in the Northeast and Central regions and exploded in the South and West regions. The difference between the actual population and the normalized population that would have existed if each region followed the growth rate of the United States makes the regional differences especially clear.

Part III moves to the states (and the District of Columbia). First, there is a profile of the states including rankings by 1990 population and growth rates. Then population growth for each state is shown compared to the normalized growth that would have existed if the state grew at the same rate as the nation starting in 1900. Ratios show the difference between the two growth rates, and these ratios are summarized and ranked at the end of Part III. Population rankings for the states in 1900, 1950, and 2000 are also shown, and the way states have moved in and out of the top rankings over the years is discussed.

Part IV shows twenty-four major cities. The list was derived by taking the top fifteen cities in population in 1900 and in 1990. Six cities appeared on both lists, and thus there is a net total of twenty-four different cities on the list. As was the case for the states, an initial table profiles the cities, individual graphs compare the growth rate of each city to the national rate, and summary tables rank the cities for population at different times and for growth rate ratios. An example of the dramatic changes in the cities is that St. Louis, Pittsburgh, and Buffalo had such sharp losses in population after 1950 that they had fewer people in 1990 than they had at the book's starting point of 1900.

The cities are not projected past 1990. States are much better indicators of expected population changes because the growth of a city can be very different from that of the state as a whole. San Francisco is a good example. It grew a little more rapidly than the nation from 1900 to 1950, and then declined slowly after 1950, even though the nation continued to grow. But the state of California grew dramatically more rapidly than the nation both before and after 1950. The growth and decline of San Francisco had no relationship at all to the growth of California.

Part V, The Future, projects which trends will continue after 2000 and what this will mean to the nation, especially in terms of political considerations. The movement of electoral control of the nation to the Sunbelt is forecasted to continue. California, Texas, and Florida will have 22 percent of the nation's electoral votes in the election of 2004, after having 11 percent in 1948 and 6 percent in 1900. If present trends continue, these three states will have 28 percent of the electoral votes in the election of 2052. No tree grows to the sky, but the present demographic trends producing the population increases in these states will not change soon. The United States continues to be the target of immigrants from around the world. This keeps the nation growing while other industrialized countries face the possibility of population declines as immigration is curtailed and birth rates fall. This high immigration rate will keep California, Texas, and Florida growing.

All parts of the book are arranged so that the discussion of each figure or table is complete on the opposing page. This means that you can turn to any region, state, or city from the list of figures or tables and find a complete discussion of the subject in one place. The states and cities are in alphabetical order in each part to help you find a specific choice readily, and the graphs for all states and cities include the official census values for every census from 1900 through 1990. Profile and summary sheets for the states and cities have lists in alphabetical and ranked order so that you can find data by state or city or by ranking position. This makes the book useful as a conventional reference source as well as a commentary on the statistical history of the population growth of the United States from 1900 through 2050.

Part I
The Nation

National Profile

Figure 1-1 shows population growth in the United States from 1900 through 2000. The actual population (solid line) is listed in column two under the graph. Actual growth rates by decade are shown next, and then the average growth rate. The last column shows the ratio of the actual rate to the average rate. A ratio greater than 1.00 means that the population grew more rapidly than average in that decade. The dashed line is the normalized population that would exist if the population grew by the average rate. From 1900, the population grew more rapidly than average if the actual line is on top, and more slowly than average if the normalized line is on top. This format is used throughout the book except that actual regional, state, or city growth rates are compared to the actual United States growth rate rather than to an average rate.

The United States grew from 76,212,168 people in 1900 to a projected level of 276,241,000 (throughout the book projected levels are rounded to thousands) in 2000. That represents an average growth rate of 13.7 percent per decade. From the 1900 baseline, the actual population grew to 92,228,496 in 1910. This was a growth rate of 21.0 percent, the highest in the century and higher than the average rate by a ratio of 1.53. This means that the nation grew 53 percent more rapidly than average in the 1900-1910 decade.

The nation grew more rapidly than average up to 1930. But in the 1930s, due to the depression and immigration law changes, the nation grew by only 7.3 percent. This was just over half the average rate, and by 1940 the actual and normalized lines were close together. This means that from 1900 through 1940 the nation grew only a little more rapidly than the average rate. The growth rate improved in the 1940s and 1950s and stayed near average in the 1960s. This kept the actual population line well ahead of the normalized line through 1970. Growth was below average after 1970, but still high compared to most developed countries. This is because of high legal and illegal immigration rates and high immigrant birthrates.

The rest of the book shows how population growth developed by region, state, and city. But first, Figure 1-2 defines the part of the nation where the highest growth took place.

National Profile

Figure 1-1. United States Population (in Millions)

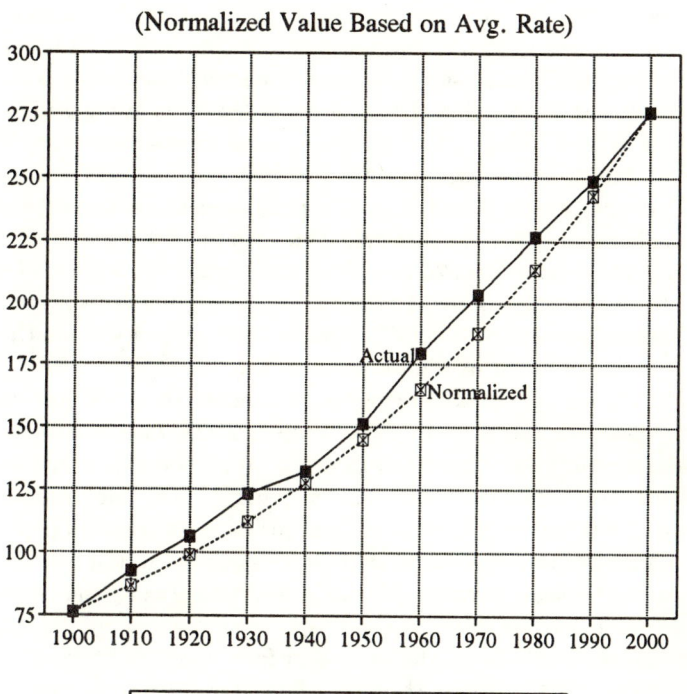

Year	Population	Growth Rate	Avg. Rate	Ratio
1900	76,212,168	--	--	--
1910	92,228,496	21.0%	13.7%	1.53
1920	106,021,537	15.0%	13.7%	1.09
1930	123,202,624	16.2%	13.7%	1.18
1940	132,164,569	7.3%	13.7%	0.53
1950	151,325,798	14.5%	13.7%	1.05
1960	179,323,175	18.5%	13.7%	1.35
1970	203,302,031	13.4%	13.7%	0.97
1980	226,542,203	11.4%	13.7%	0.83
1990	248,709,873	9.8%	13.7%	0.71
2000	276,241,000	11.1%	13.7%	0.81

Figure 1-2 shows the section of the United States where the average temperature in January is above forty degrees Fahrenheit. This line runs from the northern border of North Carolina across the northern borders of the states in sequence to the west until it curves upward through Nevada and goes across the immediate coastal portions of Oregon and Washington. The sixteen shaded states in Figure 1-2 are on most lists of "Sunbelt States." There is no formal definition of the Sunbelt, but the forty-degree line is the definition used in this book.

There has been a dramatic shift of population to the Sunbelt states, especially since 1950. The data below the map show that the population of the Sunbelt grew from 26 percent of the United States population in 1900 to 32 percent in 1950. The percentage will grow to 44 percent in 2000 and 52 percent by 2050. This means that a majority of the United States population will live in the Sunbelt states by 2050.

Not all Sunbelt states have high growth rates. Six states grew more slowly than the nation from 1950 through 2000 (low-growth states) while ten grew faster (high-growth states). With both North and South Carolina just barely exceeding the national growth rate from 1950 through 2000, only eight states account for the high population growth in the Sunbelt. But those eight states are among the fastest growing in the nation. Nevada, Arizona, Florida, California, Texas, and Georgia, in that order, had six of the top eight spots in growth rate in the nation in the 1980s (Table 3-1). The same first four states plus New Mexico and Hawaii, in that order, had six of the top nine spots in highest growth rate from 1950 through 2000 (Table 3-3).

California, Texas, and Florida are the key states that drive the growth of the Sunbelt. These states ranked 1st, 3rd, and 4th, respectively in total population in the census of 1990. But in spite of their huge size, in the 1980s Florida was 4th in growth rate, California was 5th, and Texas was 7th. These three states will have a population of 130 people by 2050. That will be almost 34 percent of the nation's population in 2050, and it is only 14 percent less than the total population of the United States in 1950.

The high-growth Sunbelt states are not the fastest growing states just because they have relatively mild winter temperatures, although that is one of the reasons. A complex set of factors drove the population away from the Northeast and Central regions of the nation and toward the Sunbelt. These factors are the key topic of the rest of the book. Part II, The Regions, shows how the population changed on a regional basis during the century.

Figure 1-2. United States Sunbelt States

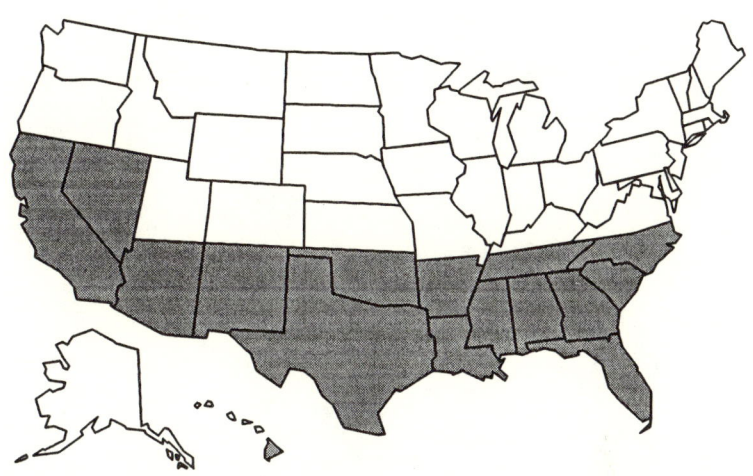

High-Growth Sunbelt States
- Arizona
- California
- Florida
- Georgia
- Hawaii
- Nevada
- New Mexico
- North Carolina
- South Carolina
- Texas

Low-Growth Sunbelt States
- Alabama
- Arkansas
- Louisiana
- Mississippi
- Oklahoma
- Tennessee

Sunbelt States Percentage of United States Population:

Year	Percent
1900	26 Percent
1950	32 Percent
2000	44 Percent
2050	52 Percent

Note:
Oregon and Washington coastal areas also meet forty-degree criteria.

Part II
The Regions

Regions Profile

Figure 2-1 shows the four population regions defined for this book (Northeast, Central, South, and West). The states (and the District of Columbia) are nearly equally divided among the regions except for the West, which has most of the larger, more sparsely populated states in the nation. The states in each region are listed in Figure 2-1. The Sunbelt states are entirely contained in the South and West regions.

The regional populations were the closest to one another they have been in this century in 1980 (Figure 2-3), as 1980 marked the transition of leadership from the Northeast and Central regions to the South and West (Figure 2-2). In 1980 the South led for the first time while the Central region fell to second for the first time. The Northeast was third and the West last. By 1990 the South and West were in first and second place, with the lead in both total population and population growth rate.

The South and West should hold the lead indefinitely (they have led in growth rate in every census since 1940). The West has been first since 1910, but it started with such a small population that it still trailed the South in total population in 1990. It is projected that the West will nearly catch up with the South by the census of 2030, then move ahead in 2040. By 2050 the West will have 33.3 percent of the nation's population, and the South will have 31.5 percent. This will give the South and West just under 65 percent of the total population, almost an exact reversal of the situation in 1900, when the Northeast and Central regions had just over 64 percent of the population (Figure 2-2).

The losers in the population race in this century are the Northeast and Central regions. They led from 1900 through 1970, with the Central region always just a little ahead of the Northeast. But the growth rate of both regions was less than the national rate in every decade from 1910 through 2000, and by 1990 they fell to third and fourth, with the Central region maintaining its small edge over the Northeast. This close tie is projected to continue into the next century, as both regions continue their slow rates of growth. The steady decline of the Northeast and Central regions through the twentieth century is nearly as big a story as the rise of the Sunbelt, and indeed one fed the other. This is shown in detail in the succeeding figures.

Figure 2-1. Population Regions

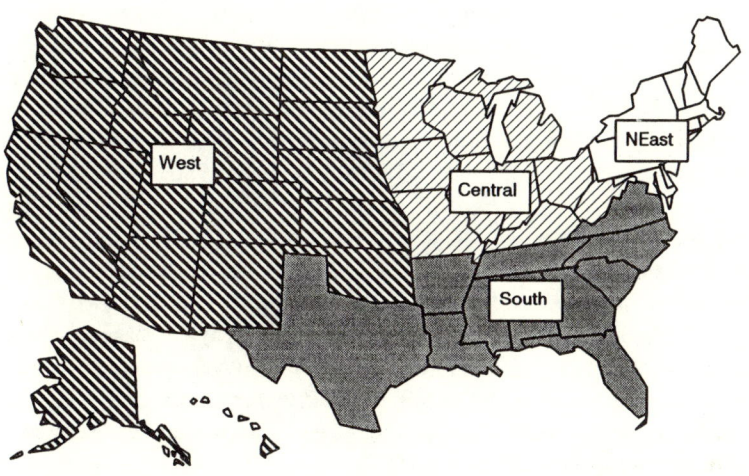

West	Central	South	Northeast
Alaska	Illinois	Alabama	Connecticut
Arizona	Indiana	Arkansas	Delaware
California	Iowa	Florida	District of
Colorado	Kentucky	Georgia	Columbia
Hawaii	Michigan	Louisiana	Maine
Idaho	Minnesota	Mississippi	Maryland
Kansas	Missouri	N. Carolina	Massachusetts
Montana	Ohio	S. Carolina	New Hampshire
Nebraska	W. Virginia	Tennessee	New Jersey
Nevada	Wisconsin	Texas	New York
New Mexico		Virginia	Pennsylvania
N. Dakota			Rhode Island
Oklahoma			Vermont
Oregon			
S. Dakota			
Utah			
Washington			
Wyoming			

Figure 2-2 shows the percentage of the nation's population in the combined Northeast and Central regions and the combined South and West regions from 1900 through 2000. The actual values are shown in the table under the graph together with the ratio of the South and West regions to the Northeast and Central regions. The ratio for 1900 shows that the South and West were only 56 percent of the Northeast and Central regions. But the ratio increased steadily until the two combined regions were almost equal at a ratio of 0.99 in 1980. The South and West took the lead in 1990 with a ratio of 1.13, meaning that the South and West were 13 percent ahead of the Northeast and Central regions.

The trend of an increasing percentage for the South and West never reversed in any decade from 1900 through 2000. This is shown clearly by the graph and the fact that the ratio constantly increased. After a sharp change in the 1900-1910 decade, the movement of population from the Northeast and Central regions to the South and West was relatively gradual from 1910 through 1940. But the rate accelerated in 1950 and jumped again in the 1970s.

As discussed in the Introduction, World War II contributed to the change in 1950. Many soldiers liked their introduction to the South and West regions during the war, and they moved there permanently soon after. This was especially true in the West. This trend continued with the first relocation of baseball franchises in fifty years in the 1950s, the growing web of interstate highways, and the national connection to the mainstream via television regardless of where a person lived.

Movement of job creation from heavy industry to the electronics, service, and information industries produced the next population shift after 1970. As Figure 2-8 shows, the actual population of the South went ahead of the normalized value for the first time in 1980. This growth rate increase in the South, added to the steady climb of the West, produced the sharp increase in the percentage of the population in the South and West after 1970 that is shown in Figure 2-2.

The Northeast and South regions grew in a similar way from 1900 through 1950, with the Central region lagging a little behind while the West grew much more rapidly from its small 1900 baseline. Growth in the West accelerated from 1950 through 1970 even as its population increased, but the other three regions did not change nearly as much from their prior trends. However, from 1970 onward there was a dramatic change in those three regions as well. Growth in the Northeast and Central regions came to a sudden halt while it exploded in the South and West. This is shown clearly in succeeding figures.

Figure 2-2. Combined Regions, Percent of Population

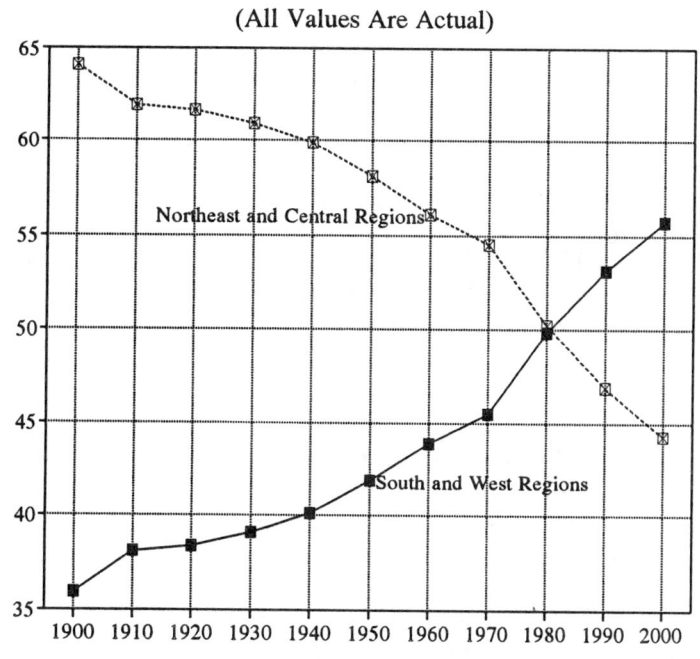

Year	NE/Central	South/West	Ratio
1900	64.1%	35.9%	0.56
1910	61.9%	38.1%	0.62
1920	61.6%	38.4%	0.62
1930	60.9%	39.1%	0.64
1940	59.9%	40.1%	0.67
1950	58.1%	41.9%	0.72
1960	56.1%	43.9%	0.78
1970	54.5%	45.5%	0.83
1980	50.2%	49.8%	0.99
1990	46.9%	53.1%	1.13
2000	44.3%	55.7%	1.26

Figure 2-3 shows the percentage of the nation's population in each region. The actual values are shown in the table under the graph. The Central region started out well ahead, then fell off a little in 1910 but held its lead with the Northeast close behind in second place. The South was 9.5 percentage points behind the Central region in third place in 1900. It stayed third up to 1970, while the Central and Northeast regions stayed first and second, respectively. But the gap between the three regions steadily grew smaller, as the South stayed nearly flat and the other two regions slowly declined. This decline was due to the constant growth of the West, which grew rapidly in the 1900-1910 decade, slowed through 1940, then accelerated from 1950 through the end of the century. But in spite of this higher rate of growth, the West stayed in last place in percentage of the total population through 1980.

The dramatic changes that took place in population distribution after 1970 produced the century's first change in rank in 1980. The South leaped into first place, a position it should hold until 2040, when it will be passed by the West. The Central region fell to second in 1980 and the Northeast to third. The West was still last, but it was much closer to the other regions than it had been since 1900 (or since the beginning of the nation, for that matter). As noted in Figure 2-1, the four regions were closer to one another in 1980 than at any time in the century. There is no reason to expect they will ever be as close again.

By 1990 the South had taken a larger lead over the Central and Northeast regions, and the West had moved into second place. The gap between the South and West will slowly close in the next century, with the West passing the South in 2040 and leading 33.3 percent to 31.5 percent by 2050. The actual percentages may vary by 2050, but the West and South will remain in the lead indefinitely. The Northeast and Central regions have fallen steadily for a hundred years and will continue to fall. The Central region should lead the Northeast by 18.2 percent to 17.1 percent in 2050 (the same 1.1 percentage point margin by which the Central region led in 1970). The decline in the percentage held by these regions could easily continue through the next century.

The percentage decline in the Northeast and Central regions does not mean that the regions are losing population. They are still growing, but the rate of increase has changed dramatically during the twentieth century. It is possible that the Central or Northeast region will become the first of the four regions to lose population from one census to another, but that possibility is decades away. The succeeding figures show actual population changes in the combined and separate regions.

Figure 2-3. Percent of Population by Region

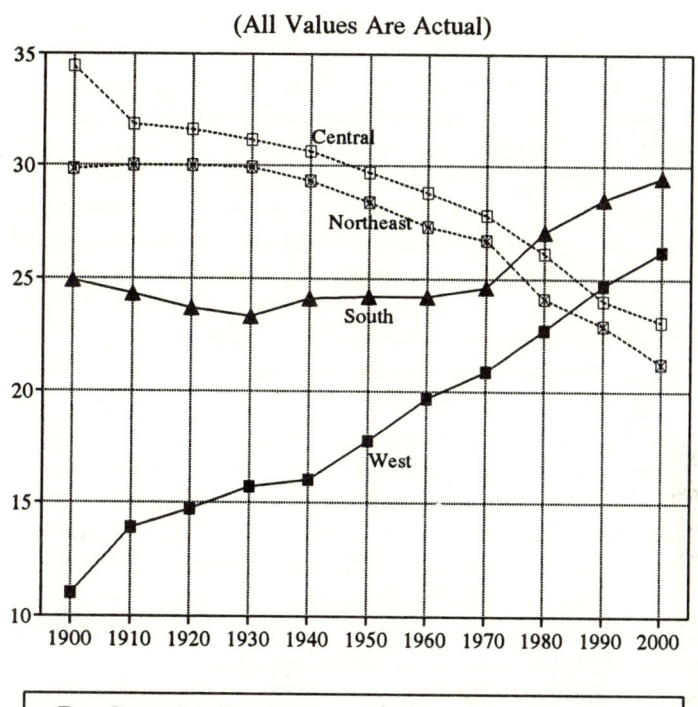

Year	Central	Northeast	South	West
1900	34.4%	29.8%	24.9%	11.0%
1910	31.8%	30.0%	24.3%	13.9%
1920	31.6%	30.0%	23.7%	14.7%
1930	31.1%	29.9%	23.3%	15.7%
1940	30.6%	29.3%	24.1%	16.0%
1950	29.7%	28.4%	24.2%	17.8%
1960	28.8%	27.3%	24.2%	19.7%
1970	27.8%	26.7%	24.6%	20.9%
1980	26.1%	24.1%	27.1%	22.7%
1990	24.0%	22.9%	28.5%	24.7%
2000	23.1%	21.2%	29.5%	26.2%

Figure 2-4 shows population in the combined Northeast and Central regions and the combined South and West regions from 1900 through 2000. Actual values are shown in the table under the graph together with the ratio of the South and West to the Northeast and Central regions. The ratio changed from 0.56 in 1900 to a projected 1.26 in 2000, meaning that the South and West will lead by 26 percent by then.

From 1900 through 1940 the combined regions seemed to move in parallel, but the constantly increasing ratio shows that the South and West regions were slowly catching up. However, from 1900 through 1940 there was not much difference in the growth rate of the combined regions. During the 1940s the South and West regions began to grow at a higher rate (mainly in the West). From 1950 through 1970 the South and West grew ever closer to the Northeast and Central regions, even though the latter regions still had a decent growth rate.

A big change came after 1970. The Northeast and Central regions made a "right turn" on the graph and their growth slowed drastically. At the same time, the South and West regions turned even more sharply upward as both regions grew more rapidly than the nation as a whole. The result was that while the Northeast and Central regions added less than 6 million people from 1970 through 1990, the South and West added almost 40 million people. This gave the South and West a lead of more than 15 million people by 1990, and the difference is projected to reach nearly 32 million by 2000.

The South and West will have nearly 3 million more people in 2000 than the United States had in 1950. These regions will almost triple in population between 1940 and 2000, while the Northeast and Central regions will grow by only 55 percent. The South and West will add over 100 million people from 1940 through 2000, while the Northeast and Central regions will add only 43 million. Between 1970 and 2000 alone, the South and West will add over 61 million people while the Northeast and Central regions add fewer than 12 million.

Compared to most Western countries, the Northeast and Central regions grew quite well in the second half of the twentieth century. The gap between these regions and the South and West regions is due to the unprecedented growth in the South and West regions. However, the Northeast and Central regions are currently entering a period of very slow growth, while the South and West are still growing rapidly, which will increase the difference between the regions in the future. This can be seen more clearly in the succeeding figure, which shows the total population from 1900 through 2000 by separate regions.

Figure 2-4. Combined Regions Population (in Millions)

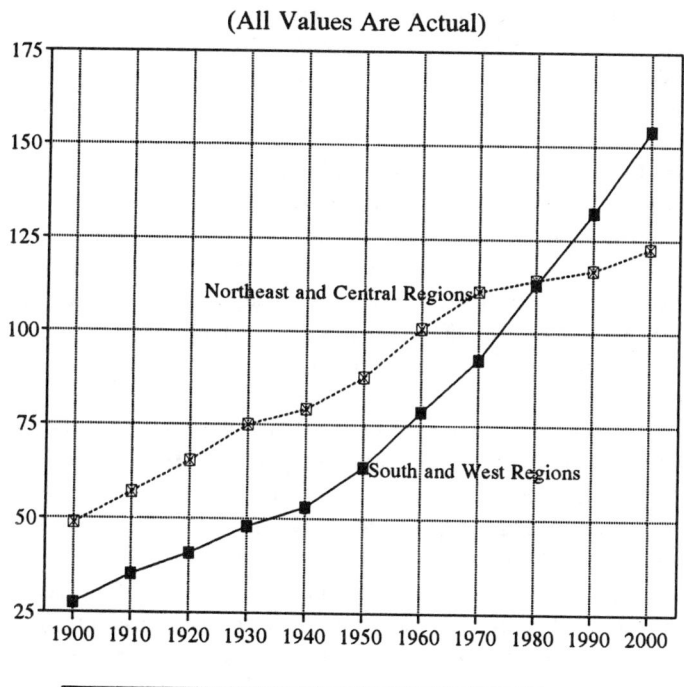

(All Values Are Actual)

Year	NE/Central	South/West	Ratio
1900	48,879,659	27,332,509	0.56
1910	57,052,769	35,175,727	0.62
1920	65,323,363	40,698,174	0.62
1930	75,089,104	48,113,520	0.64
1940	79,216,792	52,947,777	0.67
1950	87,849,185	63,476,613	0.72
1960	100,603,571	78,719,604	0.78
1970	110,825,972	92,476,059	0.83
1980	113,786,485	112,755,718	0.99
1990	116,620,407	132,089,466	1.13
2000	122,328,000	153,913,000	1.26

Figure 2-5 shows total population in the four regions. The actual values are shown in the table under the graph. The Central region led in 1900 with a population more than triple that of the last-place West, and the South in third place was more than twice as large as the West. The West grew more rapidly than the other regions, but by 1940 the Central region still had nearly twice the population of the West, and the South had 50 percent more people than the West. The Northeast region stayed closely tied to the Central region through all four decades.

In the 1940s the West added nearly 6 million people, more than any other region. This was the first time the West added more people than the other regions, even though the West still had by far the smallest population. This meant that in addition to leading in the percentage of increase, the West now had a large enough population base to lead the other regions in the increase of total population.

After 1950 the West added the most people in every decade but the 1970s. The South took the lead in population increase in the 1970s and moved into first place in population in 1980, while the growth in the Northeast and Central regions came to a halt. In the 1970s, for example, the Northeast region added less than 0.3 million people to its total of 54.3 million in 1970. The West regained the lead in people added in the 1980s, but since 1980 the South and the West have been very close together in this measure. This will continue into the next century as the West slowly catches up to the South in population.

The Northeast region slowed the most after 1970. It fell 4.6 million behind the Central region in 1980, the largest difference between these regions in the century. After starting out 3.5 million behind the Central region in 1900, the Northeast region moved to less than 2 million behind the Central in 1910. The two regions marched through the rest of the century separated by fewer than 2 million people until 1960. It is projected that the Central region will lead by more than 5 million people in 2000, an edge that will fall to 4 million by 2050.

The Northeast and Central regions will track each other in growth well into the next century as they fall ever further behind the South and West. Conditions can change over long periods of time (as they have during the twentieth century), but Figure 2-5 shows that the South and West started to pull ahead sharply after 1940, over fifty years ago, and the rate of change is still accelerating. It will take many years for the momentum to reverse (if it ever does), even in a nation of dynamic population distribution changes like the United States. The shift to the Sunbelt seems destined to continue unabated.

Figure 2-5. Population by Region (in Millions)

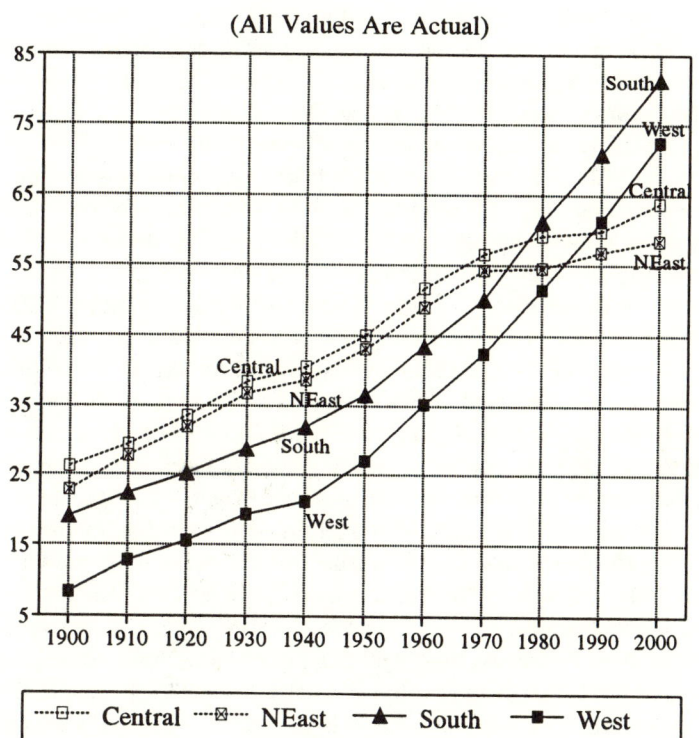

Year	Central	Northeast	South	West
1900	26,181,467	22,698,192	18,975,665	8,356,844
1910	29,355,459	27,697,310	22,392,414	12,783,313
1920	33,551,075	31,772,288	25,106,954	15,591,220
1930	38,305,238	36,783,866	28,761,024	19,352,496
1940	40,489,175	38,727,617	31,831,026	21,116,751
1950	44,907,935	42,941,250	36,550,115	26,926,498
1960	51,614,815	48,988,756	43,435,315	35,284,289
1970	56,536,789	54,289,183	50,059,900	42,416,159
1980	59,199,966	54,586,519	61,281,368	51,474,350
1990	59,756,642	56,863,765	70,767,036	61,322,430
2000	63,826,000	58,502,000	81,414,000	72,499,000

Figure 2-6 shows population growth in the Northeast compared to the nation from 1900 through 2000. As explained on page 2, the solid line is the actual population and the dashed line is the normalized population that would exist if the region grew at the national rate. This shows if the region grew more rapidly (actual line on top) or more slowly (normalized line on top) than the nation.

The Northeast grew more rapidly than the nation from 1900 through 1930. The lines on the graph are very close together during this period, but the 1.05 ratio for the 1900-1910 decade shows that the region grew more rapidly than the nation in the first decade. This edge was enough to keep the region on top in 1920 and 1930, even though the ratio fell just below 1.00 in the 1910-1920 decade and the 1920s, showing that the region grew more slowly than the nation each time.

The ratio fell to 0.73 in the 1930s, driving the actual line below the normalized line in 1940. Thus, from 1900 through 1940 the region grew more slowly than the nation. With the ratio in each decade now well below 1.00, the region regularly grew more slowly than the nation and fell further below the normalized line. The only decade in which the Northeast grew more rapidly than the nation was the first decade.

The Northeast steadily fell further behind the national growth rate from 1910 through 1970, but it was still only 10 percent below the normalized line by 1970. Then in the 1970s New York state, typically a third of the Northeast total, and the city of New York, typically half the state total, fell dramatically. The city lost 823,924 people in the 1970s and the state lost 683,226. This was the only decade in which the state lost population in the century. Many people moved to New Jersey and Connecticut, but others left the region. With Pennsylvania now barely growing at all, and Rhode Island and the District of Columbia losing population in the 1970s, the Northeast region added only 297,336 people in the decade (an increase of only 0.5 percent).

The Northeast recovered a little after the 1970s, but with more than half its population in two states (New York and Pennsylvania) that had nearly stopped growing, the region fell further behind the national growth rate in the 1980s and 1990s. By 2000 it is projected that the region will be about 29 percent below the normalized line, and it will continue to fall further behind as the region continues to trail the national growth rate well into the next century. Some individual states such as Delaware and Maryland are doing well, but much of their growth is at the expense of other states in the region. The Northeast can be expected to have continued slow growth indefinitely.

Figure 2-6. Northeast Population (in Millions)

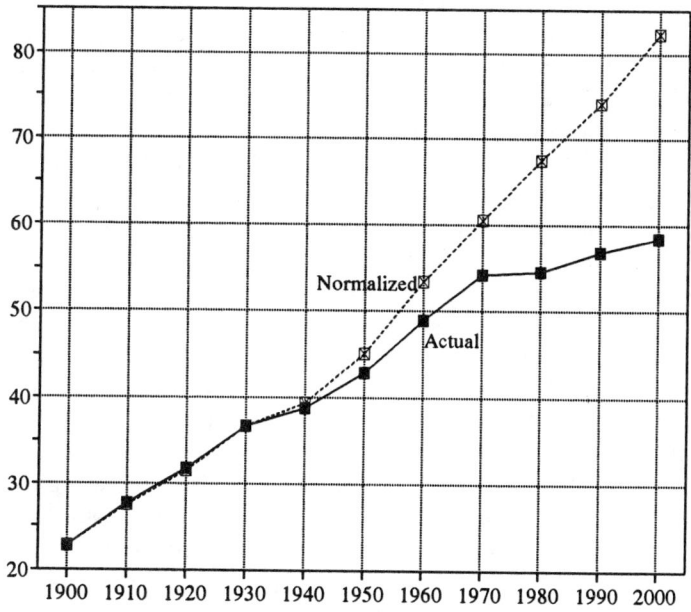

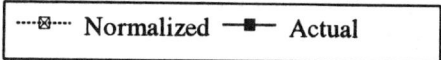

Year	Population	Growth Rate	U.S. Rate	Ratio
1900	22,698,192	--	--	--
1910	27,697,310	22.0%	21.0%	1.05
1920	31,772,288	14.7%	15.0%	0.98
1930	36,783,866	15.8%	16.2%	0.97
1940	38,727,617	5.3%	7.3%	0.73
1950	42,941,250	10.9%	14.5%	0.75
1960	48,988,756	14.1%	18.5%	0.76
1970	54,289,183	10.8%	13.4%	0.81
1980	54,586,519	0.5%	11.4%	0.05
1990	56,863,765	4.2%	9.8%	0.43
2000	58,502,000	2.9%	11.1%	0.26

Figure 2-7 shows population growth in the Central region compared to the nation from 1900 through 2000. The format is explained on pages 2 and 18. The Central region began the century growing more slowly than the nation, and it continued to do so in every decade. This is shown by the actual line's staying below the normalized line, while the ratio never grew above 1.00. The decline was relatively consistent, with the actual line falling 10 percent below the normalized line by 1930 and reaching a 20 percent deficit by 1970.

Growth slowed more sharply in the 1970s, and in the 1980s Central region growth essentially stopped. Up to 1980, the smallest population increase for the region was the addition of just over 2 million people in the depression of the 1930s. But in the 1980s, with a population more than 50 percent above 1930, the Central region added only 556,676 people. This was an increase of only 0.9 percent, making the 1980s easily the worst decade of the century for that region's growth.

The crash of the automobile business in the late 1970s and early 1980s is the key reason for the sharp decline in the 1980s. The Central region's growth has been slowed more than once by population losses in Iowa and West Virginia, and Kentucky and Missouri have grown at an unusually slow rate even if not actually losing population. These four states are the primary reason for the slow growth of the region through the century. Michigan is the only state in the region that kept ahead of the national growth rate after 1910, and its dynamic growth as a result of its position as the prime automobile manufacturing state in the nation was the one bright spot in the Central region. But the car industry crash halted Michigan's growth in the 1980s.

Ohio, also a key player in the automobile industry, stayed just below the national growth rate through 1970, then stopped growing in the 1980s. Illinois grew more slowly than Ohio while following nearly the same pattern. Illinois, Ohio, and Michigan had 52.8 percent of the population of the Central region in 1990, and they accounted for 60.1 percent of its population increase since 1900. When growth in all three came to a halt in the 1970s and 1980s, the Central region's growth stopped as well. With job creation now mainly outside the arena of heavy industry, Central region growth will be slow for many years.

The region also suffers from the fact that it is landlocked with no shoreline other than those of the Great Lakes. Its winters are cold and its summers hot and humid. There is no strong tourist industry to offset the loss of industrial jobs, and, except for the Chicago area, it is not a popular target for immigrants. This is a recipe for slow growth.

Figure 2-7. Central Population (in Millions)

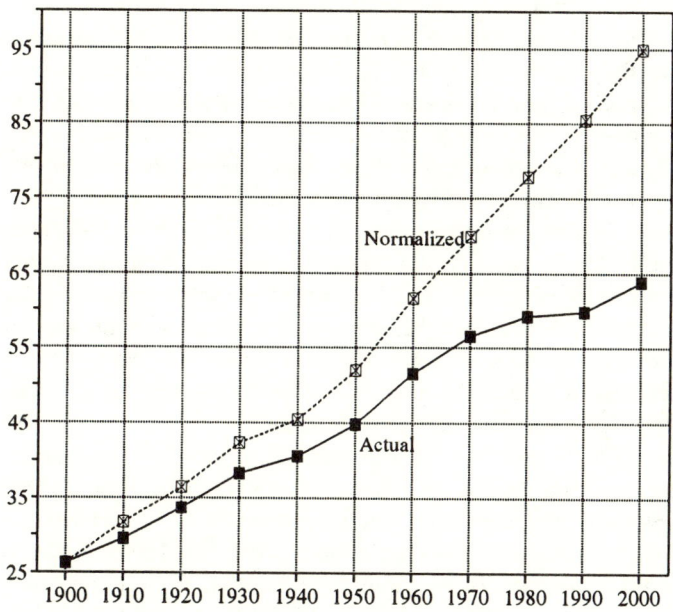

Year	Population	Growth Rate	U.S. Rate	Ratio
1900	26,181,467	--	--	--
1910	29,355,459	12.1%	21.0%	0.58
1920	33,551,075	14.3%	15.0%	0.96
1930	38,305,238	14.2%	16.2%	0.87
1940	40,489,175	5.7%	7.3%	0.78
1950	44,907,935	10.9%	14.5%	0.75
1960	51,614,815	14.9%	18.5%	0.81
1970	56,536,789	9.5%	13.4%	0.71
1980	59,199,966	4.7%	11.4%	0.41
1990	59,756,642	0.9%	9.8%	0.10
2000	63,826,000	6.8%	11.1%	0.62

Figure 2-8 shows population growth in the South region compared to the nation from 1900 through 2000. The format is explained on pages 2 and 18. The South began the century growing more slowly than the nation, as shown by the first three ratios' being below 1.00 and the actual line's falling below the normalized line. The South grew more rapidly than the nation in the 1930s (the ratio was 1.47), and it has grown more rapidly in every decade since. But the difference in the growth rate between the South and the nation was so small after 1940 that the actual population line stayed a little below the normalized line until 1970. However, after 1970 the actual line shot ahead.

The 1970s increase was fueled by migration from the Northeast and especially the Central regions, and immigration from the Caribbean nations that began after 1965, as discussed in the Introduction. Before 1970 the South was roughly in equal balance with the nation, as migration by blacks to the industrialized cities of the North (and West) was countered by retirees and others heading south. In both periods Texas and Florida were the growth leaders.

In 1990 Texas had 16 percent and Florida 3 percent of the population in the South. In 1950 Texas had 21 percent and Florida 8 percent, and together they had accounted for 39 percent of the population increase in the region since 1900. By 2000 the two states will hold 43 percent of the South's population (Florida will be at 19 percent), and they will have accounted for 51 percent of the increase since 1900. Both states are growing due to the creation of new jobs in the electronics, service, and information industries, and both are targets of immigration (legal and illegal) from nations south of the United States. Both states will be key factors in the growth of the United States in the next century. Together with California they will dominate population growth and cultural trends.

Only six of the eleven states in the South were growing more rapidly than the nation in the census of 1990, with three states in the top ten: Florida in 4th place, Texas in 7th, and Georgia in 8th (Table 3-1). Georgia grew more slowly than the nation up to 1960 due to heavy migration out of the state after 1920. But an improved business climate made it one of the fastest growing states after 1970. Virginia showed a similar pattern. North Carolina grew at almost the same rate as the nation up to 1970, then moved ahead afterwards. These states and South Carolina should continue to grow more rapidly than the nation, while the other states in the region more slowly than the nation. Just being in the South does not guarantee a state good growth.

Regions vs. Nation

Figure 2-8. South Population (in Millions)

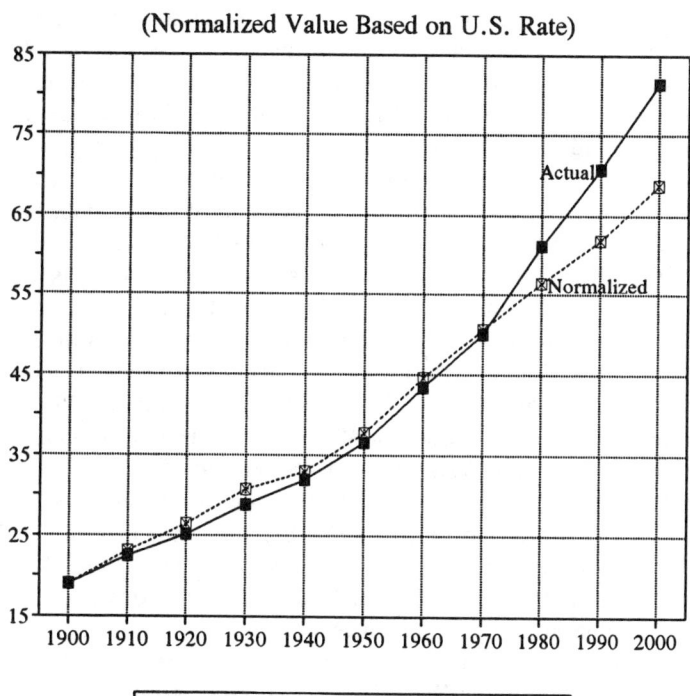

(Normalized Value Based on U.S. Rate)

Year	Population	Growth Rate	U.S. Rate	Ratio
1900	18,975,665	--	--	--
1910	22,392,414	18.0%	21.0%	0.86
1920	25,106,954	12.1%	15.0%	0.81
1930	28,761,024	14.6%	16.2%	0.90
1940	31,831,026	10.7%	7.3%	1.47
1950	36,550,115	14.8%	14.5%	1.02
1960	43,435,315	18.8%	18.5%	1.02
1970	50,059,900	15.3%	13.4%	1.14
1980	61,281,368	22.4%	11.4%	1.96
1990	70,767,036	15.5%	9.8%	1.58
2000	81,414,000	15.0%	11.1%	1.36

Figure 2-9 shows population growth in the West region compared to the nation from 1900 through 2000. The format is explained on pages 2 and 18. The West region began the century growing more rapidly than the nation, and it has continued to do so for the full one hundred years. This is shown by the ratios' being much greater than 1.00 in every decade, as the actual line soared ahead of the normalized line. The ratio was 2.52 in 1910, meaning that the West grew 2.52 times as fast as the nation in the first decade of the century. This was partly due to the low population baseline of the West in 1900, but the West has continued to grow rapidly at all population levels. Even with over 50 million people in 1980, the West grew nearly twice as rapidly as the nation in the next decade, as shown by the 1.95 ratio for 1990.

The growth of the West region was primarily due to California for most of the century. California had only 18 percent of the total population of the West region in 1900, but by 1950 it had 39 percent of the total and had accounted for 49 percent of the population increase since 1900. By 1980 California had 46 percent of the total and had accounted for 52 percent of the increase in the region since 1900. The next biggest state in the region is Washington, and, if it is added to California, the two together had 54 percent of the population in the West region in 1980, and they had accounted for 60 percent of the added population in the region since 1900.

But other states in the West region recently have also reflected the shift of population to the West. In 1990 Nevada, Alaska, and Arizona occupied the first three places on the list of the highest-growth states in the nation (Table 3-1). California was 5th, with Utah, Washington, New Mexico, Hawaii, and Colorado taking five of the six spots from 9th through 14th. That means that West region states had nine of the top fourteen spots on the high growth list, including four of the top five. These nine states are keeping the West region at the top of the national growth list, and they all have good prospects for continued high growth in the next century.

The other nine states in the West region were all growing more slowly than the rest of the nation as of the 1990 census. In fact, Montana, South Dakota, and Nebraska were barely growing at all, while North Dakota and Wyoming were losing population. But these five states had less than 7 percent of the West region's population in 1990. Thus, they have little impact on the continuing rapid growth of the region. They do show, however, as in the South region, that merely being located in the West does not guarantee a state good growth.

Regions vs. Nation

Figure 2-9. West Population (in Millions)

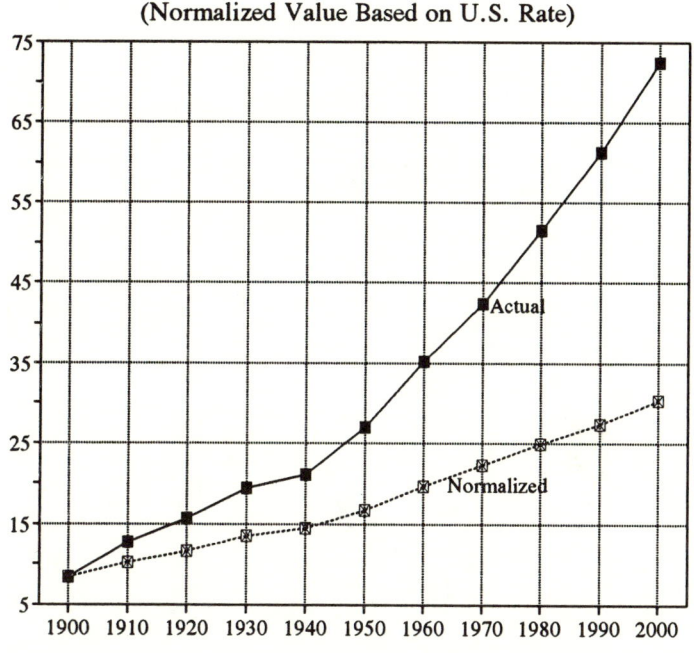

(Normalized Value Based on U.S. Rate)

Year	Population	Growth Rate	U.S. Rate	Ratio
1900	8,356,844	--	--	--
1910	12,783,313	53.0%	21.0%	2.52
1920	15,591,220	22.0%	15.0%	1.47
1930	19,352,496	24.1%	16.2%	1.49
1940	21,116,751	9.1%	7.3%	1.25
1950	26,926,498	27.5%	14.5%	1.90
1960	35,284,289	31.0%	18.5%	1.68
1970	42,416,159	20.2%	13.4%	1.51
1980	51,474,350	21.4%	11.4%	1.87
1990	61,322,430	19.1%	9.8%	1.95
2000	72,499,000	18.2%	11.1%	1.65

Part III
The States

States Profile

Table 3-1 shows the population and growth rates for the fifty states and the District of Columbia (D.C.) as of the 1990 census. The states and D.C. are listed alphabetically in the first set of columns. They are ranked by population in the middle columns and by growth rate for the 1980s in the third set of columns. California was first in population with 29,760,021 people (12 percent of the nation's total). The top ten states had 54.5 percent of total population in 1990. They had 50.8 percent in 1900 and 53.0 percent in 1950 (Table 3-2). In 2050 they will have 56.3 percent (Table 5-1). This steady increase is a result of the fact that several of the largest states also have high growth rates.

The concentration of population in the larger states explains why only seventeen states in Table 3-1 exceed the average of 4.9 million for the fifty-one states (including D.C.). Of the top twelve states for population, five also rank among the top twelve for growth (California, Texas, Florida, Georgia, and Virginia). But of the bottom twelve states for population, only two (New Hampshire and Alaska) rank in the top twelve for growth. To make the nation even more top-heavy, three of the top four states in population (California, Texas, and Florida), rank 4th, 5th, and 7th in growth. The result of this top-heavy effect is that although the growth rate for the nation in the 1980s was 9.8 percent, the growth rate ranking list shows that only nineteen states exceeded this level for the decade. This means that thirty-two of the fifty-one states grew more slowly than the nation as a whole.

California, Texas, and Florida will continue to grow well. With the mobile population that exists in the United States, people can (and do) move to states that have the most favorable combination of job creation and climate. Immigrants do the same, and once they are established future immigrants go where a support system already exists in terms of language and culture. Large states that are growing slowly (such as New York, Pennsylvania, Illinois, and Ohio) are already so big that they will stay near the top for decades to come. This is because even slow growth in such states adds a larger number of people than that added by smaller states with higher growth rates. Thus, the percentage of the total population in the top ten states will continue to increase.

Table 3-1. States Population Profile (1990 Census)

State	Population	Growth Rate %	State	Population	State	Growth Rate %
Alabama	4,040,587	3.8	1. California	29,760,021	1. Nevada	50.1
Alaska	550,043	36.9	2. New York	17,990,455	2. Alaska	36.9
Arizona	3,665,228	34.9	3. Texas	16,986,510	3. Arizona	34.9
Arkansas	2,350,725	2.8	4. Florida	12,937,936	4. Florida	32.7
California	29,760,021	25.7	5. Penn.	11,881,643	5. California	25.7
Colorado	3,294,394	14.0	6. Illinois	11,430,602	6. New Hamp.	20.5
Connecticut	3,287,116	5.8	7. Ohio	10,847,115	7. Texas	19.4
Delaware	666,168	12.1	8. Michigan	9,295,297	8. Georgia	18.6
D.C.	606,900	-4.9	9. New Jer.	7,730,188	9. Utah	17.9
Florida	12,937,926	32.7	10. N.Carolina	6,628,637	10. Washington	17.8
Georgia	6,478,216	18.6	11. Georgia	6,478,216	11. New Mex.	16.2
Hawaii	1,108,229	14.9	12. Virginia	6,187,358	12. Virginia	15.7
Idaho	1,006,749	6.6	13. Mass.	6,016,425	13. Hawaii	14.9
Illinois	11,430,602	0.0	14. Indiana	5,544,159	14. Colorado	14.0
Indiana	5,544,159	1.0	15. Missouri	5,117,073	15. Maryland	13.4
Iowa	2,776,755	-4.7	16. Wisconsin	4,891,769	16. N.Carolina	12.7
Kansas	2,477,574	4.8	17. Tennessee	4,877,185	17. Delaware	12.1
Kentucky	3,685,296	0.7	18. Washington	4,866,692	18. S.Carolina	11.7
Louisiana	4,219,973	0.3	19. Maryland	4,781,468	19. Vermont	10.0
Maine	1,227,928	9.1	20. Minnesota	4,375,099	20. Maine	9.1
Maryland	4,781,468	13.4	21. Louisiana	4,219,973	21. Oregon	7.9
Mass.	6,016,425	4.9	22. Alabama	4,040,587	22. Minnesota	7.3
Michigan	9,295,297	0.4	23. Kentucky	3,685,296	23. Idaho	6.6
Minnesota	4,375,099	7.3	24. Arizona	3,665,228	24. Tennessee	6.2
Mississippi	2,573,216	2.1	25. S.Carolina	3,486,703	25. Rhode Isl.	5.9
Missouri	5,117,073	4.1	26. Colorado	3,294,394	26. Connecticut	5.8
Montana	799,065	1.6	27. Connecticut	3,287,116	27. New Jer.	5.0
Nebraska	1,578,385	0.5	28. Oklahoma	3,145,585	28. Mass.	4.9
Nevada	1,201,833	50.1	29. Oregon	2,842,321	29. Kansas	4.8
New Hamp.	1,109,252	20.5	30. Iowa	2,776,755	30. Missouri	4.1
New Jer.	7,730,188	5.0	31. Mississippi	2,573,216	31. Oklahoma	4.0
New Mex.	1,515,069	16.2	32. Kansas	2,477,574	32. Wisconsin	4.0
New York	17,990,455	2.5	33. Arkansas	2,350,725	33. Alabama	3.8
N.Carolina	6,628,637	12.7	34. W.Virginia	1,793,477	34. Arkansas	2.8
N.Dakota	638,800	-2.1	35. Utah	1,722,850	35. New York	2.5
Ohio	10,847,115	0.5	36. Nebraska	1,578,385	36. Mississippi	2.1
Oklahoma	3,145,585	4.0	37. New Mex.	1,515,069	37. Montana	1.6
Oregon	2,842,321	7.9	38. Maine	1,227,928	38. Indiana	1.0
Penn.	11,881,643	0.1	39. Nevada	1,201,833	39. S.Dakota	0.8
Rhode Isl.	1,003,464	5.9	40. New Hamp.	1,109,252	40. Kentucky	0.7
S.Carolina	3,486,703	11.7	41. Hawaii	1,108,229	41. Nebraska	0.5
S.Dakota	696,004	0.8	42. Idaho	1,006,749	42. Ohio	0.5
Tennessee	4,877,185	6.2	43. Rhode Isl.	1,003,464	43. Michigan	0.4
Texas	16,986,510	19.4	44. Montana	799,065	44. Louisiana	0.3
Utah	1,722,850	17.9	45. S.Dakota	696,004	45. Penn.	0.1
Vermont	562,758	10.0	46. Delaware	666,168	46. Illinois	0.0
Virginia	6,187,358	15.7	47. N.Dakota	638,800	47. N.Dakota	-2.1
Washington	4,866,692	17.8	48. D.C.	606,900	48. Wyoming	-3.4
W.Virginia	1,793,477	-8.0	49. Vermont	562,758	49. Iowa	-4.7
Wisconsin	4,891,769	4.0	50. Alaska	550,043	50. D.C.	-4.9
Wyoming	453,588	-3.4	51. Wyoming	453,588	51. W.Virginia	-8.0

Figure 3-1 shows population growth in Alabama compared to the nation from 1900 through 2000. The format is explained on pages 2 and 18. Alabama grew more slowly than the nation in every decade from 1900 through 1970 (ratios less than 1.00), as the actual population line fell steadily farther below the normalized line. Alabama grew more rapidly than the nation only in the 1970s. It is projected to match the national rate in the 1990s and then fall behind again in the first half of the next century. By 2000 the actual line will be 32 percent below the normalized line, meaning that Alabama's growth ratio was 32 percent of that of the nation from 1900 through 2000.

Alabama demonstrates how states of even moderate size tend to stay in the same place in the rankings over long periods of time due to population momentum. Alabama was the 18th largest state in the nation in 1900, with a population of 1.8 million (Table 3-2). In spite of being only 33rd in growth ratio from 1900 through 1950 (Table 3-3), Alabama moved up to 17th place in the 1950 population rankings. This was because the states close to it in the rankings did not exceed its growth by a large enough factor to surpass it in population. California moved past Alabama, but Alabama passed Kentucky and Iowa, both of which had very slow growth and moved down the list. Alabama thus had a net gain of one place in the rankings from 1900 through 1950.

Momentum cannot overcome slow growth indefinitely, and with Alabama staying at 33rd in growth from 1950 through 2000, it will be 21st on the population ranking list in 2000, a drop of four places from 1950. But by staying reasonably close to the national growth rate in the first half of the next century, Alabama will be still be 22nd in 2050 (Table 5-2), a drop of only one place from 2000.

Although it is in the Sunbelt, Alabama's growth ratio was 20 percent below that of the nation from 1950 through 2000. Alabama has the disadvantage of being located next to Georgia to the east and Florida to the south. These are rapidly growing states with high capital investment already in place to attract jobs and thus population. Alabama is not a target for immigrants (they prefer Florida to the south and Texas to the west), and this also limits its population growth.

Alabama's largest city, Birmingham, fell 8.0 percent in population in the 1980s, ending at 265,347 in 1990, which was 6.6 percent of the population of the state. The Birmingham metropolitan area grew by 3.0 percent to 840,140 in 1990, representing 20.8 percent of the state's population. But the area grew less than the state's rate of 3.8 percent for the decade, another sign that Alabama is a low-growth state.

Alabama

Figure 3-1. Alabama Population (in Millions)

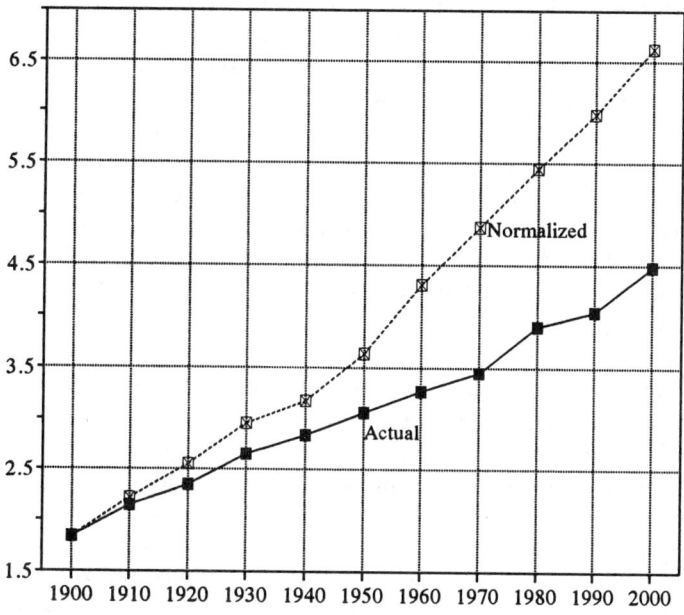

Year	Population	Growth Rate	U.S. Rate	Ratio
1900	1,828,697	--	--	--
1910	2,138,093	16.9%	21.0%	0.80
1920	2,348,174	9.8%	15.0%	0.66
1930	2,646,248	12.7%	16.2%	0.78
1940	2,832,961	7.1%	7.3%	0.97
1950	3,061,743	8.1%	14.5%	0.56
1960	3,266,740	6.7%	18.5%	0.36
1970	3,444,354	5.4%	13.4%	0.41
1980	3,894,025	13.1%	11.4%	1.14
1990	4,040,587	3.8%	9.8%	0.38
2000	4,485,000	11.0%	11.1%	0.99

Figure 3-2 shows population growth in Alaska compared to the nation from 1900 through 2000. The format is explained on pages 2 and 18. Census data were recorded for Alaska starting in 1880, even though it did not become a state until 1959. Alaska grew more slowly than the nation from 1900 through 1930 (it lost population in the 1920s, as shown by the negative ratio), but it grew three times as fast as the nation in the 1930s and has grown much more rapidly in every decade since. Alaska had a small initial population, and thus the addition of relatively few people could produce a high growth rate. But Alaska maintained a high growth rate even as its population increased. In 1990 Alaska had the second highest growth rate in the nation at 36.9 percent (Table 3-1), even though its population in 1980 was its highest ever.

Alaska ranked 23rd on the growth list from 1900 through 1950 (Table 3-3), and the fact that the actual line was barely above the normalized line by 1950 means that Alaska barely grew more rapidly than the nation over that period. But Alaska was 4th on the growth list from 1950 through 2000, with a growth ratio that was nearly three times as high as that of the nation. Alaska's high growth rates are due to its being perceived as a place offering a new beginning. That perception helped to bring people west early in the century, and not surprisingly Alaska's unofficial nickname is "The Last Frontier."

Alaska is a good example of the other side of the coin of population momentum. In spite of its outstanding growth rates, Alaska has moved very slowly up the population ranking list. Even a high growth rate on a small population takes a long time to produce a large population. Alaska was just ahead of Nevada in 1900 (Table 3-2) and then fell to last in 1950 because Nevada led the nation in growth rate during the century and went ahead of Alaska. By 1990 Alaska passed Wyoming and moved out of last place. In 2000 Alaska is projected to move up three places to 47th, a good jump for just one decade. It will take another fifty years, however, for Alaska to move up to 45th, even though it will continue to grow more rapidly than the nation.

Alaska's largest city is Anchorage, a city with a respectable population even for a state much more populous than Alaska. Anchorage's population jumped by 30 percent in the 1980s, reaching a total of 226,338 in 1990, which represented 41 percent of the population of the state. The metropolitan area of Anchorage is not greatly different from the city itself, because the city has a huge area of 1732 square miles, almost four times the size of Los Angeles. It is a city with a physical size that properly fits the state.

Figure 3-2. Alaska Population (in Millions)

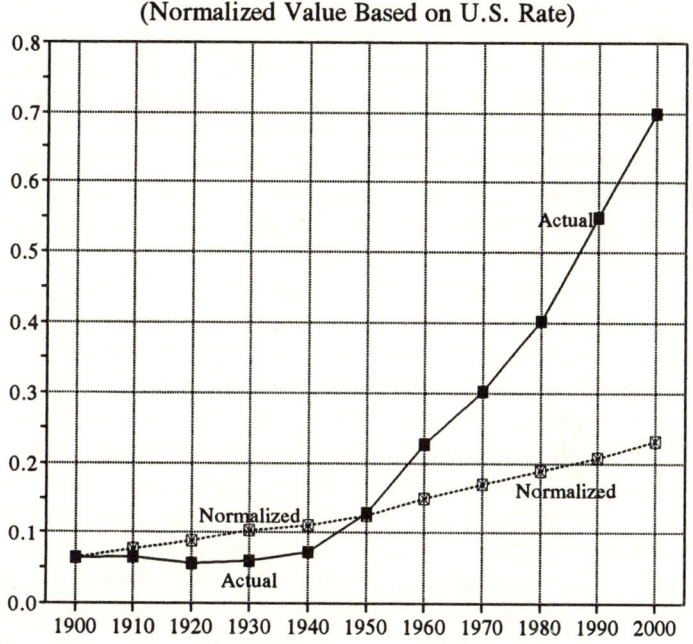

(Normalized Value Based on U.S. Rate)

Year	Population	Growth Rate	U.S. Rate	Ratio
1900	63,592	--	--	--
1910	64,356	1.2%	21.0%	0.06
1920	55,036	-14.5%	15.0%	-0.97
1930	59,278	7.7%	16.2%	0.48
1940	72,524	22.3%	7.3%	3.07
1950	128,643	77.4%	14.5%	5.34
1960	226,167	75.8%	18.5%	4.10
1970	302,583	33.8%	13.4%	2.53
1980	401,851	32.8%	11.4%	2.87
1990	550,043	36.9%	9.8%	3.77
2000	699,000	27.1%	11.1%	2.45

Figure 3-3 shows population growth in Arizona compared to the nation from 1900 through 2000. The format is explained on pages 2 and 18. Arizona grew at a rapid rate even before becoming a state in 1912. In the 1900-1910 decade, its growth rate was three times higher than the national growth rate (ratio of 3.15). It has maintained its dramatic growth rate through the century. Table 3-3 shows that Arizona ranks 2nd to California in growth ratio from 1900 through 1950, and 2nd to Nevada both from 1950 through 2000 and from 1900 through 2000. But Arizona started with a population almost three times as large as that of Nevada in 1900. From 1900 through 2000 Arizona will grow more than ten times as fast as the nation.

In 1900 Arizona ranked 48th in population (Table 3-2). It moved to 38th in 1950, 24th in 1990, and it will be 23rd in 2000. Arizona's gain of fifteen positions in the population rankings from 1950 through 2000 (Table 3-4) is just behind Florida's gain of sixteen for the largest increase in the nation over that period. Arizona also trails only Florida for the largest increase during the century, with Florida moving twenty-nine places up the rankings ladder while Arizona moved up twenty-five.

In the first half of the next century Arizona will continue to grow more rapidly than the nation. By 2050 Arizona will be the 14th largest state in the nation in population (Table 5-1). By then Arizona will have 7.6 million people and will be larger in population than such states as Maryland, Tennessee, Missouri, Massachusetts, and Indiana, all of which Arizona will have trailed in 2000. Arizona has the prime combination of high job creation rates and fine climate that has propelled the high-growth Sunbelt states to the top of the nation in population and influence. It is a target state for immigrants (legal and illegal), and this will continue to fuel its growth into the next century.

Arizona's largest city is Phoenix, which has the highest growth rate of the twenty-four cities shown in Part IV for all periods measured in the book (1900-1950, 1950-2000, and 1900-2000). Arizona had a very high growth rate, as noted above, but Phoenix grew six times as fast as the state during the century. It is a nearly perfect match of city and state in a high-growth environment. Phoenix grew by 24.5 percent in the 1980s. This gave it a population of 983,403 in 1990, making it the ninth largest city in the nation. Phoenix held 27 percent of the population of the state in 1990. But the Phoenix metropolitan area, which includes the city of Mesa, had over 2.2 million people in 1990. This was a huge 61 percent of the state's population, confirming the tight tie between the growth of the state and the growth of the city.

Arizona

Figure 3-3. Arizona Population (in Millions)

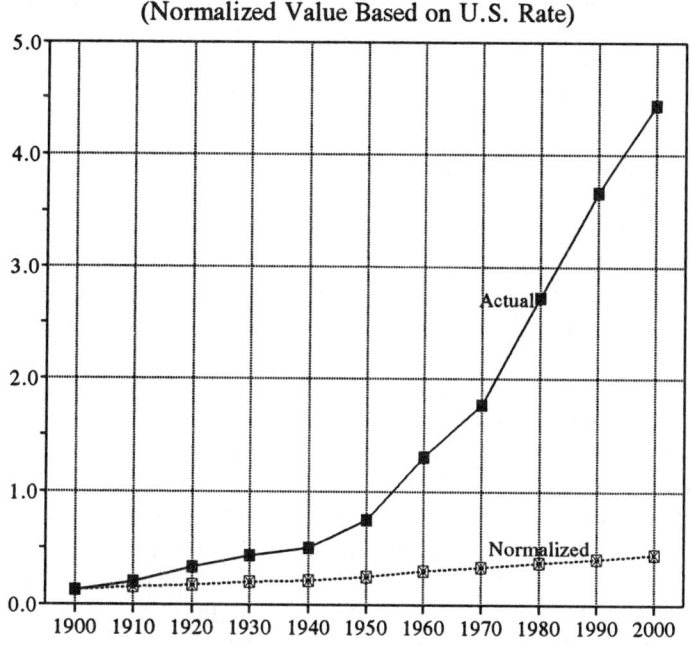

Year	Population	Growth Rate	U.S. Rate	Ratio
1900	122,931	--	--	--
1910	204,354	66.2%	21.0%	3.15
1920	334,162	63.5%	15.0%	4.25
1930	435,573	30.3%	16.2%	1.87
1940	499,261	14.6%	7.3%	2.01
1950	749,587	50.1%	14.5%	3.46
1960	1,302,161	73.7%	18.5%	3.98
1970	1,775,399	36.3%	13.4%	2.72
1980	2,716,546	53.0%	11.4%	4.64
1990	3,665,228	34.9%	9.8%	3.57
2000	4,437,000	21.1%	11.1%	1.90

Figure 3-4 shows population growth in Arkansas compared to the nation from 1900 through 2000. The format is explained on pages 2 and 18. Arkansas grew more slowly than the nation in every decade from 1900 through 1970, as shown by the string of ratios under 1.00 and the fact that the actual line always trailed the normalized line. Arkansas lost population in the 1940s and 1950s (negative ratios). As a result, its population in 1960 was lower than it was in 1930 and barely higher than it was in 1920. There was an increase in the 1960s, but the growth rate was still below that of the nation. Arkansas had a spurt in growth in the 1970s, as the ratio climbed over 1.00 for the first and only decade in the century. This was a result of the population outflow from the Northeast and Central regions that began in the 1970s, as described in the Introduction. However, Arkansas grew much more slowly than the nation in the 1980s, and it is projected to grow more slowly than the nation in the 1990s and on into the next century.

Arkansas was 25th on the population list in 1900 (Table 3-2), but it fell to 30th in 1950 because it was only 42nd on the growth ratio list from 1900 through 1950 (Table 3-3). Arkansas will fall to 33rd on the population ranking list in 2000. It will be only 40th on the growth ratio ranking list from 1950 through 2000, just barely better than it was from 1900 through 1950. In 2050 (Table 5-1), Arkansas is projected to rank 32nd in population, one place better than in 2000. Arkansas will be growing more slowly than the nation after 2000, but some states near it on the ranking list will grow even more slowly.

Arkansas is a slow-growth Sunbelt state because it has a marginal climate for such a state, and it currently has a very low job creation rate. It is landlocked in the middle of the six low-growth Sunbelt states and is not likely to attract the capital investment necessary to make it a higher growth state. This is especially true with a high-growth dynamo like Texas on its southwest border offering a preferred place for investment in the immediate area.

The largest city by far in Arkansas is Little Rock, which increased by 10.9 percent in population in the 1980s, reaching 175,727 in 1990, which was 7.5 percent of the population of the state. The third most populous city in Arkansas in 1990 was North Little Rock, with 61,829 people. This concentration of population around Little Rock meant that the Little Rock metropolitan area had 513,117 people in 1990, 22 percent of the population of the state. But the metropolitan area increased in population by only 8.1 percent in the 1980s, nearly three percentage points less than the growth rate for the city itself.

Arkansas

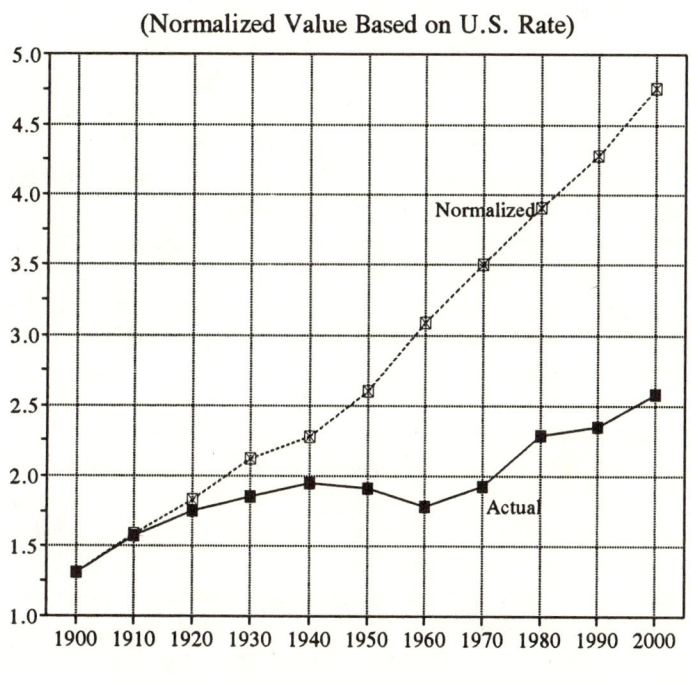

Figure 3-4. Arkansas Population (in Millions)

Year	Population	Growth Rate	U.S. Rate	Ratio
1900	1,311,564	--	--	--
1910	1,574,449	20.0%	21.0%	0.95
1920	1,752,204	11.3%	15.0%	0.75
1930	1,854,482	5.8%	16.2%	0.36
1940	1,949,387	5.1%	7.3%	0.70
1950	1,909,511	-2.0%	14.5%	-0.14
1960	1,786,272	-6.5%	18.5%	-0.35
1970	1,923,322	7.7%	13.4%	0.57
1980	2,286,357	18.9%	11.4%	1.65
1990	2,350,725	2.8%	9.8%	0.29
2000	2,578,000	9.7%	11.1%	0.87

Figure 3-5 shows population growth in California compared to the nation from 1900 through 2000. The format is explained on pages 2 and 18. California is the "Golden State" of growth in terms of both growth rate and population added. It had a growth rate of 60.1 percent in the 1900-1910 decade, 2.86 times the national rate. It continued growing at double-digit rates through the century, even as its population became the largest in the nation. By 2000 California will have added over 33 million people since 1900, 17 percent of the total added by the nation. From 1950 through 2000 California will provide over 19 percent of the total population increase in the nation. It will have grown six times as fast as the nation from 1900 through 2000 (Table 3-3), even though its population base in 1900 was a substantial 1.5 million.

California now dominates the nation in the way New York City did before 1950, when the city was the focus of financial and cultural activities. By 2010 California will be bigger than the next two states combined, a first in the nation's history. It is projected to increase its lead through 2050. California has been the prime influence in the nation for decades in trends (and fads), and it can claim to be a major player in the electronics, service, and information industries that drive the country. It is also the prime agricultural force, one of the many benefits of its climate. California has what is probably the culture of the future, with an amalgam of Hispanic, Asian, and other immigrants making "minorities" a majority. Its problems in managing its huge growth will become the problems of all growing states.

California already has a population as large as many nations in the world, and it is projected to surpass 70 million by 2050 (Table 5-1). As high as it is, this population estimate could be low. A lawsuit regarding the method of taking the census resulted in a recent court decision that, if implemented, would add a million to California's 1990 total. At a minimum the lawsuit should result in a new way of counting minorities that increases the count in states like California. It seems likely that California's future growth will be as unprecedented as its past.

The largest city in California is Los Angeles, the nation's second largest city at 3,485,557 in 1990. The Los Angeles metropolitan area had 14.5 million people in 1990, 49 percent of the population in the state. As immigrants (legal and illegal) pour into the area, it will become the largest in the nation, passing the New York City metropolitan area in the first half of the next century. California then will have the largest metropolitan area to go with the highest number of large cities (Los Angeles, San Diego, San Jose, and San Francisco).

California

Figure 3-5. California Population (in Millions)

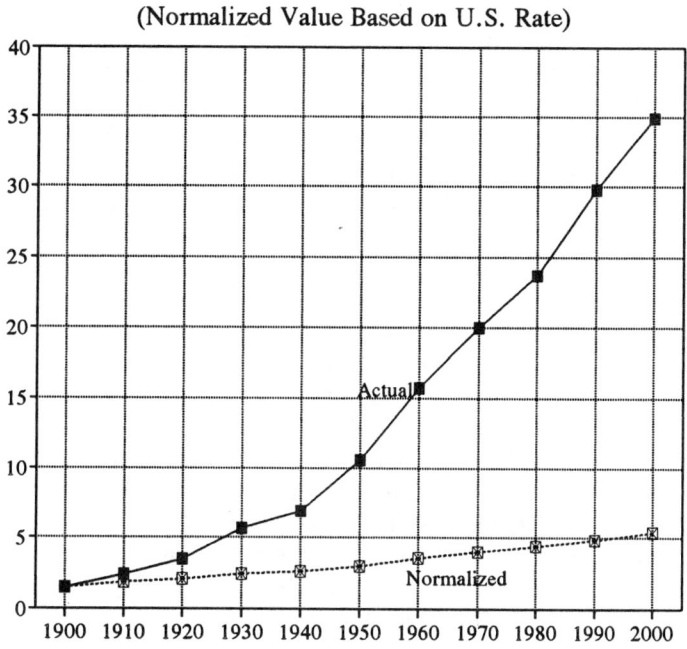

Year	Population	Growth Rate	U.S. Rate	Ratio
1900	1,485,053	--	--	--
1910	2,377,549	60.1%	21.0%	2.86
1920	3,426,861	44.1%	15.0%	2.95
1930	5,677,251	65.7%	16.2%	4.05
1940	6,907,387	21.7%	7.3%	2.98
1950	10,586,223	53.3%	14.5%	3.67
1960	15,717,204	48.5%	18.5%	2.62
1970	19,971,069	27.1%	13.4%	2.02
1980	23,667,764	18.5%	11.4%	1.62
1990	29,760,021	25.7%	9.8%	2.63
2000	34,888,000	17.2%	11.1%	1.56

Figure 3-6 shows population growth in Colorado compared to the nation from 1900 through 2000. The format is explained on pages 2 and 18. Colorado grew at nearly the same rate as the nation from 1910 through 1950. Initially, it grew 2.29 times as fast as the nation in the 1900-1910 decade. But in three of the four decades after 1910 the ratio was only a little greater than 1.00, and it was much lower in the 1920s. By 1950 the actual line was above the normalized line by little more than it was in 1910. This means that Colorado matched the nation's growth from 1910 through 1950. But Colorado benefited greatly from the population redistribution that began in the United States after 1950.

Colorado grew more rapidly than the nation in every decade from 1950 through 2000, with a big surge in the 1970s. Colorado was a favorite target of the emigration from the Northeast and Central regions in the 1970s. From 1950 through 2000, Colorado grew 68 percent more rapidly than the nation, putting it in 7th place on the growth ratio list (Table 3-3). Colorado fell from 32nd place in 1900 to 34th place in 1950 on the population ranking list (Table 3-2), then moved up to 26th in 1990 (Table 3-1). It will be 24th by 2000. This is an improvement of ten places from 1950 through 2000 (Table 3-4). Only three states moved farther up the ranking list during that period.

Energy exploration and development was a principal reason for Colorado's growth after 1950, but as the search for energy sources slowed after the big slide in oil prices in the 1980s, growth also slowed in Colorado. Following the good growth shown in the 1990s, Colorado is projected to grow at the same rate as the nation in the first half of the next century. But by 2050 Colorado is projected to fall one place on the population ranking list, making it 25th in 2050 (Table 5-2).

Colorado borders the Sunbelt states. It has lots of sunshine (it claims 310 sunny days per year), but its average temperature is lower than that of the Sunbelt states due to the winters that provide the skiing for which it is famous. Colorado has been known for its managed growth (or antigrowth) legislation. This is one reason that Colorado is not projected to grow more rapidly than the nation in the next century.

Denver is Colorado's largest city. It fell 5.1 percent in the 1980s to 467,610 in 1990. But the Denver metropolitan area grew by 13.7 percent in the 1980s, meaning the city loss was just movement to the suburbs. Denver had 14 percent of the state's population in 1990, but the metropolitan area, with 2.0 million people, held 60 percent. With the next biggest city, Colorado Springs, only seventy miles away, Colorado's population is heavily concentrated in one area.

Colorado

Figure 3-6. Colorado Population (in Millions)

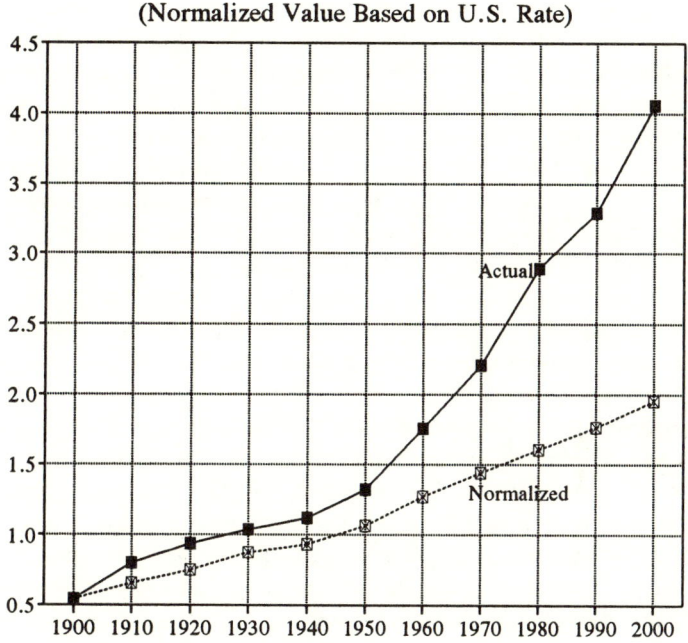

(Normalized Value Based on U.S. Rate)

Year	Population	Growth Rate	U.S. Rate	Ratio
1900	539,700	--	--	--
1910	799,024	48.0%	21.0%	2.29
1920	939,629	17.6%	15.0%	1.18
1930	1,035,791	10.2%	16.2%	0.63
1940	1,123,296	8.4%	7.3%	1.16
1950	1,325,089	18.0%	14.5%	1.24
1960	1,753,947	32.4%	18.5%	1.75
1970	2,209,596	26.0%	13.4%	1.94
1980	2,889,735	30.8%	11.4%	2.69
1990	3,294,394	14.0%	9.8%	1.43
2000	4,059,000	23.2%	11.1%	2.10

Figure 3-7 shows population growth in Connecticut compared to the nation from 1900 through 2000. The format is explained on pages 2 and 18. Connecticut will grow at the same rate as the nation from 1900 through 2000, as the actual population line rejoins the normalized line after spending most of the century ahead. The state reached its peak in growth in 1970, when the actual line led by 26 percent and the population passed 3 million, a 50 percent increase from 1950. Growth stopped in the 1970s with the start of the population outflow from the Northeast, as described in the Introduction. The state is projected to lose population in the 1990s for the first time in the century.

Connecticut benefited from the stagnation of the population of New York City from 1950 through 1970. Many people leaving the city moved across the state border to Connecticut for better schools and lower taxes, while staying within a reasonable commute of their jobs in the New York area. But the huge outflow from New York City in the 1970s did not help Connecticut's population growth in that decade. The state added only 75,347 people during the 1970s, its lowest increase in the century to that date, even though it had more people in 1970 than ever before. People left the entire region in the 1970s.

Connecticut went from 29th in population in 1900 to 28th in 1950, and will go back to 29th in 2000 (Table 3-2). It was 19th on the growth list from 1900 through 1950, but it will fall to 25th from 1950 through 2000 (Table 3-3) due to its population loss in the 1990s. Connecticut is projected to grow more slowly than the nation after 2000, but it should remain 29th on the population ranking list in 2050 (Table 5-1). None of the states behind it is growing fast enough to catch it by then.

Connecticut was a high growth state until the 1970s, but it turned into a very slow growth state with the population shifts than began in that decade. It is far from the Sunbelt and is not a target for immigrants, who prefer New York City and its immediate area due to the support groups already existing there. These factors will keep Connecticut a slow-growth state in the future.

The largest city in Connecticut is Bridgeport, which declined slightly in the 1980s to 141,686 in 1990. This left it barely ahead of Hartford at 139,739 and a little farther ahead of New Haven at 130,474. These cities each held about 4 percent of the state's population in 1990. With southern Connecticut included in the New York City metropolitan area, the major metropolitan area in the state is centered on Hartford. The Hartford area had a little under 1.2 million people in 1990, about 35 percent of the population of the state.

Figure 3-7. Connecticut Population (in Millions)

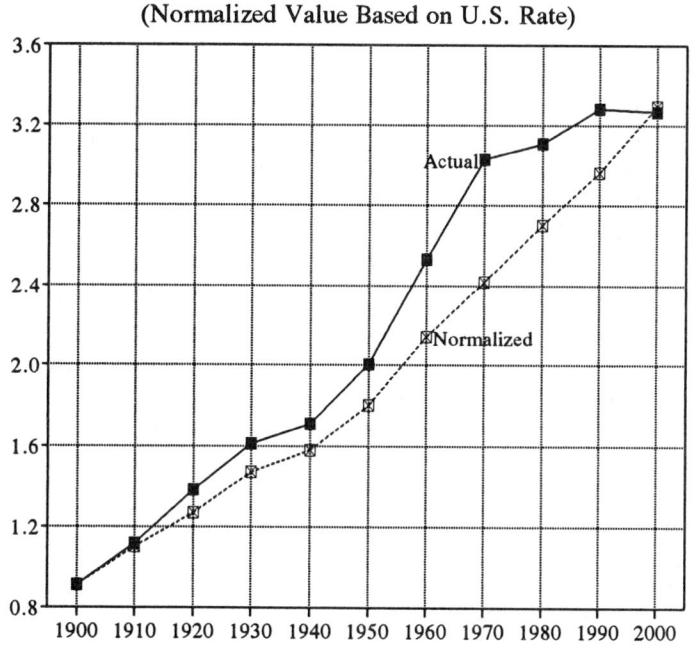

(Normalized Value Based on U.S. Rate)

Year	Population	Growth Rate	U.S. Rate	Ratio
1900	908,420	--	--	--
1910	1,114,756	22.7%	21.0%	1.08
1920	1,380,631	23.9%	15.0%	1.59
1930	1,606,903	16.4%	16.2%	1.01
1940	1,709,242	6.4%	7.3%	0.88
1950	2,007,280	17.4%	14.5%	1.20
1960	2,535,234	26.3%	18.5%	1.42
1970	3,032,217	19.6%	13.4%	1.47
1980	3,107,564	2.5%	11.4%	0.22
1990	3,287,116	5.8%	9.8%	0.59
2000	3,271,000	-0.5%	11.1%	-0.04

Figure 3-8 shows population growth in Delaware compared to the nation from 1900 through 2000. The format is explained on pages 2 and 18. Delaware grew more slowly than the nation from 1900 through 1930, as shown by the ratios during that period staying well below 1.00 and the actual line falling steadily below the normalized line. But the ratios went over 1.00 from 1930 through 1970 as Delaware grew faster than the nation. The actual line overtook the normalized line by 1960 and moved well ahead by 1970. The population outflow from the Northeast that began in the 1970s, as described in the Introduction, temporarily slowed Delaware's growth, but it rebounded in the 1980s and 1990s, with growth rates well above those of the nation.

Delaware was 12th on the growth ratio list from 1950 through 2000 (Table 3-3) after being only 31st from 1900 through 1950, due to its bad start from 1900 through 1930. Delaware's actual population will be 11 percent above the normalized line in 2000, meaning that Delaware will grow 11 percent more rapidly than the nation from 1900 through 2000. But in spite of its good growth after 1930, Delaware fell on the population ranking list because most of the small states that were behind it on the list in 1900 grew at a faster pace. Delaware was 45th in population in 1900 (Table 3-2), but it fell to 48th in 1950. It will be 46th in 2000 thanks to its good growth from 1950 through 2000. It is projected to grow more slowly than the nation after 2000, but it will grow rapidly enough to stay in 46th place in 2050 (Table 5-2).

Delaware has benefited from the population outflow of its massive neighbor, Pennsylvania. It is located close enough to the Philadelphia area for people to move across the state border while staying within commuting range of their jobs. But because of its small population base, its location outside the Sunbelt, and the fact that it is not a target for immigrants, Delaware will remain one of the smallest states indefinitely. Its position of 46th on the projected population ranking list in 2050 will be one place farther back than it was 150 years earlier.

Wilmington is Delaware's major city. It had a population of 71,529 in 1990, a small increase from 1980. But this is less than the 76,508 it had in 1900. Wilmington peaked in 1940 at 112,504, and it lost 36 percent of its population from 1940 through 1990. This is a common story for large cities in the Northeast region, and it made Delaware one of only eight states without a city of at least 100,000. As small as it is, Wilmington had 11 percent of the population of the state in 1990. The metropolitan area, of course, had more, but Wilmington is included in the Philadelphia metropolitan area by the Bureau of the Census.

Figure 3-8. Delaware Population (in Millions)

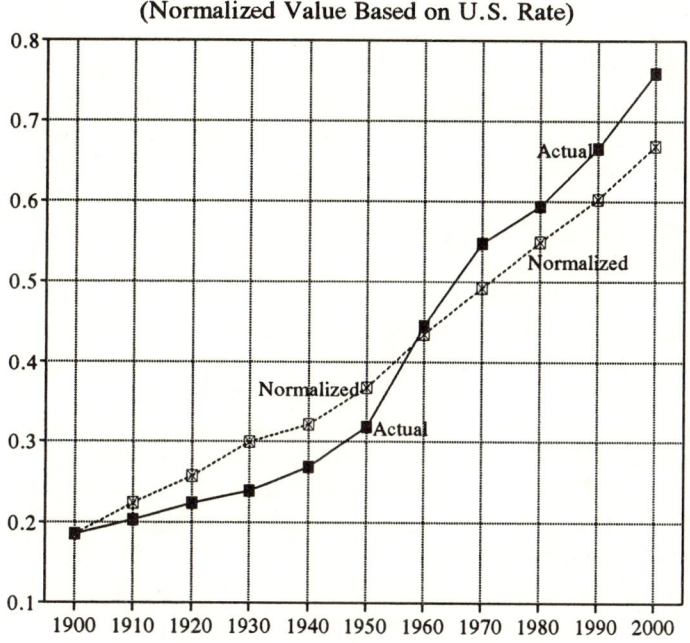

Year	Population	Growth Rate	U.S. Rate	Ratio
1900	184,735	--	--	--
1910	202,322	9.5%	21.0%	0.45
1920	223,003	10.2%	15.0%	0.68
1930	238,380	6.9%	16.2%	0.43
1940	266,505	11.8%	7.3%	1.62
1950	318,085	19.4%	14.5%	1.33
1960	446,292	40.3%	18.5%	2.18
1970	548,104	22.8%	13.4%	1.71
1980	594,338	8.4%	11.4%	0.74
1990	666,168	12.1%	9.8%	1.23
2000	759,000	13.9%	11.1%	1.26

Figure 3-9 shows population growth in the District of Columbia compared to the nation from 1900 through 2000. The format is explained on pages 2 and 18. The District is included as a "state" in this book because the District is a separate entity in the census and has three electoral votes in presidential elections. The population totals and rankings for the fifty states agree with the census only when the District is included. In that sense, when we talk about rankings, we are talking about "fifty-one states." The District was given the vote in presidential elections in 1964, but it has been part of the census since 1800. It is in both the State and City parts of the book for consistency.

The District's history is similar to that of most eastern cities. It grew more rapidly than the nation from 1900 through 1950, with sharp increases in the 1930s and 1940s as the government grew rapidly to fight the depression and World War II. The population of the District increased by 65 percent from 1930 through 1950 (it grew five times as fast as the nation in the 1930s), and by 1950 the actual line was 45 percent above the normalized line. This means that the District grew 45 percent faster than the nation from 1900 through 1950. But 1950 was the peak, as it was for twelve of the fifteen cities that were the fifteen biggest in the nation in 1900.

The government did not shrink after 1950, but the District did, and for the same reasons as the other cities. As described in the Introduction, an influx of minorities, school integration, and high welfare costs drove people from the old cities of the Northeast and Central regions in large numbers after 1950. The District lost population in every census after 1950 (negative ratios). It was 11th on the growth list from 1900 through 1950 (Table 3-3), but it was last from 1950 through 2000. It went from 41st on the population ranking list in 1900 to 36th in 1950 (Table 3-2). It will fall to 50th in 2000, ahead of only Wyoming, after being larger than fifteen states in 1950. In the 1990 census (Table 3-1), the District was 50th on the growth list, and its loss of 4.9 percent of its population was exceeded only by West Virginia, with an 8.0 percent loss.

By 2000 the District will have 265,178 fewer people than it had at its peak in 1950, a loss of 33 percent. It is projected to start gaining population again in the next century, but its growth rate will still be low and it will still be next to last in population in 2050 (Table 5-2). The surrounding states of Maryland and Virginia will continue to be the main beneficiaries of the combined growth of government workers and the hordes of lobbyists that call on them.

District of Columbia

Figure 3-9. District of Columbia Pop. (in Millions)

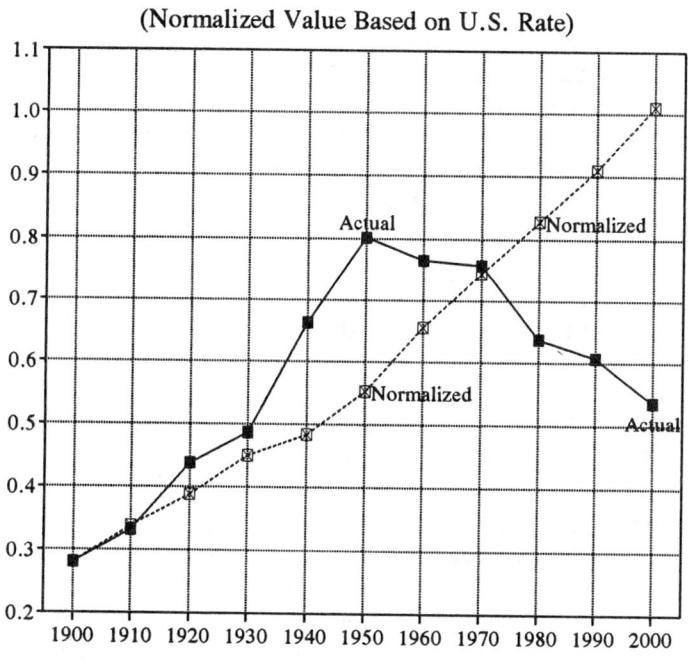

Year	Population	Growth Rate	U.S. Rate	Ratio
1900	278,718	--	--	--
1910	331,069	18.8%	21.0%	0.89
1920	437,571	32.2%	15.0%	2.15
1930	486,869	11.3%	16.2%	0.70
1940	663,091	36.2%	7.3%	4.98
1950	802,178	21.0%	14.5%	1.45
1960	763,956	-4.8%	18.5%	-0.26
1970	756,668	-1.0%	13.4%	-0.07
1980	638,432	-15.6%	11.4%	-1.37
1990	606,900	-4.9%	9.8%	-0.50
2000	537,000	-11.5%	11.1%	-1.04

Figure 3-10 shows population growth in Florida compared to the nation from 1900 through 2000. The format is explained on pages 2 and 18. Florida is one state that can be mentioned in the same breath with California for high growth rates and added population. Florida grew more rapidly than the nation in every decade from 1900 through 2000, with ratios from 1.66 to 4.25 (meaning that Florida grew from 1.66 to 4.25 times faster than the nation), and it continues to grow rapidly even as its population increases. Florida was 3rd on the growth list behind California and Arizona from 1900 through 1950 (Table 3-3), 3rd behind Nevada and Arizona from 1950 through 2000, and 3rd overall from 1900 through 2000 (also behind Nevada and Arizona).

This growth rate moved Florida from 33rd on the population ranking list in 1900 (Table 3-2) to 20th in 1950 and to 4th in 2000. The increase of twenty-nine places on the ranking list from 1900 through 2000 is the highest of all the states (Table 3-4). Florida's added population of almost 15 million from 1900 through 2000 is just behind that of Texas, which shows an increase of 17 million during the same period. Both states are far behind California, which increased by over 33 million from 1900 through 2000, but both states are well ahead of New York, which is next in added population at 11 million. No other state is even near double digits in millions of added population.

The Bureau of the Census projects a growth rate of 18.4 percent in the 1990s for Florida. However, a lawsuit concerning the method of taking the census could increase the rate. With a continued inflow of immigrants (legal and illegal) and retirees who come to join the support systems already existing in Florida, and with Florida's attraction as a Sunbelt state with a strong economy, the state may do better than the 15.3 million projected for 2000. Florida is projected also to grow well in the next century, and by 2050 its population should exceed 25 million (Table 5-1). Florida will pass New York by 2020, becoming the 3rd largest state in the nation. It will still hold that position in 2050, when it will be about 6 million people ahead of New York and nearly 80 percent larger than the 5th largest state at that time, Illinois.

Jacksonville is the largest city in Florida. It had 672,971 people in 1990, 88 percent more than second-place Miami at 358,648. But the Miami metropolitan area had 3.2 million people (25 percent of the state's population), the Tampa-St. Petersburg area had 2.1 million, and the Orlando area had 1.2 million. The Jacksonville metropolitan area trailed behind with 0.9 million. These four areas combined had 57 percent of the state's population.

Florida

Figure 3-10. Florida Population (in Millions)

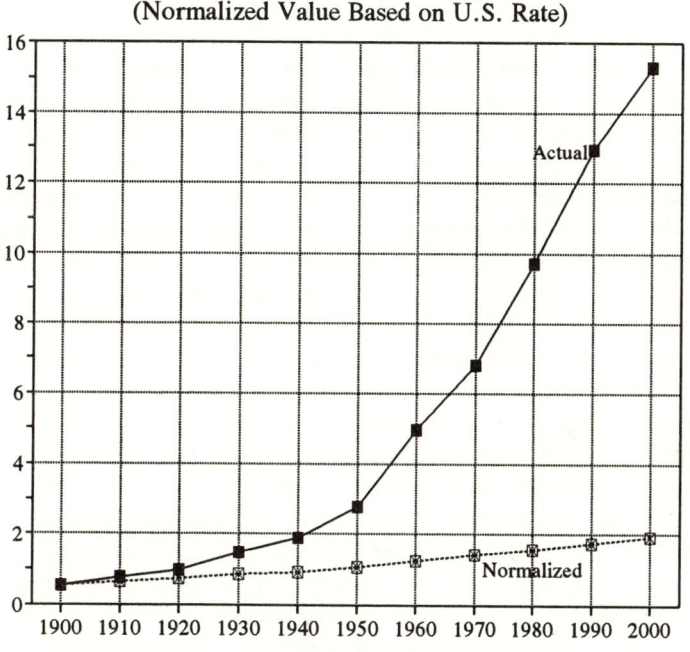

(Normalized Value Based on U.S. Rate)

Year	Population	Growth Rate	U.S. Rate	Ratio
1900	528,542	--	--	--
1910	752,619	42.4%	21.0%	2.02
1920	968,470	28.7%	15.0%	1.92
1930	1,468,211	51.6%	16.2%	3.18
1940	1,897,414	29.2%	7.3%	4.02
1950	2,771,305	46.1%	14.5%	3.18
1960	4,951,560	78.7%	18.5%	4.25
1970	6,791,418	37.2%	13.4%	2.78
1980	9,746,961	43.5%	11.4%	3.81
1990	12,937,926	32.7%	9.8%	3.34
2000	15,313,000	18.4%	11.1%	1.66

Figure 3-11 shows population growth in Georgia compared to the nation from 1900 through 2000. The format is explained on pages 2 and 18. Georgia has two different growth histories. It began the century as the 11th most populous state (Table 3-2), but it grew more slowly than the nation from 1900 through 1920, with ratios of 0.84 and 0.73 in the first two decades. A substantial outflow from the state started in the 1920s as blacks began to migrate north. Georgia barely grew at all in the 1920s, while the nation grew by over 16 percent. The outflow paused during the depression, in the sense that the state's slow growth exceeded that of the nation, but in the next two decades Georgia once again grew more slowly than the nation. By 1960 the actual line was about 25 percent below the normalized line, meaning that Georgia had grown 25 percent more slowly than the nation through 1960.

Georgia ranked 41st on the growth list from 1900 through 1950 (Table 3-3), and it fell to 13th on the population ranking list in 1950. But the dramatic change in the nation's population distribution that began in the 1950s, as described in the Introduction, ultimately created a new phase in Georgia's growth history. Georgia joined with other Sunbelt states in making it easier for new companies to locate in the state and bring jobs with them. Favorable tax and regulatory laws, together with low-cost housing and mild winter weather, began to attract companies from all over the United States to states like Georgia. In the 1960s Georgia had its highest growth rate since the first decade of the century.

The outflow of population from the Northeast and Central areas in the 1970s resulted in the highest decade growth rate in the century for Georgia (19.1 percent), and rates continued high into the 1990s. Georgia was in 15th on the growth ratio list from 1950 through 1990, and will be 10th in total population in 2000. By then Georgia will nearly match the growth rate of the nation for the century, as the actual and normalized lines nearly touch again. Georgia is projected to grow more rapidly than the nation after 2000, and by 2050 it will be 7th on the population ranking list, with 11.7 million people (Table 5-1).

Atlanta is Georgia's largest city. It lost 7.3 percent of its population in the 1980s, falling to 393,929. This was a drop of 20 percent from its 1970 peak. But Atlanta was still more than twice as large as Columbus, the second largest city. The Atlanta metropolitan area had 3.0 million people in 1990, an increase of 33 percent since 1980, showing that the loss in the city was simply movement to the suburbs. The area held 46 percent of the state's population in 1990.

Georgia

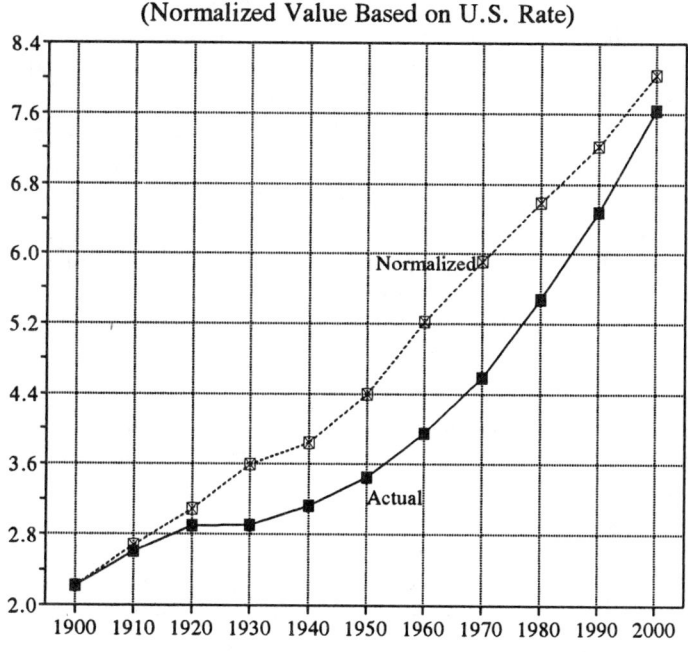

Figure 3-11. Georgia Population (in Millions)

Year	Population	Growth Rate	U.S. Rate	Ratio
1900	2,216,331	--	--	--
1910	2,609,121	17.7%	21.0%	0.84
1920	2,895,832	11.0%	15.0%	0.73
1930	2,908,506	0.4%	16.2%	0.03
1940	3,123,723	7.4%	7.3%	1.02
1950	3,444,578	10.3%	14.5%	0.71
1960	3,943,116	14.5%	18.5%	0.78
1970	4,587,930	16.4%	13.4%	1.22
1980	5,462,982	19.1%	11.4%	1.67
1990	6,478,216	18.6%	9.8%	1.90
2000	7,637,000	17.9%	11.1%	1.62

Figure 3-12 shows population growth in Hawaii compared to the nation from 1900 through 2000. The format is explained on pages 2 and 18. Hawaii has been included in the census since 1900, although it did not become a state until 1959, when it rounded out the total at fifty. Hawaii grew 1.17 times as rapidly as the nation in the 1900-1910 decade, and it never grew that slowly again in the century. Its highest rate was in the 1920s when it grew 43.9 percent, 2.71 times as rapidly as the nation. But it has grown at double-digit rates in every decade, and always much more rapidly than the nation.

Hawaii was 9th on the growth list from 1900 through 1950 (Table 3-3), and it will be 9th again on the list from 1950 through 2000, putting it in 8th place from 1900 through 2000. The combination of a strong tourist industry, the crucial location of Pearl Harbor, and lucrative agricultural production (mainly sugar and pineapple) kept Hawaii growing rapidly. The small population in 1900 made it easier to record high growth rates, but, like most high growth-states, Hawaii continued to grow at a fast pace even as its population increased.

In spite of its high growth rates (Table 3-2), Hawaii moved only from 47th on the population ranking list in 1900 to 46th in 1950. This was due to its small population base. But Hawaii will rank 39th in 2000. This increase of 7 places will make Hawaii 6th in the ranking change list from 1950 through 2000 (Table 3-4). Hawaii will continue to grow much more rapidly than the nation after 2000, but it will move up only two places to 37th on the ranking list by 2050 (Table 5-2). States ahead of it with population momentum will slow Hawaii's gains.

Hawaii is a high-growth Sunbelt state. It offers the same incentives for growth as other such states except for its distance from the mainland. The fact that this distance has not hindered Hawaii's growth is a good example of how the excellent transportation and communication infrastructure in the United States extends 2,000 miles past the mainland. Hawaii is also unique in that its population is over 60 percent Asian or Pacific Islanders. It is the only state in which whites are not a majority of the population. But with the continuing growth of immigration to the United States, other states may follow Hawaii in this respect in the next century.

Honolulu is Hawaii's largest city, and it is ten times larger than the second largest city, Hilo. Honolulu had 365,272 people in 1990 (33 percent of the state's population), but the Honolulu metropolitan area had 836,231 people, over 75 percent of the state's population. As goes Honolulu, so goes Hawaii.

Hawaii

Figure 3-12. Hawaii Population (in Millions)

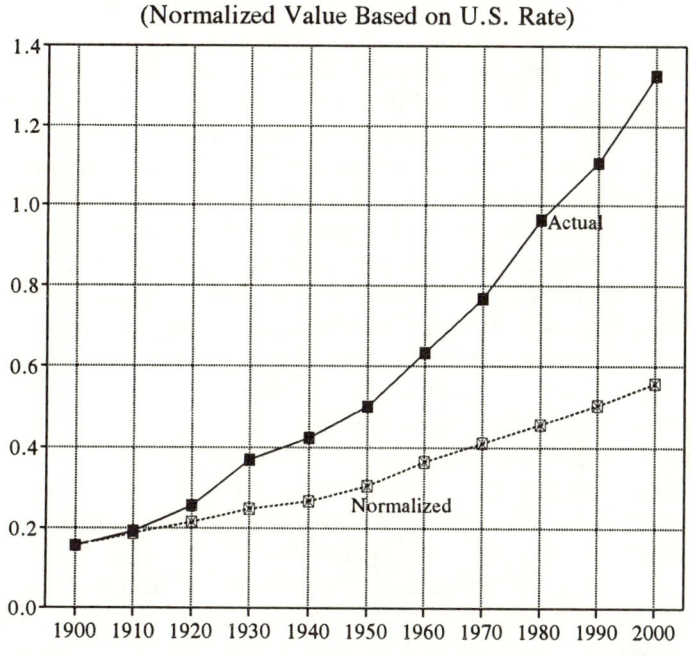

Year	Population	Growth Rate	U.S. Rate	Ratio
1900	154,001	--	--	--
1910	191,874	24.6%	21.0%	1.17
1920	255,881	33.4%	15.0%	2.23
1930	368,300	43.9%	16.2%	2.71
1940	422,770	14.8%	7.3%	2.03
1950	499,794	18.2%	14.5%	1.26
1960	632,772	26.6%	18.5%	1.44
1970	769,913	21.7%	13.4%	1.62
1980	964,691	25.3%	11.4%	2.21
1990	1,108,229	14.9%	9.8%	1.52
2000	1,327,000	19.7%	11.1%	1.78

Figure 3-13 shows population growth in Idaho compared to the nation from 1900 through 2000. The format is explained on pages 2 and 18. Idaho has an unusual boom-and-bust growth history. It grew nearly five times as rapidly as the nation in the 1900-1910 decade (ratio of 4.82), more than doubling in population. It grew more than twice as rapidly as the nation in the 1910-1920 decade, nearly stopped growing in the 1920s, then soared again in the 1930s. This put the actual line about 87 percent above the normalized line by 1940, meaning that Idaho grew 87 percent faster than the nation from 1900 through 1940.

Idaho grew more slowly than the nation in each of the next three decades, with the growth ratio falling off sharply in the 1960s. But the huge outflow of people from the Northeast and Central regions in the 1970s, as described in the Introduction, boosted Idaho as it did so many other states outside those two regions. Idaho grew by 32.4 percent in the 1970s, nearly three times as rapidly as the nation. This put the actual line twice as high as the normalized line, meaning that Idaho had double the national growth ratio from 1900 through 1980.

Idaho's growth slowed greatly in the 1980s, but in the 1990s it is projected to continue its boom-and-bust pattern and grow rapidly again. Idaho was 7th on the growth ratio list from 1900 through 1950 (Table 3-3), but it will fall to 16th from 1950 through 2000, making it 10th overall from 1900 through 2000. Idaho was 46th in population in 1900 (Table 3-2), and it was only 44th in 1950 in spite of its high growth in the first part of the century. It will move four places up the ranking list to 40th in 2000, and it is projected to move up one more place to 39th in 2050 (Table 5-1) as it grows more rapidly than the nation after 2000.

Idaho is another state with good growth that moves only slowly up the ranking list due to its small population base. Although it is far from the Sunbelt and off the immigrant track, Idaho has been helped in recent decades by electronics manufacturers who located in the state to take advantage of its favorable laws, cheap housing, and lack of congestion. The degree to which the state can continue to attract such investment will determine its future growth rates.

The largest city in Idaho is Boise. It had a population of 125,551 in 1990, an increase of 23 percent from 1980. Boise had 12 percent of the population of the state in 1990. The metropolitan area had more, but it was too small to be ranked in the top eighty-five list, which cuts off at 400,000. However, Idaho's population is well distributed along the interstate highways in the south of the state, and there is no great concentration in just one area.

Idaho

Figure 3-13. Idaho Population (in Millions)

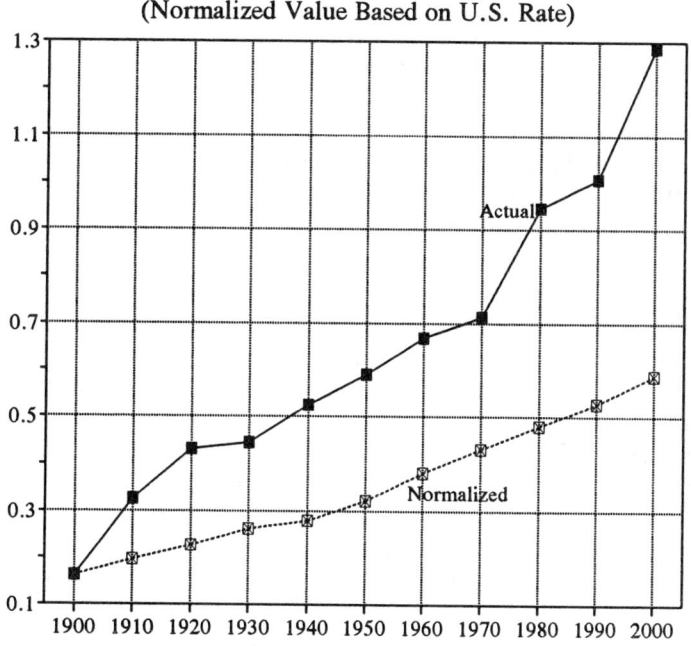

Year	Population	Growth Rate	U.S. Rate	Ratio
1900	161,772	--	--	--
1910	325,594	101.3%	21.0%	4.82
1920	431,866	32.6%	15.0%	2.18
1930	445,032	3.0%	16.2%	0.19
1940	524,873	17.9%	7.3%	2.47
1950	588,637	12.1%	14.5%	0.84
1960	667,191	13.3%	18.5%	0.72
1970	713,015	6.9%	13.4%	0.51
1980	944,127	32.4%	11.4%	2.84
1990	1,006,749	6.6%	9.8%	0.68
2000	1,290,000	28.1%	11.1%	2.54

Figure 3-14 shows population growth in Illinois compared to the nation from 1900 through 2000. The format is explained on pages 2 and 18. Illinois went from moderate growth to low growth to no growth as the century progressed. For the first three decades it tracked the growth of the nation very well, falling behind in the 1900-1910 decade (ratio of 0.81), but catching up in the next decade and then growing more rapidly (ratio of 1.09) in the 1920s. The result was that by 1930 the actual line was slightly below the normalized line, meaning that Illinois had grown slightly more slowly than the nation.

In the depression of the 1930s, Illinois grew only half as rapidly as the nation, and for the next three decades it had ratios in the range of 0.71 to 0.85. This made it a slow-growth state, but one with still steadily increasing population. By 1970 the actual line was about 14 percent below the normalized line, meaning that Illinois had grown about 14 percent more slowly than the nation up to that point. Its growth from 1900 through 1950 was only 29th best in the nation (Table 3-3), but its population ranking dropped just one place from 3rd in 1900 to 4th in 1950 as it was passed by California (Table 3-2).

Growth stopped for Illinois in the 1970s and 1980s, when the entire Central region stopped growing, as described in the Introduction. The crash of the car business and the poor job creation of heavy manufacturing generally cut Illinois's growth rate to 2.9 percent in the 1970s. In the 1980s Illinois added only 3,193 people to its base of 11.4 million, a growth rate of 0.0 percent to the first decimal. Illinois will be 36th in growth from 1950 through 2000, and it will fall to 6th on the population ranking list by 2000 as it is passed by Florida and Texas. Although it will continue to grow very slowly after 2000, by 2050 Illinois is projected to move up one place on the ranking list past Pennsylvania, which will grow even more slowly than Illinois.

Chicago is by far the largest city in Illinois. It had 35 percent of the population of the state in 1900 and 42 percent in 1950. But Chicago fell to 24 percent of the state in 1990, when its population reached 2,783,726. This was down 23 percent from the 1950 peak. The Chicago metropolitan area gained 1.5 percent in the 1980s, passing 8.2 million. The metropolitan area includes parts of Indiana and Wisconsin, and thus it can not be counted as a percentage of the state's population. Since Chicago itself has 24 percent of the state's population, the Chicago metropolitan area within Illinois has easily more than half of the state's population. That is why the area's slow growth played a big role in making Illinois a slow-growth state.

Illinois

Figure 3-14. Illinois Population (in Millions)

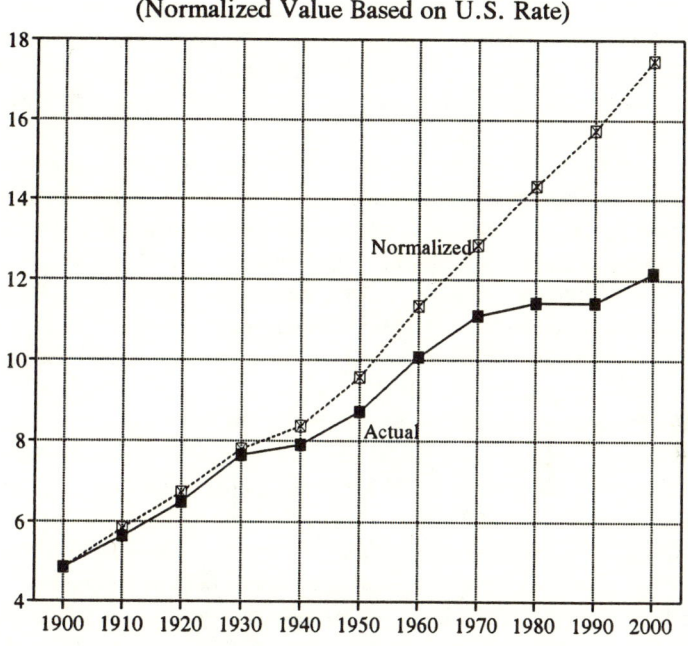

Year	Population	Growth Rate	U.S. Rate	Ratio
1900	4,821,550	--	--	--
1910	5,638,591	16.9%	21.0%	0.81
1920	6,485,280	15.0%	15.0%	1.00
1930	7,630,654	17.7%	16.2%	1.09
1940	7,897,241	3.5%	7.3%	0.48
1950	8,712,176	10.3%	14.5%	0.71
1960	10,081,158	15.7%	18.5%	0.85
1970	11,110,285	10.2%	13.4%	0.76
1980	11,427,409	2.9%	11.4%	0.25
1990	11,430,602	0.0%	9.8%	0.00
2000	12,168,000	6.5%	11.1%	0.58

Figure 3-15 shows population growth in Indiana compared to the nation from 1900 through 2000. The format is explained on pages 2 and 18. Indiana was a slow-growth state for nearly the full century. The ratio was less than 1.00 (meaning that the state grew more slowly than the nation) in all but two decades. The exceptions were the 1940s, when Indiana grew just 2 percent more rapidly than the nation (ratio of 1.02), and the 1950s, when Indiana matched the national growth rate. Indiana started slowly, built up to equal the national rate in the middle decades, then fell to its lowest growth rates of the century in the 1980s. It should rebound a little in the 1990s. By 2000 the actual line will be 34 percent below the normalized line, meaning that Indiana's growth ratio was 34 percent below that of the nation from 1900 through 2000.

Indiana was hurt by its location. Illinois to the west and Ohio to the east grew well in the early part of the century, and Michigan to the north was a very high growth state up to the collapse of Central (and Northeast) region population growth in the 1970s (as described in the Introduction). Thus, incremental capital investments after the turn of the century in the geographical area that included Indiana were more likely to go to one of these states than to Indiana. As a result, immigrants who moved inland from the eastern seaboard were more likely to follow the flow of capital investment (and jobs) than to settle in Indiana. Immigrants who were farmers moved even farther west.

Indiana was the 8th ranked state in population in 1900 (Table 3-2), but it was a lowly 40th in growth from 1900 through 1950 (Table 3-3). The result was that its population ranking fell to 12th in 1950. It will move up in the growth rankings to 30th from 1950 through 2000, but its population ranking will fall to 14th by 2000. Indiana is projected to continue to grow very slowly after 2000, and it will fall to 19th place in population by 2050 (Table 5-1).

The largest city in Indiana is Indianapolis. Partly by merging with its suburbs after 1960, Indianapolis grew to the 12th largest city in the nation in 1990, with a population of 741,952. It held 13.4 percent of the population of the state in 1990, exactly double the 6.7 percent it held in 1900. The Indianapolis metropolitan area in 1990 was a little under 1.4 million people, corresponding to 25 percent of the state's population. In 1990 Indianapolis was more than four times as large as Fort Wayne, Indiana's second largest city. Except for the concentration of population in the northwest corner of the state that is included in the Chicago metropolitan area, Indiana's population is well distributed outside the Indianapolis area.

Indiana

Figure 3-15. Indiana Population (in Millions)

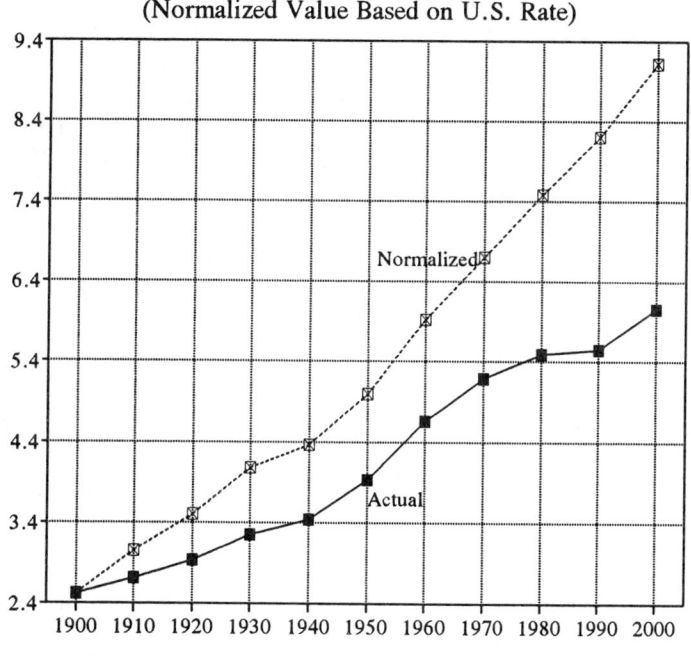

(Normalized Value Based on U.S. Rate)

Year	Population	Growth Rate	U.S. Rate	Ratio
1900	2,516,462	--	--	--
1910	2,700,876	7.3%	21.0%	0.35
1920	2,930,390	8.5%	15.0%	0.57
1930	3,238,503	10.5%	16.2%	0.65
1940	3,427,796	5.8%	7.3%	0.80
1950	3,934,224	14.8%	14.5%	1.02
1960	4,662,498	18.5%	18.5%	1.00
1970	5,195,392	11.4%	13.4%	0.85
1980	5,490,214	5.7%	11.4%	0.50
1990	5,544,159	1.0%	9.8%	0.10
2000	6,045,000	9.0%	11.1%	0.82

Figure 3-16 shows population growth in Iowa compared to the nation from 1900 through 2000. The format is explained on pages 2 and 18. Iowa will fall farther in the population rankings from 1900 through 2000 (and from 1900 through 1950) than any other state (Table 3-4). In 1900 Iowa was the 10th most populous state (Table 3-2). But from 1900 through 1950 it was 50th in growth (Table 3-3), and it fell to 22nd in 1950 on the population ranking list. This loss of twelve places was the worst in the nation. By 2000 Iowa will rank 30th in population, a loss of twenty places since 1900, easily the worst in the nation. Kentucky is next, with a loss of thirteen places. Only the fourteen places lost by the District of Columbia from 1950 through 2000 will outrank Iowa over that period. Iowa will rank 35th in population in 2050.

Iowa will have the lowest growth ratio from 1900 through 2000. Nebraska is just ahead of Iowa on the list, but the gap between Iowa in last place and Nebraska in next-to-last place is the same as the gap between Nebraska and Pennsylvania, and Pennsylvania is ten places ahead of Nebraska. Iowa stands alone in recording slow growth in the twentieth century. It will be one of the four slowest growth states after 2000 as well (Table 5-1).

The normalized population line shows that if Iowa had grown at the same rate as the nation from 1900 through 2000, it would have 8 million people in 2000 and still be the 10th largest state. One reason that Iowa was able to fall so many places in the rankings was that it was high in the rankings in 1900. A state far down the rankings list cannot fall too much farther, by definition. Iowa is unique in its combination of large starting size and very slow growth.

The 1910-1920 decade was the best for Iowa. It grew by 8.1 percent, just over half the national rate (ratio of 0.54). Iowa lost population in the 1900-1910 decade and the 1980s (negative ratios). Iowa was hurt by the revolution in farming techniques that drove over a third of the nation's farm workers off the farms from 1948 through 1960, as outlined in the Introduction. But Iowa was a slow-growth state long before 1948. The lack of nonagricultural jobs and the harsh weather make Iowa unattractive to new residents.

Iowa's largest city is Des Moines, which had 193,189 people in 1990 (80th in the nation). This was 7.6 percent below its 1960 peak and 7.0 percent of the state's population. The Des Moines metropolitan area is not in the top eighty-five list, meaning that it has fewer than 400 thousand people, and it has below 15 percent of the state's population.

Figure 3-16. Iowa Population (in Millions)

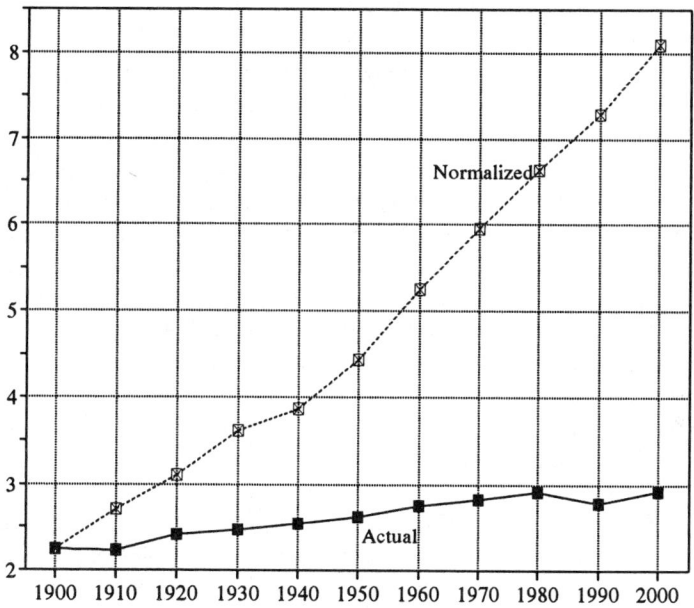

(Normalized Value Based on U.S. Rate)

Year	Population	Growth Rate	U.S. Rate	Ratio
1900	2,231,853	--	--	--
1910	2,224,771	-0.3%	21.0%	-0.02
1920	2,404,021	8.1%	15.0%	0.54
1930	2,470,939	2.8%	16.2%	0.17
1940	2,538,268	2.7%	7.3%	0.37
1950	2,621,073	3.3%	14.5%	0.22
1960	2,757,537	5.2%	18.5%	0.28
1970	2,825,368	2.5%	13.4%	0.18
1980	2,913,808	3.1%	11.4%	0.27
1990	2,776,755	-4.7%	9.8%	-0.48
2000	2,930,000	5.5%	11.1%	0.50

Figure 3-17 shows population growth in Kansas compared to the nation from 1900 through 2000. The format is explained on pages 2 and 18. Kansas grew more slowly than the nation in every decade (all ratios less than 1.00), and in the depression it lost population. It was 46th on the growth list from 1900 through 1950 (Table 3-3), and it will be 35th on the list from 1950 through 2000. It moved down the population ranking list (Table 3-2) from 22nd place in 1900 to 31st in 1950, and it will drop to 32nd by 2000. The only encouraging note is that Kansas will grow a little more rapidly (compared to the nation) from 1950 through 2000 than it did from 1900 through 1950.

Kansas is projected to continue to grow more slowly than the nation after 2000, but it will move up to 30th in the population rankings by 2050 (Table 5-1). By then Kansas will have a population of 3.6 million. It will be passed by some higher-growth states below it, but it will also move ahead of some slower-growth states currently ahead of it, for a net gain of two places. This gain is possible because a majority of the states grow more slowly than the nation. Table 3-3 shows that only twenty-two states grew more rapidly than the nation from 1900 through 2000. Thus Kansas is able to move up the ranking list with a relatively stable growth rate, even if that rate is lower than that of the nation.

Kansas has problems common to states in the center of the nation. Job creation from agriculture has disappeared and a strong new source of job creation has not developed. The weather is unattractive compared to Sunbelt states, and there are no coastal or shoreline cities where immigrants tend to accumulate. The result is permanent slow growth.

One positive development in Kansas is the growth of its largest city, Wichita. Unlike most large cities in slow-growth states, Wichita has increased in population in every decade in the century, and it grew to 304,017 people in 1990. This gave it a rank of 51st in the nation and 12.3 percent of the population of Kansas. The Wichita metropolitan area had 485,270 people in 1990, 19.6 percent of the state's population. Wichita had less than 1.7 percent of the state's population in 1900, and thus the city grew more than seven times as fast as the state from 1900 through 1990.

Wichita is more than twice as large as Kansas City, the second largest city in Kansas. But Kansas City is part of a much larger metropolitan area that includes Kansas City, Missouri, its namesake just across the border. Kansas City, Kansas, however, was larger than Wichita in 1940. It obviously has grown much more slowly than Wichita since then, to fall to only half the size of Wichita in 1990.

Kansas

Figure 3-17. Kansas Population (in Millions)

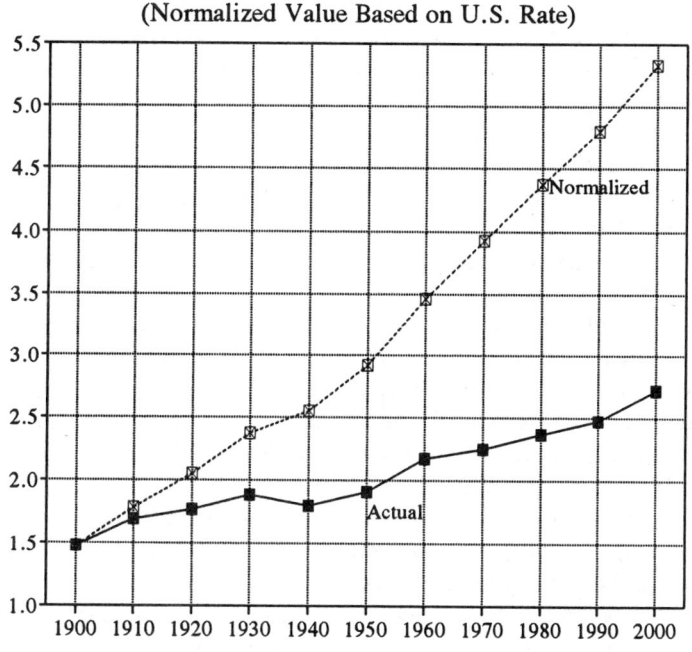

Year	Population	Growth Rate	U.S. Rate	Ratio
1900	1,470,495	--	--	--
1910	1,690,949	15.0%	21.0%	0.71
1920	1,769,257	4.6%	15.0%	0.31
1930	1,880,999	6.3%	16.2%	0.39
1940	1,801,028	-4.3%	7.3%	-0.58
1950	1,905,299	5.8%	14.5%	0.40
1960	2,178,611	14.3%	18.5%	0.78
1970	2,249,071	3.2%	13.4%	0.24
1980	2,364,236	5.1%	11.4%	0.45
1990	2,477,574	4.8%	9.8%	0.49
2000	2,722,000	9.9%	11.1%	0.89

Figure 3-18 shows population growth in Kentucky compared to the nation from 1900 through 2000. The format is explained on pages 2 and 18. Kentucky was a very slow growth state during the century, and it is 2nd in places lost on the population ranking list from 1900 through 2000 (Table 3-4). Kentucky ranked 12th in population in 1900 (Table 3-2), but it was 44th in growth from 1900 through 1950 (Table 3-3), and it fell to 19th on the population ranking list in 1950. It will be 39th in growth from 1950 through 2000, and it will rank 25th in population by 2000. This loss of thirteen places on the ranking list from 1900 through 2000 is topped only by Iowa's huge loss of twenty places.

Kentucky grew at only about a third of the national rate in the first two decades (ratios of 0.32 and 0.37), then improved to about half in the 1920s and grew more rapidly than the nation in the 1930s (ratio of 1.22). But Kentucky immediately fell to about a fifth of the national growth rate in the next two decades. By 1960 the actual population line was about 40 percent below the normalized population line, meaning that Kentucky had a growth ratio 40 percent below the national rate from 1900 through 1960.

Kentucky grew a little better from 1960 through 1980, but, in step with nearly every other Central region state, it had its slowest growth decade of the century in the 1980s. Kentucky is projected to grow even more slowly after 2000, and by 2050 it will fall three more steps on the population ranking list to 28th place (Figure 5-1).

With three large industrial states all touching its northern border (Illinois, Ohio, and Indiana), Kentucky has had difficulty in attracting the capital investment necessary to create jobs. As a landlocked state too far north to be in the Sunbelt, tourism has not been a source of job creation either, and the same factors make Kentucky an unlikely target of immigrants. The result is very slow population growth.

The largest city in Kentucky during the century was Louisville, but it may be about to lose its number one ranking. Louisville had 269,555 people in 1990, a decline of 10 percent since 1980 and 31 percent since its 390,639 peak in 1960. Lexington (officially now Lexington-Fayette) had 225,366 people in 1990, an increase of 10 percent since 1980 and close to four times its 1960 level. In metropolitan areas, the Louisville area had 948,829 people in 1990, but its area includes part of Indiana just across the Ohio River. The Lexington area had 405,936 people in 1990. However, the cities are only seventy-five miles apart, and this gives the north-central section of the state where they both are located the majority of the state's total population.

Kentucky

Figure 3-18. Kentucky Population (in Millions)

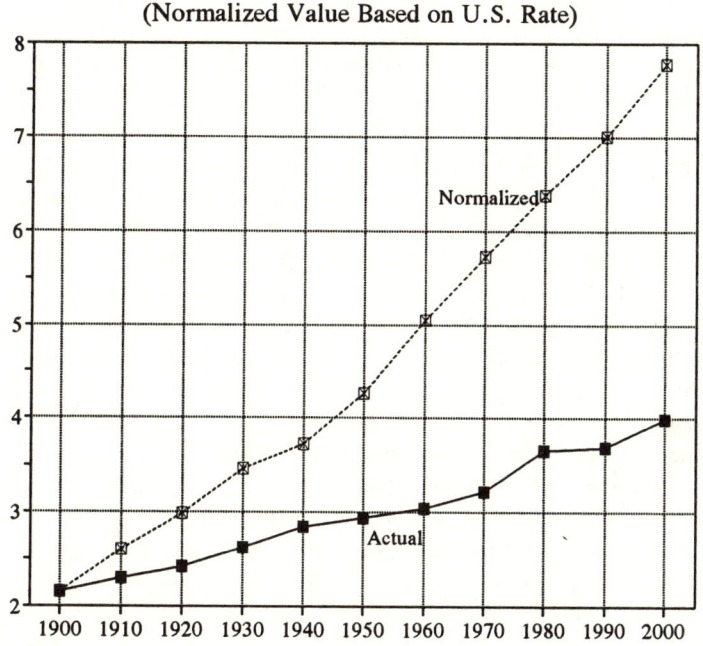

(Normalized Value Based on U.S. Rate)

Year	Population	Growth Rate	U.S. Rate	Ratio
1900	2,147,174	--	--	--
1910	2,289,905	6.6%	21.0%	0.32
1920	2,416,630	5.5%	15.0%	0.37
1930	2,614,589	8.2%	16.2%	0.51
1940	2,845,627	8.8%	7.3%	1.22
1950	2,944,806	3.5%	14.5%	0.24
1960	3,038,156	3.2%	18.5%	0.17
1970	3,220,711	6.0%	13.4%	0.45
1980	3,660,324	13.6%	11.4%	1.19
1990	3,685,296	0.7%	9.8%	0.07
2000	3,989,000	8.2%	11.1%	0.74

Figure 3-19 shows population growth in Louisiana compared to the nation from 1900 through 2000. The format is explained on pages 2 and 18. Louisiana has an unusual growth history. From 1900 through 1980 it grew at almost exactly the same rate as the nation. It had four decades below the national rate (ratios below 1.00) and four decades above. The actual line stayed close to the normalized line throughout the century, showing that growth in the state and the nation were very close. By 1980 the actual line was above the normalized line by 2 percent, after being below from 1900 through 1950. This means that from 1950 through 1980 Louisiana grew more rapidly than the nation.

But good growth stopped in 1980. In the 1980s Louisiana hardly grew at all, with a growth rate of only 0.3 percent. The lowest rate for Louisiana prior to the 1980s was 8.6 percent in the 1910-1920 decade. The low growth in the 1980s was without precedent in Louisiana. It is projected that growth will resume in the 1990s, but the rate will be only half that of the nation. This will make the 1990s Louisiana's second lowest decade for growth in the century.

Louisiana is a Sunbelt state with a major coastal city (New Orleans), a combination that often attracts immigrants. But Texas is next door and Florida not far, and both are more attractive targets. The decline in oil prices in the last decade also hurt growth in Louisiana. It will stay in the middle on the growth lists (Table 3-3), and its population ranking will go from 23rd in 1900 to 22nd in 2000. It is projected to grow better in the next century than in the last two decades of this century, but it will still be a little behind the national rate. However, it should improve by one place to 21st on the population ranking list by 2050 (Table 5-1), as its population goes past 6 million.

New Orleans is Louisiana's largest city. In 1900 and 1950 it had 21 percent of the state's population, meaning that it grew at the same rate as the state from 1900 through 1950. New Orleans lost population for the first time in the 1960s, when it fell 5.4 percent from its 1960 peak of 627,525. From 1960 through 1990, New Orleans fell 21 percent to 496,938 in 1990, which was less than 12 percent of the state's population. The New Orleans metropolitan area had just under 1.3 million in 1990, and it held 30 percent of the state's population. But it lost 1.5 percent in the 1980s, meaning that some of the people leaving New Orleans were also leaving the area. Some may have headed to Baton Rouge, the state's second largest city. It had 219,531 people in 1990, with a metropolitan area of 470,050. The area grew by 5.8 percent in the 1980s.

Figure 3-19. Louisiana Population (in Millions)

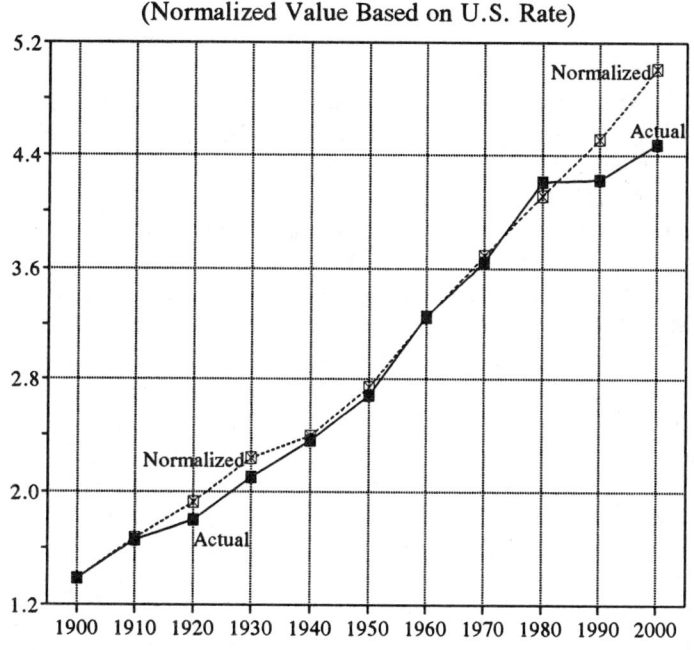

Year	Population	Growth Rate	U.S. Rate	Ratio
1900	1,381,625	--	--	--
1910	1,656,388	19.9%	21.0%	0.95
1920	1,798,509	8.6%	15.0%	0.57
1930	2,101,593	16.9%	16.2%	1.04
1940	2,363,880	12.5%	7.3%	1.72
1950	2,683,516	13.5%	14.5%	0.93
1960	3,257,022	21.4%	18.5%	1.16
1970	3,644,637	11.9%	13.4%	0.89
1980	4,206,116	15.4%	11.4%	1.35
1990	4,219,973	0.3%	9.8%	0.03
2000	4,478,000	6.1%	11.1%	0.55

Figure 3-20 shows population growth in Maine compared to the nation from 1900 through 2000. The format is explained on pages 2 and 18. Maine has a growth history that is the reverse of the Northeast region of which it is a part. While the region was growing at nearly the same rate as the nation from 1900 through 1970 (Figure 2-6), Maine was growing much more slowly than the nation. By 1970 Maine's actual line was almost 50 percent below the normalized line, meaning that through 1970 Maine had a growth ratio 50 percent below that of the nation. But when the population growth of the Northeast region collapsed after 1970, as described in the Introduction, Maine had its best growth in the century. In the 1970s Maine grew at a rate of 13.2 percent, the only decade in which it exceeded the national rate.

Maine was 45th on the growth list from 1900 through 1950 (Table 3-3), and it fell from 31st to 35th on the population ranking list (Table 3-2) over the same period. Maine will move up to 38th on the growth list from 1950 through 2000, but it will still fall to 41st on the population ranking list. This is because some of the small states behind it on the list will grow more rapidly. Maine is projected to continue to grow more slowly than the nation after 2000, and it will fall one place to 42nd on the population ranking list by 2050 (Table 5-1).

Maine's small spurt in growth in the 1970s and 1980s is similar to what happened in other small states in the Northeast region (New Hampshire, Delaware, and Vermont). As the large industrial states in the region stopped growing, the smaller states benefited from the movement of people who wanted to stay in the region but who moved into what they perceived as less frenetic (and in many cases lower tax) areas. In spite of this movement, Maine's small industrial base and its location far from the Sunbelt and the immigrant stream will keep it among the smaller states indefinitely.

The largest city in Maine is Portland, and it grew slightly in the 1980s to reach 64,358 in 1990. This made Maine one of only eight states with no cities greater than 100,000 in population. In fact, combining Portland with the next largest city in Maine (Lewiston, with a population of 39,757 in 1990), just barely exceeds the 100,000 mark in total. Even together, these two cities had only 8.5 percent of the population of the state. There is no metropolitan area in Maine large enough to make the top eighty-five list (400,000 minimum). However, Portland and Lewiston are only fifty miles apart. The area between the two cities and then south along the Atlantic coast to the border with New Hampshire has the major concentration of population in the state.

Maine

Figure 3-20. Maine Population (in Millions)

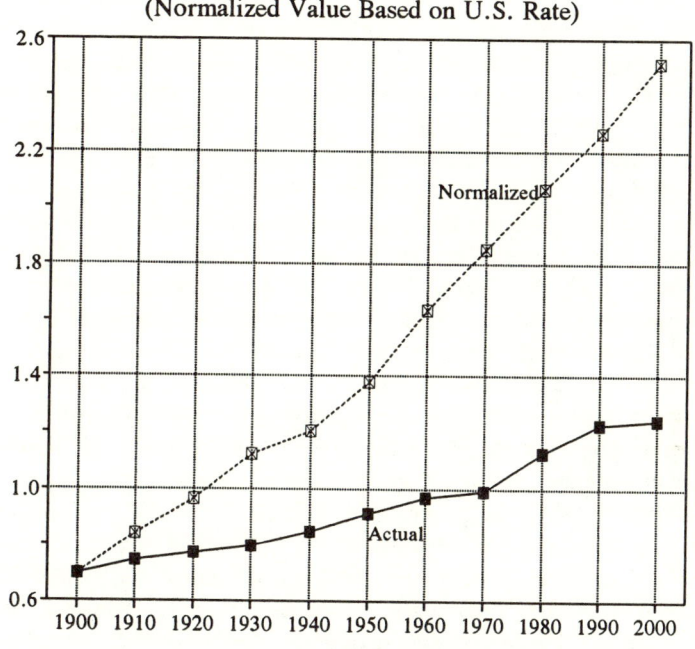

(Normalized Value Based on U.S. Rate)

Year	Population	Growth Rate	U.S. Rate	Ratio
1900	694,466	--	--	--
1910	742,371	6.9%	21.0%	0.33
1920	768,014	3.5%	15.0%	0.23
1930	797,423	3.8%	16.2%	0.24
1940	847,226	6.2%	7.3%	0.86
1950	913,774	7.9%	14.5%	0.54
1960	969,265	6.1%	18.5%	0.33
1970	993,722	2.5%	13.4%	0.19
1980	1,125,043	13.2%	11.4%	1.16
1990	1,227,928	9.1%	9.8%	0.93
2000	1,240,000	1.0%	11.1%	0.09

Figure 3-21 shows population growth in Maryland compared to the nation from 1900 through 2000. The format is explained on pages 2 and 18. Maryland is one state that definitely received benefits from the federal government, at least in terms of population growth. Maryland grew more slowly than the nation in the first three decades (ratios less than 1.00), and by 1930 the actual line was about 15 percent below the normalized line. This means that Maryland had a growth ratio 15 percent lower than that of the nation up to 1930. But in the 1930s Maryland grew at a rate 60 percent higher than the nation (ratio of 1.60), and nearly double the national rate in the 1940s. These were the decades when the federal government grew explosively to fight the depression and World War II. By 1950 Maryland had matched the national growth rate as the actual and normalized lines came together.

Maryland maintained very high growth rates through the second half of the century, falling behind the national rate only in the 1970s, when the entire Northeast region grew by only 0.5 percent. But Maryland grew fifteen times faster than the region even if it was behind the national rate. Maryland grew as people moved into the state to work for and lobby the government in Washington, and others left the city to move into the surrounding areas of Maryland at the same time.

Maryland was 24th on the growth list from 1900 through 1950 (Table 3-3), but it will move up to 13th place from 1950 through 2000. It also moved up the population ranking list (Table 3-2), going from 26th in 1900 to 24th in 1950, and it is projected to be in 19th place by 2000. By 2050 Maryland is projected to move up to 15th place as it continues to grow as rapidly as the nation.

Maryland grew rapidly in spite of the decline of Baltimore, its major city. Baltimore had 43 percent of the population of the state in 1900 and 41 percent in 1950. Baltimore fell off sharply after 1950, as did all the major cities along the East Coast. It went from a peak of 949,708 in 1950 to 736,014 in 1990. By 1990 it had only 15 percent of the population of the state, although it still had nearly ten times as many people as the second largest city in Maryland. But most of this loss was just movement to the suburbs. The Baltimore-Washington metropolitan area covers parts of four states and thus cannot be expressed in terms of a percentage of the population of any of them. But it was the fourth largest metropolitan area in the nation in 1990, with 6.7 million people. Most notably, it grew by a substantial 16.2 percent in the 1980s. The loss of population in Baltimore proper had no effect on the growth of Maryland.

Figure 3-21. Maryland Population (in Millions)

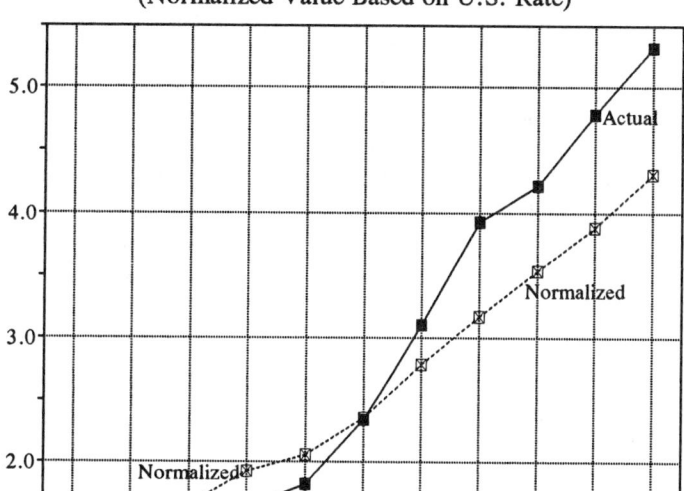

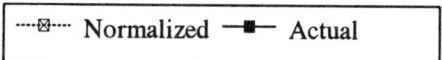

Year	Population	Growth Rate	U.S. Rate	Ratio
1900	1,188,044	--	--	--
1910	1,295,346	9.0%	21.0%	0.43
1920	1,449,661	11.9%	15.0%	0.80
1930	1,631,526	12.5%	16.2%	0.77
1940	1,821,244	11.6%	7.3%	1.60
1950	2,343,001	28.6%	14.5%	1.98
1960	3,100,689	32.3%	18.5%	1.75
1970	3,923,897	26.5%	13.4%	1.99
1980	4,216,933	7.5%	11.4%	0.65
1990	4,781,468	13.4%	9.8%	1.37
2000	5,322,000	11.3%	11.1%	1.02

Figure 3-22 shows population growth in Massachusetts compared to the nation from 1900 through 2000. The format is explained on pages 2 and 18. Massachusetts will grow more slowly than the nation in every decade in the century (all ratios less than 1.00). It was close to the nation for the first two decades, then fell off sharply afterwards. It is projected to lose population in the 1990s for the first time, and by 2000 the actual line will be more than 40 percent below the normalized line. This means that its growth ratio will be more than 40 percent less than the national ratio from 1900 through 2000. Massachusetts was 34th on the growth list from 1900 through 1950 (Table 3-3), and it will be 42nd from 1950 through 2000. It fell from 7th place on the population ranking list in 1900 (Table 3-2) to 9th in 1950, and it will fall to 15th by 2000. It will fall three more places to 18th in 2050 (Table 5-1), as its growth rate continues well below that of the nation.

The loss of industrial base has hurt growth in Massachusetts. For many years this was due to the moving of mills from the state to the South for lower wage (and lower tax) locations. But the effect has also been felt by the high-technology businesses that grew up after World War II on Route 128 around Boston and its excellent colleges. Places like the Silicon Valley in California and the new electronics centers in Florida and Texas offer the same kind of opportunity, with much more favorable weather. These three states also have much better existing support systems for the immigrants who are attracted to the high-technology areas of electronics and the information industry.

This erosion of the industrial base of the state, its location out of the new immigrant stream and the Sunbelt, and the high taxes that provided its liberal welfare benefits (Massachusetts has been known as "Taxachusetts" for at least the last forty years), all combined to produce a low population growth rate. It is a litany that can be read for many of the states in the Northeast and Central regions.

The major city in the state, Boston, fell 28 percent from its 1950 peak of 801,444 to 574,283 in 1990. This reduced Boston from 20 percent of the state's population in 1900 (and 17 percent in 1950) to 9.5 percent in 1990. Much of Boston's population loss of 227,161 was a net state loss, as many people moved across the northern border to New Hampshire to lower their taxes while staying in commuting range. The Boston metropolitan area includes most of those people because the area stretches over three other states (Maine, New Hampshire, and Connecticut). The total area grew by 6.5 percent to 5.4 million in 1990, but its growth did not help that of the state of Massachusetts.

Figure 3-22. Massachusetts Population (in Millions)

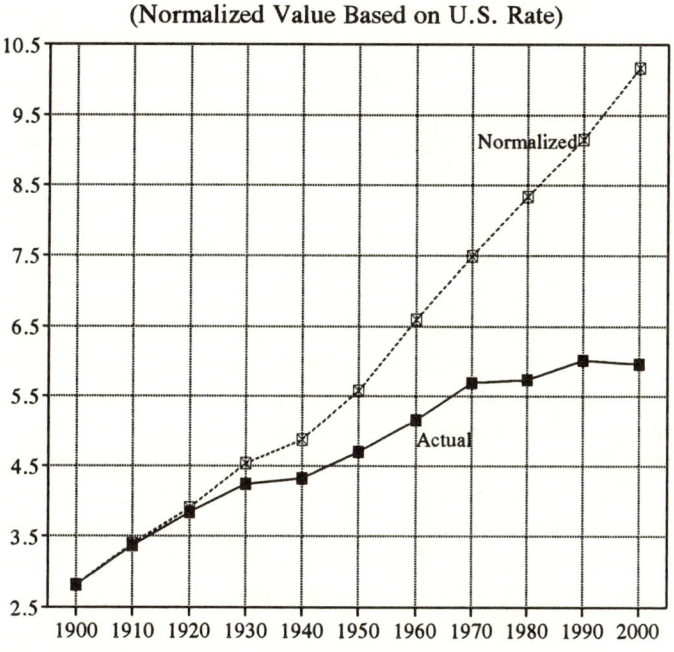

Year	Population	Growth Rate	U.S. Rate	Ratio
1900	2,805,346	--	--	--
1910	3,366,416	20.0%	21.0%	0.95
1920	3,852,356	14.4%	15.0%	0.96
1930	4,249,614	10.3%	16.2%	0.64
1940	4,316,721	1.6%	7.3%	0.22
1950	4,690,514	8.7%	14.5%	0.60
1960	5,148,578	9.8%	18.5%	0.53
1970	5,689,170	10.5%	13.4%	0.79
1980	5,737,093	0.8%	11.4%	0.07
1990	6,016,425	4.9%	9.8%	0.50
2000	5,950,000	-1.1%	11.1%	-0.10

Figure 3-23 shows population growth in Michigan compared to the nation from 1900 through 2000. The format is explained on pages 2 and 18. Michigan was the star performer for the Central region. It was behind the nation in the 1900-1910 decade, then exploded in population from 1910 through 1970 as people flocked to the state to take part in the creation and expansion of the nation's automobile manufacturing industry. Henry Ford provided the impetus in 1914 by offering the then startling amount of five dollars for an eight-hour day.

Michigan was 13th on the growth list from 1900 through 1950 (Table 3-3), and it moved up the population ranking list (Table 3-2) from 9th in 1900 to 7th in 1950. It continued to soar in the 1950s, and by 1960 the actual line was 35 percent above the normalized line, meaning that Michigan's growth ratio exceeded that of the nation by 35 percent from 1900 through 1960. But that was the peak. Growth slowed in the 1960s, and with the car industry crash of the late 1970s and early 1980s, as described in the Introduction, Michigan's growth stopped.

Michigan will fall to 31st on the growth list from 1950 through 2000, and by 2000 it will drop to 8th place on the population ranking list. By 2050 Michigan will be 10th on the ranking list as it continues to grow very slowly after 2000 (Table 5-1). The shift of job creation away from heavy industry and towards the electronics, information, and service industries, like those in most Sunbelt states, has hit states like Michigan hard. It will remain as one of the most populous states due to population momentum, but its high growth period is over.

Michigan's early growth was due to the growth of its major city, Detroit. Detroit had 12 percent of state population in 1900, but it grew more rapidly than the state as the car industry mushroomed, and it held 29 percent in 1950. Detroit accounted for 42 percent of the state's population increase from 1900 through 1950. It was the nation's 5th largest city, with 1,849,568 people in 1950, but it declined sharply after 1950 with the other major eastern cities. Detroit lost 44 percent of its population from 1950 through 1990, falling to 1,027,974. By then it held only 11 percent of the state's population. But the Detroit metropolitan area, even after falling 2.0 percent in the 1980s to 5.2 million in 1990, held 56 percent of the state's population. Michigan's 2nd largest city is Grand Rapids (189,126 in 1990). Its metropolitan area increased by 11.5 percent to 937,891 in 1990, but it held only 10 percent of the state's population. This shows the extent to which the state's population is still concentrated in the Detroit area, the center of the world in the golden days of the automobile manufacturing industry.

Figure 3-23. Michigan Population (in Millions)

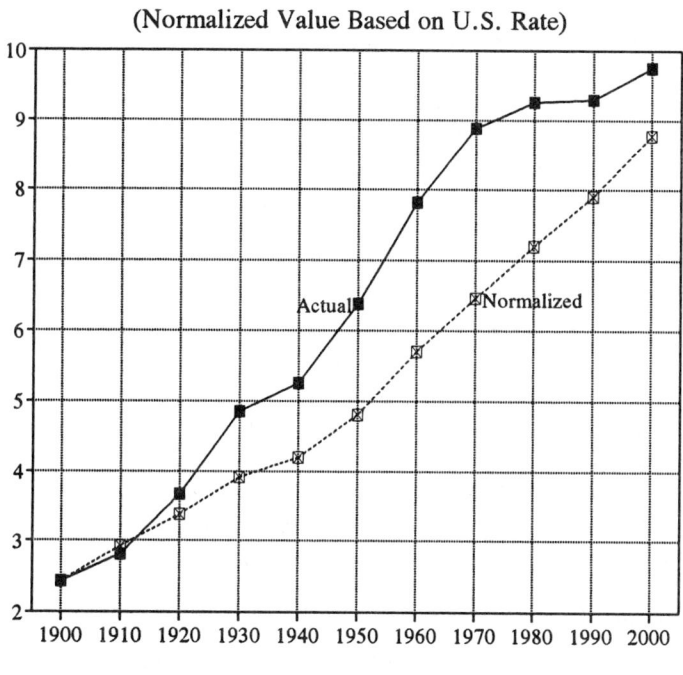

Year	Population	Growth Rate	U.S. Rate	Ratio
1900	2,420,982	--	--	--
1910	2,810,173	16.1%	21.0%	0.76
1920	3,668,412	30.5%	15.0%	2.04
1930	4,842,325	32.0%	16.2%	1.97
1940	5,256,106	8.5%	7.3%	1.18
1950	6,371,766	21.2%	14.5%	1.46
1960	7,823,194	22.8%	18.5%	1.23
1970	8,881,826	13.5%	13.4%	1.01
1980	9,262,044	4.3%	11.4%	0.37
1990	9,295,297	0.4%	9.8%	0.04
2000	9,759,000	5.0%	11.1%	0.45

Figure 3-24 shows population growth in Minnesota compared to the nation from 1900 through 2000. The format is explained on pages 2 and 18. Minnesota grew steadily during the century, even though it grew more slowly than the nation in all but two decades. It matched the nation in the 1910-1920 decade, then exceeded it in the 1930s by 23 percent (1.23 ratio). Its lowest growth ratio, 0.46 in the 1920s, is high for a worst decade. Minnesota has slowly fallen behind the national rate, but has never had a period when growth completely stalled.

Minnesota was 32nd on the growth list from 1900 through 1950 (Table 3-3), but it moved up the population ranking list (Table 3-2) from 19th in 1900 to 18th in 1950. It will be 26th on the growth list from 1950 through 2000, but will fall two places on the population ranking list to 20th in 2000. It is a good example of how the growth rates of states nearby on the ranking list are as important as a state's growth rate in determining changes in ranking position. Minnesota will fall three places to 23rd on the population ranking list in 2050 as it continues to grow steadily but even more slowly after 2000 (Table 5-1).

When the population outflows in the Central and Northeast regions took place after 1970, as described in the Introduction, Minnesota performed much better than the Central region of which it is a part. The Central region grew by only 4.7 percent in the 1970s, then nearly stopped growing at 0.9 percent in the 1980s (Figure 2-7). Minnesota, however, grew by 7.1 percent and 7.3 percent, respectively, in those decades. Its growth ratios of 0.62 and 0.75, respectively, were not far from its average decade ratio of 0.80 for the century. This confirms that Minnesota tends to be an insular state, growing at a consistent (slow) rate. National trends, such as new immigration patterns and changes in the industries producing job creation, have little effect.

Minneapolis was Minnesota's major city in 1990 with 368,383 people, while its sister city St. Paul had 272,235 people. The two cities together had 21 percent of the state's population in 1900, and this increased to 28 percent in 1950. The two cities accounted for 38 percent of the population increase in the state from 1900 through 1950. They fell to 15 percent of the state's population in 1990, declining like most other major cities in the Central and Northeast regions. But the Minneapolis-St. Paul metropolitan area increased by 15.5 percent to 2.5 million in 1990. Although the area includes part of Wisconsin just across the St. Croix and Mississippi Rivers, the 58 percent of the state's population it held in 1990 is a fair representation of the concentration of state population in the metropolitan area.

Minnesota

Figure 3-24. Minnesota Population (in Millions)

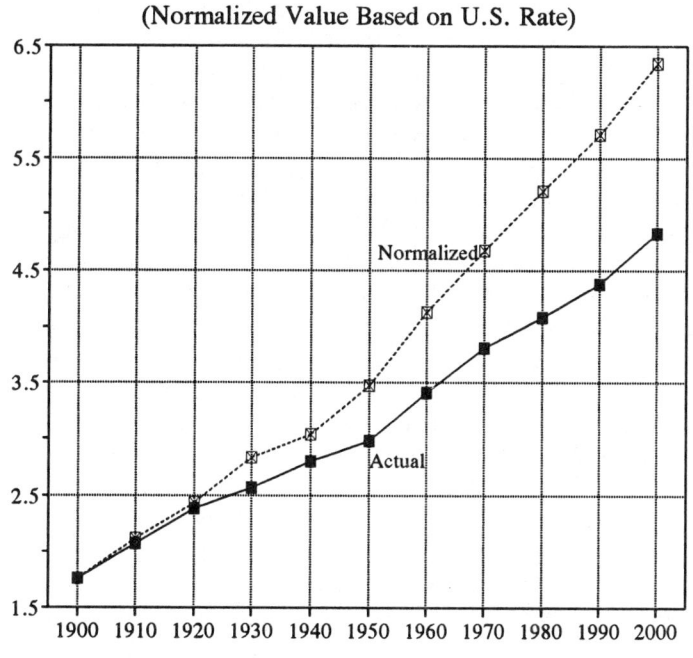

Year	Population	Growth Rate	U.S. Rate	Ratio
1900	1,751,394	--	--	--
1910	2,075,708	18.5%	21.0%	0.88
1920	2,387,125	15.0%	15.0%	1.00
1930	2,563,953	7.4%	16.2%	0.46
1940	2,792,300	8.9%	7.3%	1.23
1950	2,982,483	6.8%	14.5%	0.47
1960	3,413,864	14.5%	18.5%	0.78
1970	3,806,103	11.5%	13.4%	0.86
1980	4,075,970	7.1%	11.4%	0.62
1990	4,375,099	7.3%	9.8%	0.75
2000	4,824,000	10.3%	11.1%	0.93

Figure 3-25 shows population growth in Mississippi compared to the nation from 1900 through 2000. The format is explained on pages 2 and 18. Mississippi has been a slow-growth state throughout the century. It had two decades of good growth, exceeding the national rate by about 20 percent in the 1930s and 1970s. But it lost population in three decades (as shown by the negative ratios), and it had two very slow growth decades in the 1960s and 1980s. Part of this slow growth was due to the strong outflow of blacks from Mississippi to the industrial cities of the North and West, as described in the Introduction. The actual population line for Mississippi will fall to less than half the normalized line by 2000, meaning that Mississippi's growth ratio was less than half that of the nation from 1900 through 2000.

Mississippi was 43rd on the growth list from 1900 through 1950 (Table 3-3), falling six places on the population ranking list (Table 3-2) from 20th in 1900 to 26th in 1950. Mississippi will stay at 43rd on the growth list from 1950 through 2000, and it will fall five places on the population ranking list to 31st by 2000. Its loss of eleven places from 1900 to 2000 is a total exceeded by only three states (Table 3-4). Overall, Mississippi will be 47th on the growth list from 1900 through 2000. All these results confirm its position as one of the slowest growing states in the nation during the century. By 2050 Mississippi is projected to fall two more places to 33rd on the population ranking list (Table 5-1) as it continues to grow much more slowly than the nation.

Mississippi is a good example of a low-growth Sunbelt state. Simply being in the Sunbelt is not a guarantee of high growth. The only feature Mississippi shares with high-growth Sunbelt states is mild winter weather. Mississippi is in the middle of the block of low-growth Sunbelt states (Figure 1-2), and it offers few incentives for the capital investment that generates jobs. It also is not a target for immigration (either legal or illegal), as its present lack of immigrant populations means that there are few support systems in place for new immigrants. These two factors make Mississippi a permanent slow-growth state.

The largest city in Mississippi is Jackson, which had a population of 196,637 in 1990. This represented only 7.6 percent of the population of the state, but it is actually a big jump from 4.5 percent in 1950 and 0.5 percent in 1900. The Jackson metropolitan area is not big enough to make the top eighty-five list of the Bureau of the Census (minimum 400,000 people), but the majority of people in the state live in an area defined by a line running east from Jackson to Meridian, and then 150 miles south to the small shoreline the state has on the Gulf of Mexico.

Mississippi

Figure 3-25. Mississippi Population (in Millions)

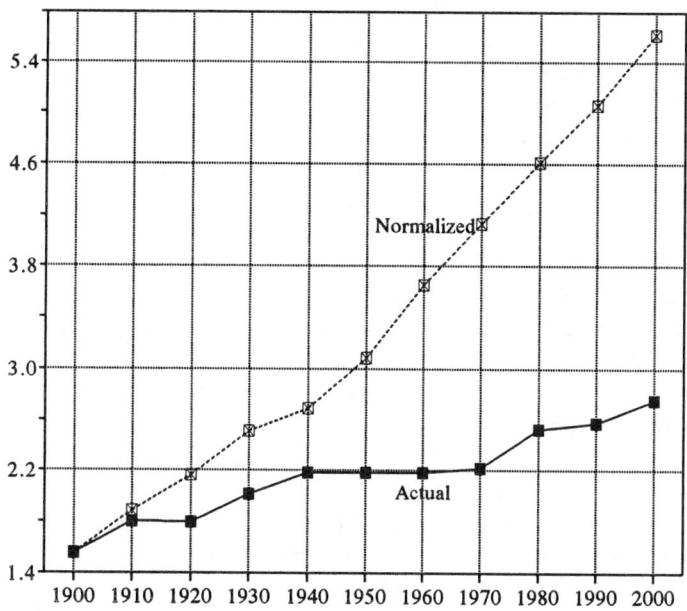

(Normalized Value Based on U.S. Rate)

Year	Population	Growth Rate	U.S. Rate	Ratio
1900	1,551,270	--	--	--
1910	1,797,114	15.8%	21.0%	0.75
1920	1,790,618	-0.4%	15.0%	-0.02
1930	2,009,821	12.2%	16.2%	0.76
1940	2,183,796	8.7%	7.3%	1.19
1950	2,178,914	-0.2%	14.5%	-0.02
1960	2,178,141	-0.0%	18.5%	-0.00
1970	2,216,994	1.8%	13.4%	0.13
1980	2,520,770	13.7%	11.4%	1.20
1990	2,573,216	2.1%	9.8%	0.21
2000	2,750,000	6.9%	11.1%	0.62

Figure 3-26 shows population growth in Missouri compared to the nation from 1900 through 2000. The format is explained on pages 2 and 18. Only three states grew more slowly than Missouri during the century. But its growth was quite consistent, even if very slow. Missouri has an average decade growth ratio of 0.44, meaning that it will grow a little less than half as rapidly as the nation from 1900 through 2000. The decade ratios ranged from a low of 0.22 (the 1910-1920 decade) to a high of 0.62 in the 1960s. Few states match Missouri in consistency, just as few states match it in such slow growth.

Missouri was 48th on the growth list from 1900 through 1950 (Table 3-3), falling six places on the population ranking list (Table 3-2) from 5th in 1900 to 11th in 1950. Missouri will be 37th on the growth list from 1950 through 2000, but it will fall six places on the population list to 17th by 2000. Its loss of twelve places from 1900 through 2000 is exceeded only by Kentucky and Iowa (Table 3-4). From 1900 through 2000 Missouri will be 48th on the growth list. Missouri is projected to remain 17th on the population ranking list by 2050 (Table 5-1), even though it will continue to grow more slowly than the nation.

Ranking 5th in population, Missouri was an important state in 1900. Its major city, St. Louis (the nation's 4th largest), was the gateway to the West because of its position at the juncture of the Missouri and Mississippi Rivers. But trains replaced rivers as the key mode of transportation, manufacturing replaced agriculture as the key source of job creation, and the key way West no longer led through St. Louis. As a result, both city and state steadily declined in importance.

St. Louis lost so many people after 1950 that Kansas City became the largest city in the state in 1990. St. Louis went from holding 19 percent of the state's population in 1900 to 22 percent in 1950, accounting for a third of the state's small growth during the period. But St. Louis collapsed as people poured out of the major cities of the Central and Northeast regions after 1950. It went from 856,796 in 1950 to 396,685 in 1990 (a 54 percent loss), and it fell to 7.8 percent of state population. St. Louis was 10 percent smaller in 1990 than it was 100 years earlier in 1890. But the St. Louis metropolitan area, which includes part of Illinois across the Mississippi River, grew to 2.5 million in 1990. Kansas City had 434,829 people in 1990, and its metropolitan area, including Kansas City, Kansas, had 1.6 million. These relative sizes represent well the relative concentrations of population in the state. Two-thirds of the population live in the two city areas and the corridor along Interstate 70 that connects them.

Figure 3-26. Missouri Population (in Millions)

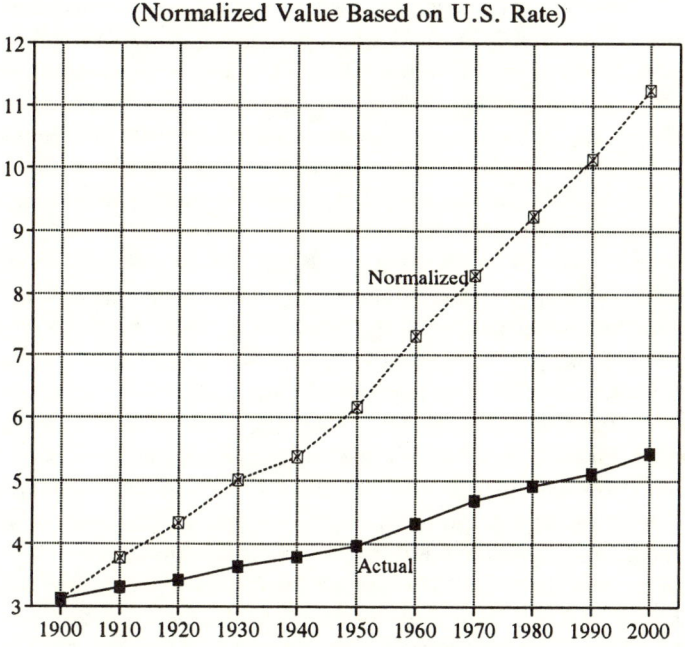

Year	Population	Growth Rate	U.S. Rate	Ratio
1900	3,106,665	--	--	--
1910	3,293,335	6.0%	21.0%	0.29
1920	3,404,055	3.4%	15.0%	0.22
1930	3,629,367	6.6%	16.2%	0.41
1940	3,784,664	4.3%	7.3%	0.59
1950	3,954,653	4.5%	14.5%	0.31
1960	4,319,813	9.2%	18.5%	0.50
1970	4,677,623	8.3%	13.4%	0.62
1980	4,916,766	5.1%	11.4%	0.45
1990	5,117,073	4.1%	9.8%	0.42
2000	5,437,000	6.3%	11.1%	0.56

Figure 3-27 shows population growth in Montana compared to the nation from 1900 through 2000. The format is explained on pages 2 and 18. Montana will match the national growth rate for the century, but this is due mostly to the large percentage increases in population that took place from 1900 through 1920, when Montana had a small population base. In those decades Montana grew nearly three times as rapidly as the nation, even though it added only 300,000 people in total. Montana lost population in the next decade (negative ratio), then grew very slowly for the next forty years. But just as the normalized and actual lines were about to touch, Montana grew more rapidly than the nation in the 1970s. It was a beneficiary of the population outflow from the Northeast and Central regions, as described in the Introduction. Montana stopped growing in the 1980s, but another spurt of growth is projected for the 1990s. This will give Montana a growth ratio just ahead of the national growth ratio from 1900 through 2000.

Montana was 18th on the growth list from 1900 through 1950 (Table 3-3), but it was 43rd on the population ranking list (Table 3-2) in both 1900 and 1950, due to its small population base. Montana will fall to 29th on the growth list from 1950 through 2000, and it will fall one place on the population list to 44th by 2000. Montana will be 22nd on the growth list from 1900 through 2000, making it the last state on the list to have a growth ratio higher than that of the nation for that period. It is projected that Montana will move up one place to 43rd on the ranking list by 2050 (Table 5-1), even though it will grow a little more slowly than the nation in the first half of the next century.

Montana's surge in growth early in the century was due to booms in mining exploration and cattle ranching. These are long since over, and Montana is a long way from the Sunbelt and not at all a target for legal or illegal immigration. This suggests very low population growth, but Montana is attractive to some because of its open space (it is the fourth largest state in geographical size) and lack of congestion.

The largest city in Montana is Billings. It had 81,125 people in 1990, an increase of 21 percent from 1980. Montana was one of only eight states in 1990 with no city over 100,000 people, and it had no metropolitan area large enough to make the top eighty-five list of the Bureau of the Census (minimum of 400,000). In spite of its good growth in the 1980s, Billings had only 10 percent of the state's population in 1990. In fact, combining the five most populous cities in Montana still adds up to less than 30 percent of the state's population. Cities are not what attracts people to Montana.

Montana

Figure 3-27. Montana Population (in Millions)

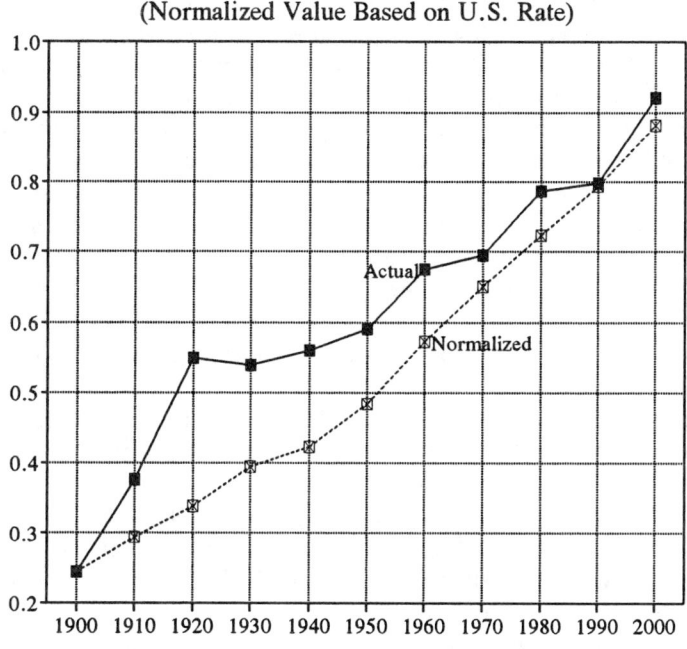

(Normalized Value Based on U.S. Rate)

Year	Population	Growth Rate	U.S. Rate	Ratio
1900	243,329	--	--	--
1910	376,053	54.5%	21.0%	2.59
1920	548,889	46.0%	15.0%	3.07
1930	537,606	-2.1%	16.2%	-0.13
1940	559,456	4.1%	7.3%	0.56
1950	591,024	5.6%	14.5%	0.39
1960	674,767	14.2%	18.5%	0.77
1970	694,409	2.9%	13.4%	0.22
1980	786,690	13.3%	11.4%	1.16
1990	799,065	1.6%	9.8%	0.16
2000	920,000	15.1%	11.1%	1.37

Figure 3-28 shows population growth in Nebraska compared to the nation from 1900 through 2000. The format is explained on pages 2 and 18. Only Iowa will grow more slowly than Nebraska from 1900 through 2000, and Nebraska's growth ratio will be 44 percent of that of the nation (the actual line will be 44 percent of the normalized line by 2000). Nebraska grew more slowly than the nation in every decade. It grew by 11.8 percent in the 1910-1920 decade with a growth ratio of 0.56, and it is projected to grow by 8.0 percent in the 1990s, with a growth ratio of 0.72. These are its best two decades. Nebraska lost population in the 1930s (as shown by the negative ratio), and it did not surpass its 1930 population until 1960.

Nebraska was 49th on the growth list from 1900 through 1950 (Table 3-3), and it fell from 27th on the population ranking list in 1900 (Table 3-2) to 33rd in 1950. Nebraska will be 41st on the growth list from 1950 through 2000, and will fall four places on the population list to 37th by 2000. Only four states will have a greater drop from 1900 through 2000 (Table 3-4). Nebraska will be 50th on the growth list from 1900 through 2000, and it will grow even more slowly after 2000, falling to 38th on the ranking list by 2050 (Table 5-1).

Nebraska was hit by the revolution in farming techniques that drove over a third of the nation's farm workers off the farms from 1948 through 1960 alone, as outlined in the Introduction. Nebraska is far from the Sunbelt, with harsh winter weather, and it is not a target for immigrants. Its industrial base is too small to replace the lost agricultural jobs, and even the location of the Strategic Air Command in the state will be less helpful with the easing of the cold war. Thus Nebraska runs far behind the national average in population growth.

Omaha is the largest city in Nebraska, and it had 335,719 people in 1990. But Lincoln, the next largest city at 191,972, is only fifty miles away. These cities accounted for 80 percent of the population increase in the state from 1900 through 1950, growing to 350,001 in combined population in 1950 after starting at 142,724 in 1900. They accounted for 92 percent of the increase in the state from 1950 through 1970, reaching 496,447 in combined population in 1970. But Omaha lost population from 1970 through 1990, and the two together grew by only 6.3 percent during that period. The Omaha metropolitan area includes Council Bluffs, Iowa, just across the Missouri River, and it had 639,580 people in 1990. If Omaha and Lincoln were defined as a metropolitan area, they would be bigger than the Omaha area, and they would hold half the state's population.

Figure 3-28. Nebraska Population (in Millions)

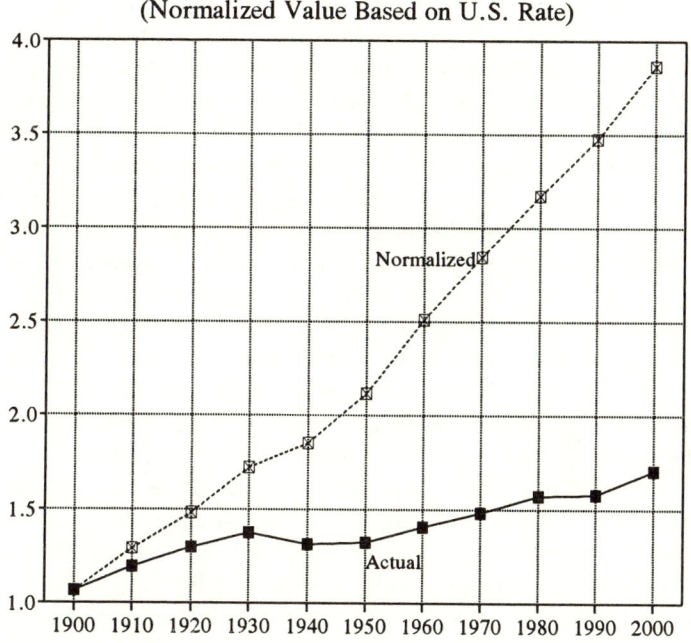

Year	Population	Growth Rate	U.S. Rate	Ratio
1900	1,066,300	--	--	--
1910	1,192,214	11.8%	21.0%	0.56
1920	1,296,372	8.7%	15.0%	0.58
1930	1,377,963	6.3%	16.2%	0.39
1940	1,315,834	-4.5%	7.3%	-0.62
1950	1,325,510	0.7%	14.5%	0.05
1960	1,411,330	6.5%	18.5%	0.35
1970	1,485,333	5.2%	13.4%	0.39
1980	1,569,825	5.7%	11.4%	0.50
1990	1,578,385	0.5%	9.8%	0.06
2000	1,704,000	8.0%	11.1%	0.72

Figure 3-29 shows population growth in Nevada compared to the nation from 1900 through 2000. The format is explained on pages 2 and 18. Due to mining booms and busts, Nevada in 1900 had fewer people than it did in 1870 (it became a state in 1864). It nearly doubled its population in the first decade of the twentieth century, partly due to miners chasing new silver and gold discoveries they hoped would be as successful as the famous Comstock Lode had been in the previous century. As these hopes faded for most, the state lost population in the 1910-1920 decade (as shown by the negative ratio). But after 1920 Nevada started an explosion in growth that is unmatched by any state.

Nevada was only a little ahead of the nation's growth rate in the 1920s (ratio of 1.09), but it had a ratio of 2.90 in the 1930s. It increased the ratio in each subsequent decade, hitting a peak of 5.58 in the 1970s. Nevada "slowed" to 5.12 in the 1980s, and is projected to be at 3.68 in the 1990s. The mineral wealth of Nevada was the attraction at first, but the wealth to be found in the gaming palaces of Las Vegas and Reno kept the boom going later in the century.

In spite of its 1910-1920 dip, Nevada was 5th on the growth list from 1900 through 1950 (Table 3-3). But its small population base limited its rise on the population ranking list from 51st in 1900 to 50th in 1950 (Table 3-2). Nevada will top the growth list from 1950 through 2000, and it will move twelve places up the ranking list to 38th place by 2000. Only Florida and Arizona will move up more places from 1950 through 2000 (Table 3-4). Nevada will also top the growth list from 1900 through 2000, growing eleven times as fast as the nation. Nevada is projected to continue to grow more rapidly than the nation after 2000, and it will be 36th on the population ranking list by 2050.

Nevada's largest city is Las Vegas. It had 258,204 people in 1990, an increase of 57 percent from 1980. The Las Vegas metropolitan area is the 5th fastest growing metropolitan area in the United States, and it reached 852,737 people in 1990. This represents over 70 percent of the state's population, but the metropolitan area includes part of Arizona just across the Colorado River. It is indicative, however, of the concentration of population near Las Vegas. The city itself had more than ten times as many people in 1990 as it had in 1950, and it more than doubled its population just since 1970. Its dynamic growth is symbolic of the growth of Nevada. It is a classic Sunbelt state with weather, resorts, resources, available capital investment, and a favorable business climate that will support strong growth in the city and the state for many years to come.

Figure 3-29. Nevada Population (in Millions)

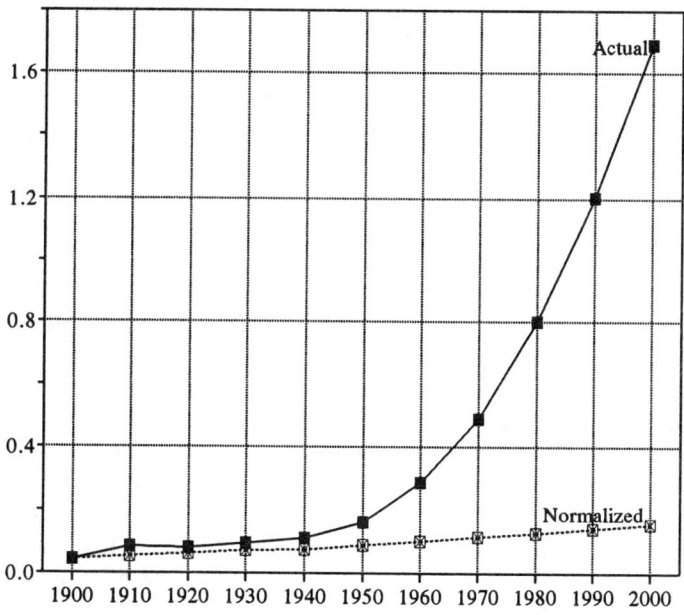

Year	Population	Growth Rate	U.S. Rate	Ratio
1900	42,335	--	--	--
1910	81,875	93.4%	21.0%	4.44
1920	77,407	-5.5%	15.0%	-0.36
1930	91,058	17.6%	16.2%	1.09
1940	110,247	21.1%	7.3%	2.90
1950	160,083	45.2%	14.5%	3.12
1960	285,278	78.2%	18.5%	4.23
1970	488,738	71.3%	13.4%	5.33
1980	800,508	63.8%	11.4%	5.58
1990	1,201,833	50.1%	9.8%	5.12
2000	1,691,000	40.7%	11.1%	3.68

Figure 3-30 shows population growth in New Hampshire compared to the nation from 1900 through 2000. The format is explained on pages 2 and 18. New Hampshire grew very slowly in the first half of the century. Its best period of growth was 1960 through 1990, when many people moved into New Hampshire from Massachusetts, its large neighbor to the south. New Hampshire was seen as a more desirable place in terms of local schools and taxes (Massachusetts was not called "Taxachusetts" for nothing), and yet Boston metropolitan area jobs were in easy commuting range of New Hampshire. Not unexpectedly, population growth in Massachusetts stagnated as New Hampshire's population increased to its highest rates in the century. It is projected that this flow will temporarily slow in the 1990s.

New Hampshire was 47th on the growth list from 1900 through 1950 (Table 3-3), and as a result it fell eight places on the population ranking list from 37th in 1900 to 45th in 1950 (Table 3-2). Only Kansas and Iowa fell further from 1900 through 1950 (Table 3-4), while Vermont fell an equal distance. Thanks to the immigration from Massachusetts, New Hampshire will jump to 17th on the growth list from 1950 through 2000. It will grow almost 20 percent faster than the nation, and the actual line will get closer to the normalized line. The result of the improved growth is that by 2000 New Hampshire will move up 3 places on the population ranking list to 42nd place. It is projected that, after a dip in growth in the 1990s, New Hampshire will grow at about the same rate as the nation in the first half of the next century. It should move up one more place to 41st on the population ranking list by 2050 (Table 5-1).

New Hampshire is far away from the Sunbelt, and although the skiing and mountain climbing its mountains provide attract many tourists, New Hampshire will be able to keep its growth rate at the national level only by continued migration from nearby states. It is not a target for immigrants from outside the United States, and not enough capital investment is available for a high rate of job creation.

The largest city in New Hampshire is Manchester. It had 99,932 people in 1990, a total just small enough to make New Hampshire one of only eight states with no cities over 100,000. The next largest city, Nashua (79,662 in 1990), is fifteen miles south of Manchester, near the Massachusetts border. Nashua is included in the Boston metropolitan area. Combining Manchester and Nashua with all New Hampshire cities within twenty-five miles of the Massachusetts border would give a total count of more than half the population of New Hampshire.

Figure 3-30. New Hampshire Population (in Millions)

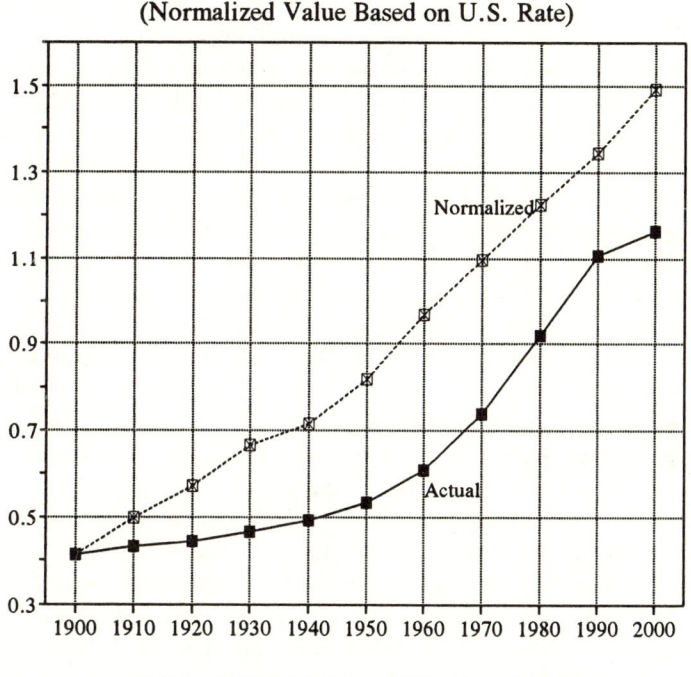

Year	Population	Growth Rate	U.S. Rate	Ratio
1900	411,588	--	--	--
1910	430,572	4.6%	21.0%	0.22
1920	443,083	2.9%	15.0%	0.19
1930	465,293	5.0%	16.2%	0.31
1940	491,524	5.6%	7.3%	0.78
1950	533,242	8.5%	14.5%	0.59
1960	606,921	13.8%	18.5%	0.75
1970	737,681	21.5%	13.4%	1.61
1980	920,610	24.8%	11.4%	2.17
1990	1,109,252	20.5%	9.8%	2.09
2000	1,165,000	5.0%	11.1%	0.45

Figure 3-31 shows population growth in New Jersey compared to the nation from 1900 through 2000. The format is explained on pages 2 and 18. New Jersey was a high-growth state from 1900 through 1970, pausing only in the depression of the 1930s. Its location between the New York and Philadelphia metropolitan areas produced a large commuter population, and its diverse economy, from heavy industry in the north to vegetable truck farms in the south (plus many tourist beaches), gave New Jersey high job creation and high population growth. But it all ended in 1970 when population flowed out of the Northeast and Central regions, as described in the Introduction.

Up to 1970 the actual population line stayed above the normalized line. The actual line led by 45 percent in 1970, meaning that the growth ratio for New Jersey was 45 percent higher than that of the nation from 1900 through 1970. But the gap closed substantially after 1970. By 2000 the actual line will be only 20 percent above the normalized line, meaning that the growth ratio for New Jersey will be only 20 percent higher than that of the nation for the full century.

New Jersey was 14th on the growth list from 1900 through 1950 (Table 3-3), and it jumped from 16th on the population ranking list in 1900 to become the 8th largest state in 1950 (Table 3-2). This increase of eight places put it behind only the high-growth states of California, Florida, Washington, and Arizona for the largest increase from 1900 through 1950 (Table 3-4). Because of its dip after 1970, New Jersey will fall to 22nd on the growth list from 1950 through 2000, and it will fall to 9th on the population ranking list by 2000. New Jersey is projected to grow more slowly than the nation after 2000, and it will fall to 13th on the population ranking list by 2050 (Table 5-1).

Newark and Jersey City are the major cities in New Jersey, and they symbolize the problems of industrial cities in the Northeast region. At its peak, Newark was the nation's 18th largest city in 1930 with 442,337 people. But by 1990, Newark was 56th with 275,221 people, a loss of 38 percent in people and thirty-eight places on the population ranking list. Jersey City also peaked in 1930 at 316,715. In 1990 it had 228,517 people, a loss of 28 percent. Newark and Jersey City in 1990 both had only 10 percent more people than they had in 1900. The cities are within ten miles of each other in the northeast corner of the state and are part of the huge New York City metropolitan area, the nation's largest. Similarly, the population concentration in the south of the state is part of the Philadelphia metropolitan area. However, the largest part of the state's population lives in the area dominated by New York City.

Figure 3-31. New Jersey Population (in Millions)

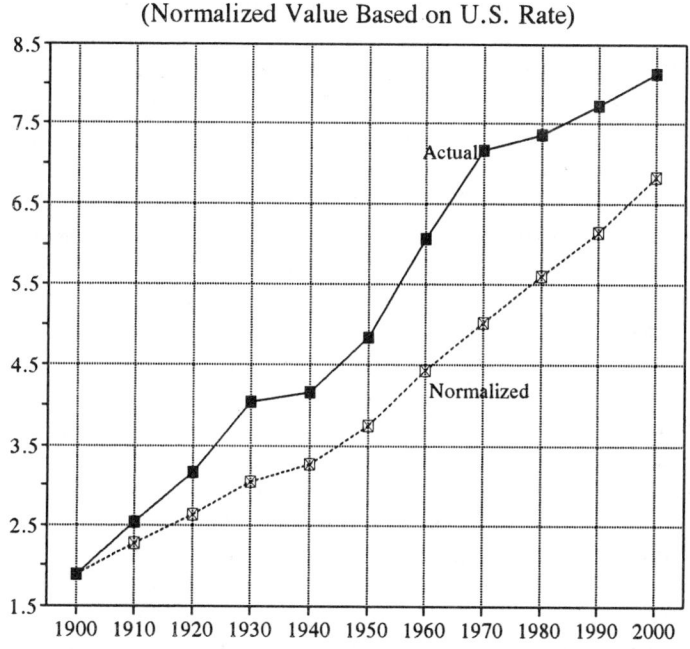

Year	Population	Growth Rate	U.S. Rate	Ratio
1900	1,883,669	--	--	--
1910	2,537,167	34.7%	21.0%	1.65
1920	3,155,900	24.4%	15.0%	1.63
1930	4,041,334	28.1%	16.2%	1.73
1940	4,160,165	2.9%	7.3%	0.40
1950	4,835,329	16.2%	14.5%	1.12
1960	6,066,782	25.5%	18.5%	1.38
1970	7,171,112	18.2%	13.4%	1.36
1980	7,365,011	2.7%	11.4%	0.24
1990	7,730,188	5.0%	9.8%	0.51
2000	8,135,000	5.2%	11.1%	0.47

Figure 3-32 shows population growth in New Mexico compared to the nation from 1900 through 2000. The format is explained on pages 2 and 18. New Mexico had high growth through the century, with only two decades below the national rate (ratios below 1.00). The first was the 1910-1920 decade (even though New Mexico became a state in 1912), and the second was in the 1960s, when New Mexico paused after its sharp rise from 1930 through 1960. The hunt for mineral wealth gave New Mexico a boost early in the century. Then the location of government facilities in the state, after the creation of the atomic bomb in Los Alamos during World War II, helped New Mexico to grow in the second part of the century. In the 1960s more than one quarter of personal income in the state came from government payrolls.

These high growth rates drove the actual population of New Mexico far above the normalized line, meaning that at each point in the century New Mexico was growing more rapidly than the nation. By 2000 the actual line will be more than 2.5 times above the normalized line. This means that New Mexico's growth ratio will be 2.5 times as high as that of the nation during the century. The population of New Mexico in 2000 will be over nine times as high as it was in 1900.

New Mexico was 8th on the growth list from 1900 through 1950 (Table 3-3), and it improved from 44th on the population ranking list in 1900 to 40th in 1950 (Table 3-2). New Mexico will stay in 8th place on the growth list from 1950 through 2000, and it will move up another four places to 36th on the population ranking list by 2000. New Mexico is projected to continue to grow much more rapidly than the nation from 2000 through 2050, and it will move up to 34th on the population ranking list by 2050 (Table 5-1). By then it will have a population of over 3 million people, more than three times its 1970 level.

New Mexico is in the Sunbelt and enjoys all the advantages of a high-growth Sunbelt state. Its population is about 40 percent Hispanic and it is an attractive target for the continuing flow of Hispanic immigrants (legal and illegal). New Mexico's major city, Albuquerque, had 384,619 people in 1990, a 16 percent increase from 1980 and 25 percent of the state's population. The metropolitan area had 589,131 people, a 21 percent increase from 1980 and 39 percent of state population. In 1900 Albuquerque held only 3.2 percent of the state's population with 6,238 people. It soared to 96,815 by 1950 and had 14 percent of state population. It grew almost twice as rapidly as the state even after 1950, and it is still growing rapidly as a symbol of the strong growth of the state around it.

Figure 3-32. New Mexico Population (in Millions)

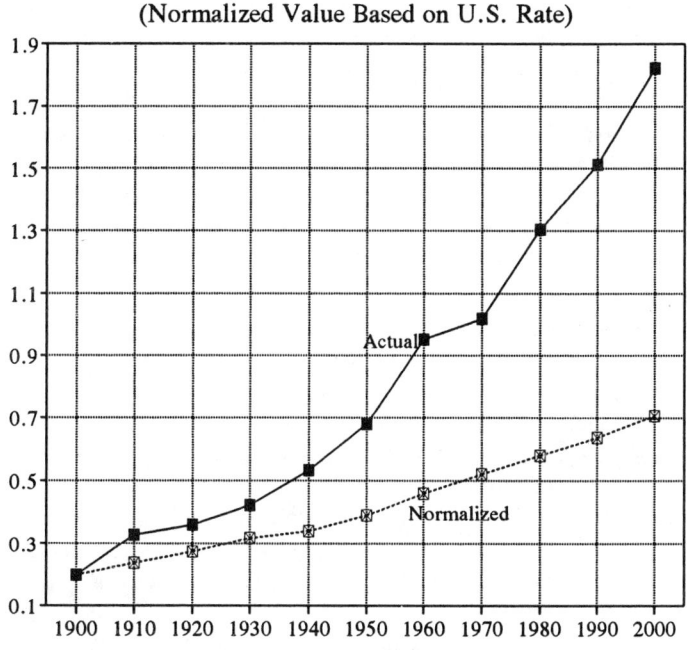

Year	Population	Growth Rate	U.S. Rate	Ratio
1900	195,310	--	--	--
1910	327,301	67.6%	21.0%	3.22
1920	360,350	10.1%	15.0%	0.67
1930	423,317	17.5%	16.2%	1.08
1940	531,818	25.6%	7.3%	3.53
1950	681,187	28.1%	14.5%	1.94
1960	951,023	39.6%	18.5%	2.14
1970	1,017,055	6.9%	13.4%	0.52
1980	1,303,302	28.1%	11.4%	2.46
1990	1,515,069	16.2%	9.8%	1.66
2000	1,823,000	20.3%	11.1%	1.84

Figure 3-33 shows population growth in New York compared to the nation from 1900 through 2000. The format is explained on pages 2 and 18. In New York, the city drives the growth of the state. The city had 47 percent of state population in 1900 and 53 percent in 1950. If the city were a separate state, it would have ranked fifth in the nation in 1900 and 1950 (coming in one spot ahead of the rest of New York state in 1950). By 1990 the city was down to 41 percent of the state, although since 1980 it has been growing more rapidly (once again) than the state as a whole. By 2000 the city still should be close to the 10th ranked state in population. The city metropolitan area spreads over four states and was the nation's largest at 19.3 million in 1990. The New York City and Los Angeles areas rank far ahead of all other areas as preferred destinations for immigrants (legal and illegal), and they keep these areas growing. It does not help the tax problems in New York City, but it keeps the state from a big net loss of population.

New York state grew at the same rate as the nation from 1900 through 1960, keeping the actual population line and the normalized line close together in that period. The actual line fell behind by 1970, then declined in the 1970s when the state lost population as part of the massive outflow from the Northeast and Central regions of the country, as described in the Introduction. The state lost 683,226 people in the 1970s, but the city lost 825,924 people, more than the 1970 population of New Hampshire. The state stopped growing in 1970, and its population in 2000 will be about 4,000 less than it was in 1970.

New York state was 22nd on the growth list from 1900 through 1950 (Table 3-3), but it stayed in 1st place on the population ranking list in both 1900 and 1950. New York will fall to 45th on the growth list from 1950 through 2000, and it will fall from 1st to 3rd on the population ranking list by 2000, being passed first by California and then by Texas. New York is projected to grow by less than 7 percent from 2000 through 2050. It will be passed by Florida in 2020, and it will be in 4th place on the population ranking list in 2050 (Table 5-1).

The state's largest cities after New York City are Buffalo and Rochester. Sixty miles apart in the "Snow Belt" along Lake Erie and Lake Ontario, they form the state's second largest population center. Buffalo had 328,175 people in 1990, a loss of 43 percent since 1950. Rochester had 230,356, a 31 percent loss. Their respective metropolitan areas were 1.2 and 1.1 million (the Syracuse area seventy-five miles east had 0.7 million). The three areas combined lost 2,386 people in the 1980s. That is why New York City determines net state growth.

New York

Figure 3-33. New York Population (in Millions)

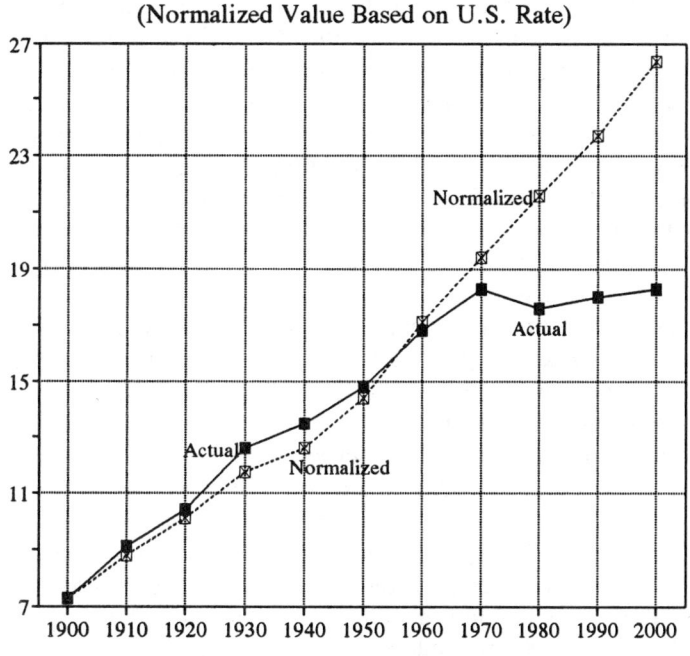

(Normalized Value Based on U.S. Rate)

Year	Population	Growth Rate	U.S. Rate	Ratio
1900	7,268,894	--	--	--
1910	9,113,614	25.4%	21.0%	1.21
1920	10,385,227	14.0%	15.0%	0.93
1930	12,588,066	21.2%	16.2%	1.31
1940	13,479,132	7.1%	7.3%	0.97
1950	14,830,192	10.0%	14.5%	0.69
1960	16,782,304	13.2%	18.5%	0.71
1970	18,241,391	8.7%	13.4%	0.65
1980	17,558,165	-3.7%	11.4%	-0.33
1990	17,990,455	2.5%	9.8%	0.25
2000	18,237,000	1.4%	11.1%	0.12

Figure 3-34 shows population growth in North Carolina compared to the nation from 1900 through 2000. The format is explained on pages 2 and 18. North Carolina tracks the growth of the nation more closely than any state. By 2000 it will have six decades above average (ratio above 1.00) and four below (ratio below 1.00). The actual line was ahead of the normalized line by 8 percent in 1950, and it will be 11 percent ahead in 2000. This means the state and nation had similar growth rates in both parts of the century. This degree of consistency before and after 1950 is as unusual as the fact that the two lines were close together throughout the century. The reasons for North Carolina's consistent growth, however, are quite different before and after 1950.

North Carolina was an agricultural state in the first half of the century, with the prime products being tobacco and cigarettes (North Carolina accounted for about half of the nation's production of each for many years). But in the 1950s the value of manufactured goods surpassed that of agriculture for the first time. North Carolina became more industrialized, and it built scientific research centers tied to its university system that symbolized its move into the new areas of job creation in the nation (as summarized in the Introduction). This adaptation to change kept the state's population steadily growing.

North Carolina was 20th on the growth list from 1900 through 1950 (Table 3-3), and it went from 15th on the population ranking list in 1900 to 10th in 1950 (Table 3-2). North Carolina will be 19th on the growth list from 1950 through 2000, but it will fall to 11th place on the population ranking list by 2000. It will be passed by Florida and by Georgia, both of which will have grown more rapidly from 1950 through 2000. North Carolina will pass Massachusetts, the state ahead of it in 1950, keeping its loss to only one position. North Carolina is projected to continue to grow at the same rate as the nation after 2000, and it will hold its 11th place population ranking in 2050 (Table 5-1).

North Carolina is the northern border of the Sunbelt on the East Coast, and it just makes the high-growth category. But its reputation as a good state for business keeps capital investment flowing. The biggest city, Charlotte, had 395,925 people in 1990, which was 26 percent larger than in 1980 and three times its 1950 size. Charlotte is nearly twice as large as the next city, Raleigh. But the Charlotte metropolitan area, which includes part of South Carolina across the border, held only 1.2 million, while the Greensboro-Winston-Salem area held 1.1 million and the Raleigh area 0.9 million. This shows that the population in the state is relatively well distributed.

Figure 3-34. North Carolina Population (in Millions)

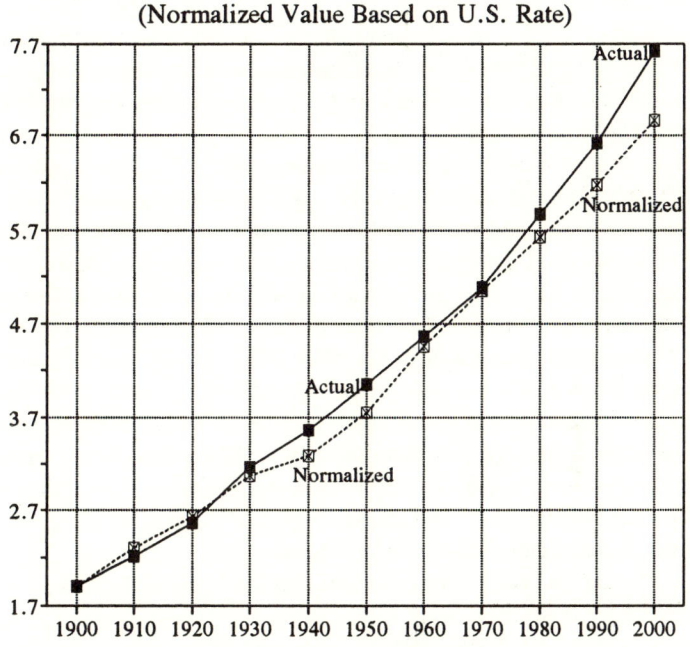

Year	Population	Growth Rate	U.S. Rate	Ratio
1900	1,893,810	--	--	--
1910	2,206,287	16.5%	21.0%	0.78
1920	2,559,123	16.0%	15.0%	1.07
1930	3,170,276	23.9%	16.2%	1.47
1940	3,571,623	12.7%	7.3%	1.74
1950	4,061,929	13.7%	14.5%	0.95
1960	4,556,155	12.2%	18.5%	0.66
1970	5,084,411	11.6%	13.4%	0.87
1980	5,880,095	15.6%	11.4%	1.37
1990	6,628,637	12.7%	9.8%	1.30
2000	7,617,000	14.9%	11.1%	1.35

Figure 3-35 shows population growth in North Dakota compared to the nation from 1900 through 2000. The format is explained on pages 2 and 18. North Dakota grew sharply in the 1900-1910 decade. It was part of the surge of homesteading that took place in the central part of the nation from late in the nineteenth century into the beginning of the 1900s. But that was the only time in the century that North Dakota grew more rapidly than the nation. Its population continued to grow at a slower rate in the two decades after 1910, and it peaked in 1930 just before the depression. North Dakota lost population in the 1930s and 1940s, and it lost population again in the 1960s and 1980s (negative ratios). Its population has not yet regained the 1930 level (it is projected to do so a little after 2010). In fact, North Dakota's population in 2000 will be less than it was in 1920, let alone 1930.

Thanks to the big jump in the 1900-1910 decade, North Dakota's actual population was well above the normalized line until 1940. But it fell below by 1950, and it has fallen farther below in each successive decade as the state's growth remains stagnant while the nation continues to grow. By 2000 North Dakota's actual population will be 55 percent of the normalized line, meaning that the state's growth ratio was 55 percent of that of the nation during the century.

North Dakota was 26th on the growth list from 1900 through 1950 (Table 3-3), falling from 40th on the population ranking list in 1900 to 42nd in 1950 (Table 3-2). North Dakota will fall to 49th on the growth list from 1950 through 2000 (only West Virginia and the District of Columbia will have slower growth for that period), and North Dakota will fall to 48th on the population ranking list by 2000. It is projected that the state will continue to grow much more slowly than the nation in the first half of the next century, and it will move down to 49th on the population ranking list by 2050 (Table 5-1). Only the District of Columbia and Vermont will have smaller populations by then.

North Dakota marks the northern border of the central United States, and it has the harsh winter weather expected from such a location. Agriculture (mainly wheat) and oil are its key products, but it is attractive mostly to people who like to live in desolate places. Its major city, Fargo, had 74,084 people in 1990, making North Dakota one of only eight states with no city over 100,000. The metropolitan area of Fargo was too small to make the top eighty-five list (minimum of 400,000), and the part of the area completely within the state (Fargo is close to the North Dakota-Minnesota border) held less than 20 percent of the state's population. The city itself held 12 percent.

Figure 3-35. North Dakota Population (in Millions)

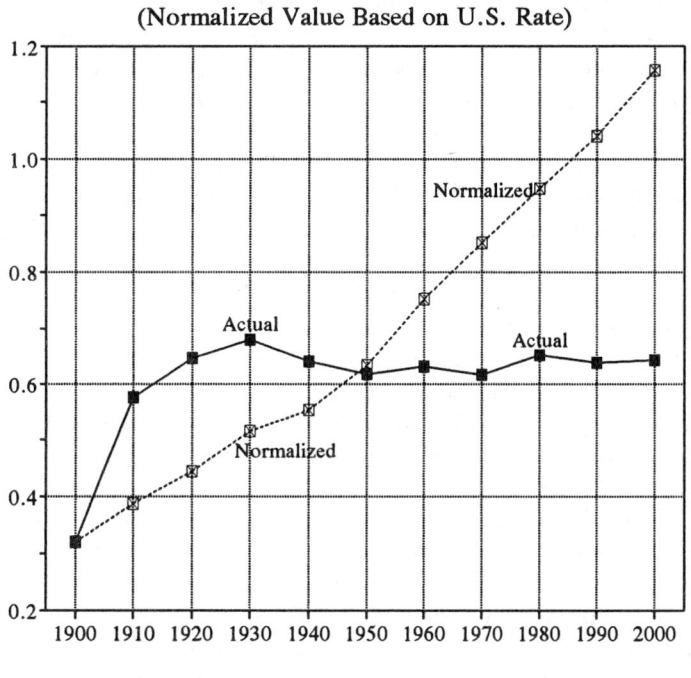

Year	Population	Growth Rate	U.S. Rate	Ratio
1900	319,146	--	--	--
1910	577,056	80.8%	21.0%	3.84
1920	646,872	12.1%	15.0%	0.81
1930	680,845	5.3%	16.2%	0.32
1940	641,935	-5.7%	7.3%	-0.79
1950	619,636	-3.5%	14.5%	-0.24
1960	632,446	2.1%	18.5%	0.11
1970	617,792	-2.3%	13.4%	-0.17
1980	652,717	5.7%	11.4%	0.49
1990	638,800	-2.1%	9.8%	-0.22
2000	643,000	0.7%	11.1%	0.06

Figure 3-36 shows population growth in Ohio compared to the nation from 1900 through 2000. The format is explained on pages 2 and 18. Ohio grew at nearly the same rate as the nation from 1900 through 1960. It fell a little behind the national rate in the 1960s, slowed in the 1970s, and stopped in the 1980s. This duplicated the pattern followed by the other states in the Central region. Ohio had its lowest growth decade in the century in the 1980s, growing by only 0.5 percent. As described in the Introduction, the car industry crash of the late 1970s and early 1980s, and the shift of job creation away from heavy industry generally, stopped population growth in states like Ohio. It was one of the nation's most important industrial states up to 1970, but the population flow from the Central region in favor of the Sunbelt will keep population growth low for an indefinite period in Ohio.

Although Ohio's actual population line and normalized line were almost superimposed in 1960 (confirming that Ohio and the nation grew at the same rate from 1900 through 1960), the actual line will be 24 percent below the normalized line by 2000. If Ohio had grown as rapidly as the nation just from 1960 through 2000, it would have had hit the 15 million mark by 2000 (as shown by the normalized line). Instead Ohio will have less than 11.5 million people in 2000.

Ohio was 27th on the growth list from 1900 through 1950 (Table 3-3). It fell from 4th on the population ranking list in 1900 to 5th in 1950 (Table 3-2) as it was passed by California. Ohio will fall to 34th on the growth list from 1950 through 2000, and it will fall to 7th on the population ranking list by 2000 as both Florida and Texas move ahead of it. Ohio is projected to grow very little in the first half of the next century, and it will fall to 8th on the population ranking list by 2050 (Table 5-1) as Georgia moves past it into 7th place.

Cleveland lost its lead as Ohio's largest city in 1990. Cleveland lost 45 percent of its population from 1950 through 1990, and was 10 percent smaller in 1990 (505,616) than it was in 1910. Cincinnati grew and declined in a similar way and was nearly the same size in 1990 (364,114) as in 1910. Columbus, the largest city in Ohio in 1990 with 632,954 people, grew by 12 percent in the 1980s, and by 68 percent from 1950 through 1990. The Cleveland-Akron metropolitan area still had a big lead with 2.9 million in 1990, while the Cincinnati area (including part of Kentucky across the Ohio River) had 1.8 million and the Columbus area 1.3 million. The Cleveland area had 26 percent of the state's population, but the area fell by 2.7 percent in the 1980s. The Columbus area gained 10.8 percent and the Cincinnati area 5.3 percent.

Figure 3-36. Ohio Population (in Millions)

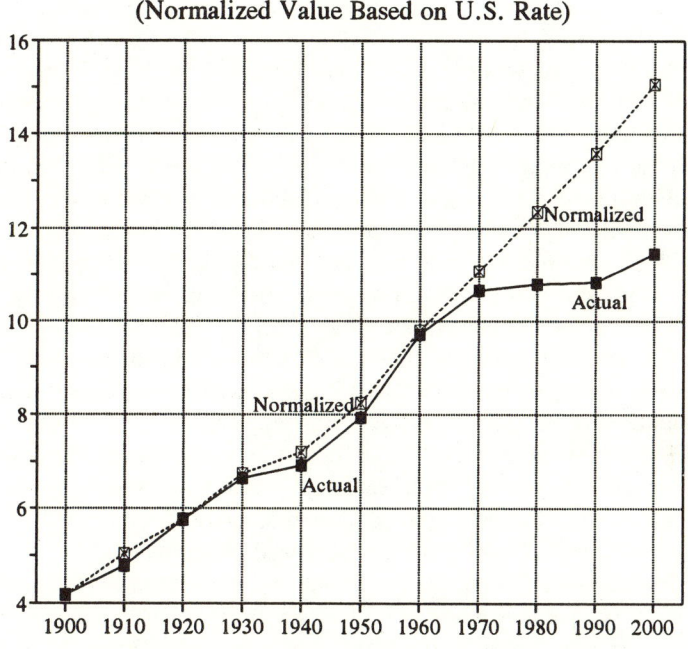

(Normalized Value Based on U.S. Rate)

Year	Population	Growth Rate	U.S. Rate	Ratio
1900	4,157,545	--	--	--
1910	4,767,121	14.7%	21.0%	0.70
1920	5,759,394	20.8%	15.0%	1.39
1930	6,646,697	15.4%	16.2%	0.95
1940	6,907,612	3.9%	7.3%	0.54
1950	7,946,627	15.0%	14.5%	1.04
1960	9,706,397	22.1%	18.5%	1.20
1970	10,657,423	9.8%	13.4%	0.73
1980	10,797,603	1.3%	11.4%	0.12
1990	10,847,115	0.5%	9.8%	0.05
2000	11,453,000	5.6%	11.1%	0.50

Figure 3-37 shows population growth in Oklahoma compared to the nation from 1900 through 2000. The format is explained on pages 2 and 18. Oklahoma grew over five times as fast as the nation in the 1900-1910 decade (ratio of 5.22), and stayed ahead up to 1930 (ratios above 1.00). This was a result of the land and oil booms that started in earnest in 1889 and ran into the early 1900s, with statehood for Oklahoma in 1907 helping the process. But drought and misuse of land produced the infamous "dust bowl" of the 1930s, and the state lost population in the 1930s and 1940s. The losses stopped in the 1950s, and recovery of some farmland and the demand for oil and natural gas put Oklahoma in position to benefit from the outflow of people from the Central and Northeastern regions in the 1970s, as described in the Introduction. The 1970s were a time of high growth for Oklahoma.

The actual population line for Oklahoma soared far above the normalized line in the 1900-1910 decade, and the actual line stayed constantly above the normalized line afterwards. This means that Oklahoma grew more rapidly than the nation at all points in the century as measured from the 1900 baseline. After 1930 the lines started coming closer together, but the growth spurt in the 1970s kept Oklahoma's overall growth rate well ahead of the nation.

Oklahoma was 12th on the growth list from 1900 through 1950 (Table 3-3), and it climbed from 30th on the population ranking list in 1900 to 25th in 1950 (Table 3-2). Oklahoma will fall to 32nd on the growth list from 1950 through 2000, and it will fall to 28th on the population ranking list by 2000. It is projected that Oklahoma will grow at almost exactly the same rate as the nation in the first half of the next century, and it will move up one place to 27th on the population ranking list by 2050 (Table 5-1).

Oklahoma is a Sunbelt state, but it is in the low-growth category because it grew more slowly than the nation from 1950 through 2000, even though it will grow more rapidly from 1900 through 2000. It tends to be overshadowed by Texas, its massive neighbor to the south, but Oklahoma's natural resources keep it near the national growth rate. Its major cities in 1990 were Oklahoma City (444,724) and Tulsa (367,302). Their respective metropolitan areas had 1.0 million and 0.7 million people. The cities are only 100 miles apart, and if their metropolitan areas were combined they would have 54 percent of the state's population. Oklahoma City and its metropolitan area both grew by over 10 percent in the 1980s, but Tulsa grew by only 1.8 percent as its metropolitan area grew by 7.9 percent.

Figure 3-37. Oklahoma Population (in Millions)

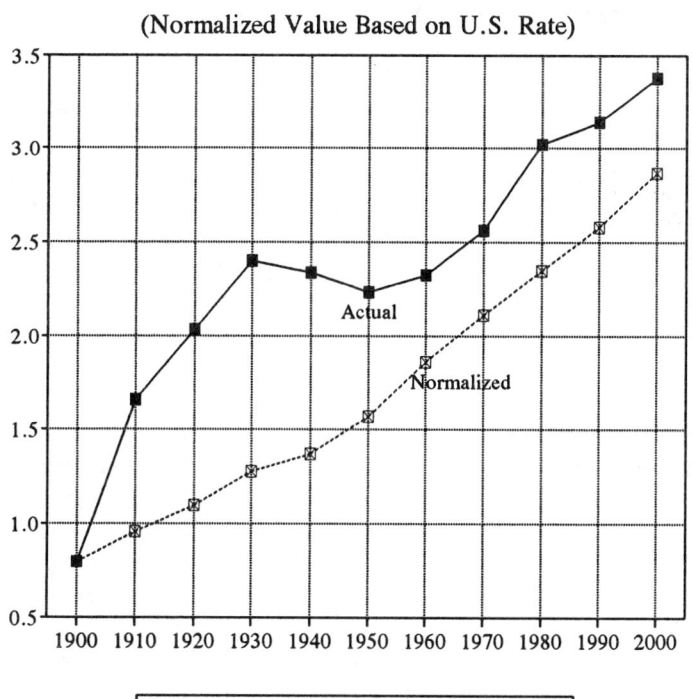

Year	Population	Growth Rate	U.S. Rate	Ratio
1900	790,391	--	--	--
1910	1,657,155	109.7%	21.0%	5.22
1920	2,028,283	22.4%	15.0%	1.50
1930	2,396,040	18.1%	16.2%	1.12
1940	2,336,434	-2.5%	7.3%	-0.34
1950	2,233,351	-4.4%	14.5%	-0.30
1960	2,328,284	4.3%	18.5%	0.23
1970	2,559,463	9.9%	13.4%	0.74
1980	3,025,487	18.2%	11.4%	1.59
1990	3,145,585	4.0%	9.8%	0.41
2000	3,382,000	7.5%	11.1%	0.68

Figure 3-38 shows population growth in Oregon compared to the nation from 1900 through 2000. The format is explained on pages 2 and 18. Oregon has been a high-growth state through the century. In the two decades during which its growth was below the national level (ratios less than 1.00), Oregon's rate was still over 80 percent of the national rate. Its growth rate benefited from a small population base in 1900, but Oregon was a sizable state when it grew over twice as rapidly as the nation in the 1970s (2.27 ratio). Its early growth was led by the lumber industry in its huge coastal forests, but its second highest decade for growth was the 1940s. World War II brought many people to the West Coast who stayed or returned after the war ended. This has been a factor in Oregon's later growth, as many people find Oregon to be a refuge from more crowded and hectic areas like California.

Oregon's actual population line jumped above the normalized line when Oregon tripled the national growth rate (ratio of 2.98) in the 1900-1910 decade. The difference between the two lines increased as the century progressed and Oregon kept growing more rapidly than the nation. By 2000 Oregon will be more than twice as large as it would have been if it had grown at the national rate, meaning that its growth ratio more than doubled the national ratio from 1900 through 2000.

Oregon was 6th on the growth ratio list from 1900 through 1950 (Table 3-3), going from 36th on the population ranking list in 1900 to 32nd in 1950 (Table 3-2). It will be 14th on the growth list from 1950 through 2000 and 27th on the population ranking list by 2000. This gain of nine places on the population ranking list from 1900 through 2000 is the 6th best in the nation (Table 3-4). Oregon will grow more rapidly than the nation after 2000, and it will move up three places to 24th on the population ranking list by 2050 (Table 5-1).

Oregon's coastal area, where most people live, qualifies as a Sunbelt state on the basis of average temperature. It also qualifies in terms of growth, resources, and capital investment. But Oregon's major city, Portland (438,802 in 1990), definitely did not look like a typical high-growth Sunbelt state city as it grew by only 17 percent from 1950 through 1990. It held 25 percent of state population in 1950, but only 15 percent in 1990. However, the Portland-Salem metropolitan area was 1.8 million in 1990, over 63 percent of state population. The area includes part of Washington across the Columbia River, but its percentage of state population fairly represents Oregon's concentration of population on the coast. The area grew by 13.3 percent in the 1980s, matching Sunbelt state expectations.

Oregon

Figure 3-38. Oregon Population (in Millions)

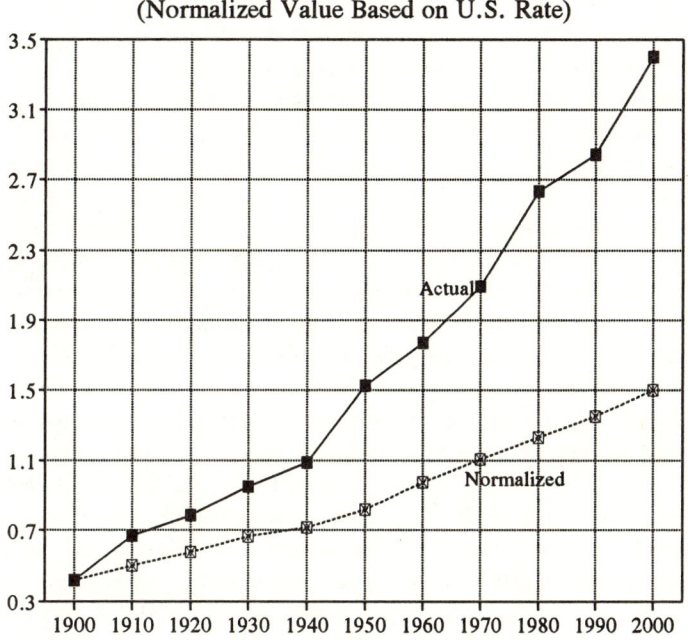

Year	Population	Growth Rate	U.S. Rate	Ratio
1900	413,536	--	--	--
1910	672,765	62.7%	21.0%	2.98
1920	783,389	16.4%	15.0%	1.10
1930	953,786	21.8%	16.2%	1.34
1940	1,089,684	14.2%	7.3%	1.96
1950	1,521,341	39.6%	14.5%	2.73
1960	1,768,687	16.3%	18.5%	0.88
1970	2,091,533	18.3%	13.4%	1.37
1980	2,633,156	25.9%	11.4%	2.27
1990	2,842,321	7.9%	9.8%	0.81
2000	3,404,000	19.8%	11.1%	1.79

Figure 3-39 shows population growth in Pennsylvania compared to the nation from 1900 through 2000. The format is explained on pages 2 and 18. Pennsylvania was the second largest state in the nation in 1900, but it grew more rapidly than the nation only in the 1900-1910 decade (all subsequent ratios below 1.00). It is a good model for the population outflow from the industrialized states of the Northeast that began in the 1940s and peaked in the 1970s, as described in the Introduction. Pennsylvania suffers from its location. People move to New Jersey, Delaware, and Maryland while staying in commuting range of Philadelphia but avoiding its taxes. These three states are the only states in the Northeast region to grow more rapidly than the nation from 1900 through 2000. Also, with New York City only ninety miles away, capital investment flows there in preference to Philadelphia.

The actual population line for Pennsylvania was above the normalized line only in the 1900-1910 decade. It fell below by 1920, and the difference increased in each decade thereafter. As shown by the normalized line, if Pennsylvania had grown at the same rate as the nation from 1900 through 2000, it would have had 23 million people in 2000, making it the 2nd largest state. But it will have just over half that total. That means that the growth ratio for Pennsylvania will be only a little more than half that of the nation from 1900 through 2000.

Pennsylvania was 35th on the growth list from 1900 through 1950 (Table 3-3), falling from 2nd on the population ranking list in 1900 (Table 3-2) to 3rd in 1950 (it was passed by California). Pennsylvania will be 47th on the growth list from 1950 through 2000, and it will fall to 5th on the population ranking list by 2000 as it is passed by Texas and Florida. Pennsylvania is projected to grow almost not at all in the first half of the next century, and it will drop to 6th on the population ranking list by 2050 (Table 5-1) as it falls behind Illinois.

Philadelphia, Pennsylvania's major city, was the nation's 3rd largest in 1900 and 1950. But it fell 23 percent from its 1950 peak to 1,585,577 in 1990, going from 20 percent of state population to 13 percent. Pittsburgh fell more rapidly, losing 45 percent from its 1950 peak to 369,879 in 1990. The Philadelphia metropolitan area had 5.9 million people in 1990, but the area includes portions of the states of New Jersey, Delaware, and Maryland, the three that absorbed many people from Pennsylvania over the century. The Pittsburgh metropolitan area had 2.4 million people in 1990 (20 percent of state population), but it had the nation's worst metropolitan area loss in the 1980s, falling by 6.9 percent.

Figure 3-39. Pennsylvania Population (in Millions)

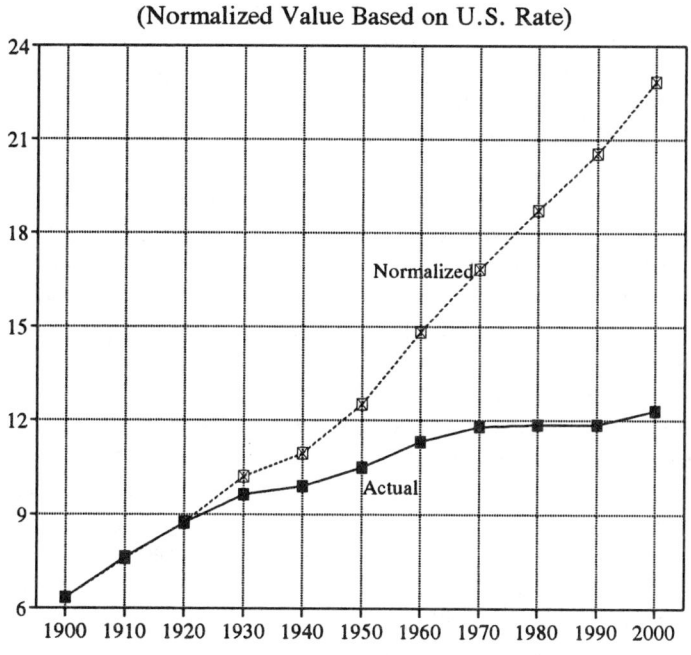

Year	Population	Growth Rate	U.S. Rate	Ratio
1900	6,302,115	--	--	--
1910	7,665,111	21.6%	21.0%	1.03
1920	8,720,017	13.8%	15.0%	0.92
1930	9,631,350	10.5%	16.2%	0.64
1940	9,900,180	2.8%	7.3%	0.38
1950	10,498,012	6.0%	14.5%	0.42
1960	11,319,366	7.8%	18.5%	0.42
1970	11,800,766	4.3%	13.4%	0.32
1980	11,864,720	0.5%	11.4%	0.05
1990	11,881,643	0.1%	9.8%	0.01
2000	12,296,000	3.5%	11.1%	0.32

Figure 3-40 shows population growth in Rhode Island compared to the nation from 1900 through 2000. The format is explained on pages 2 and 18. Rhode Island matched the nation's growth from 1900 through 1930 as an influx of immigrants came to work in the state's textile mills. But growth slowed in the depression of the 1930s, and the movement of textile mills to the lower tax and lower wage areas of the South depressed growth in Rhode Island for the next few decades. Then, in the 1970s, as explained in the Introduction, Rhode Island was hit by the same exodus as the other states in the Northeast region, and population growth essentially stopped. Rhode Island lost population in the 1970s, and it is forecasted to lose population again in the 1990s. With almost no natural resources and no influx of capital investment (the neighboring states of Massachusetts and Connecticut are much more likely targets for the investment that is available), Rhode Island is hard pressed to increase its population.

The surge in growth in the 1900-1910 decade kept Rhode Island's actual population line above the normalized line up to 1920. Even as growth slowed after 1930, the actual line stayed close to the normalized line up to 1950. But as population shifted to the Sunbelt in the 1950s, the actual line fell further behind, and when growth stopped after 1970 the gap increased dramatically. The actual line will be 35 percent below the normalized line by 2000, meaning that Rhode Island's growth ratio will be 35 percent less than that of the nation from 1900 through 2000.

Rhode Island was 28th on the growth list from 1900 through 1950 (Table 3-3), and it fell from 35th on the population ranking list in 1900 (Table 3-2) to 37th in 1950. But it will be 44th on the growth list from 1950 through 2000, and it will fall to 43rd on the population ranking list by 2000. Only Iowa and the District of Columbia will fall more places on the ranking list for that period (Table 3-4). Rhode Island is projected to continue to grow more slowly than the nation after 2000 as it falls to 44th on the population ranking list in 2050 (Table 5-1).

With industrial manufacturing the key source of job creation, Rhode Island's major city, Providence, held 41 percent of the state's population in 1900. This fell to 31 percent in 1950, and by 1990 it was down to 16 percent. Providence lost 35 percent of its population from 1950 through 1990, and with 160,728 people in 1990 it was about 10 percent smaller than it was in 1900. The Providence metropolitan area was too small to make the top eighty-five list (400,000 minimum), but if the cities reasonably close to Providence are combined, the total is about 400,000, representing 40 percent of the population of the state.

Figure 3-40. Rhode Island Population (in Millions)

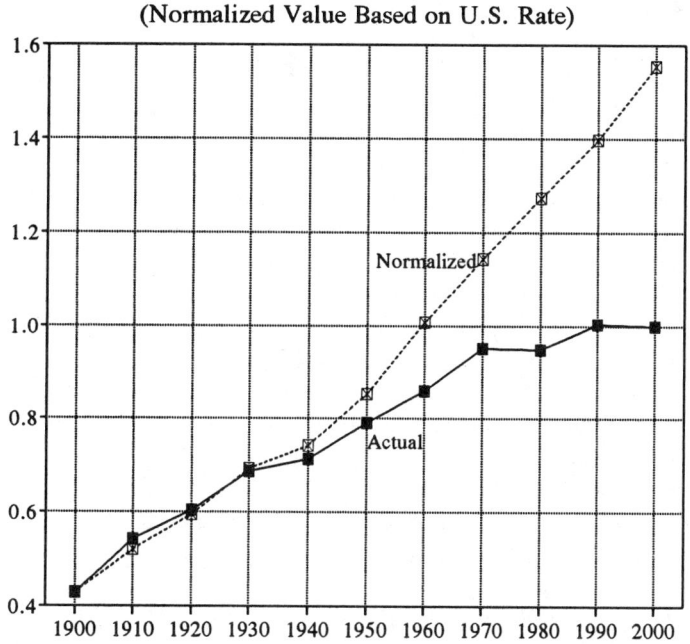

Year	Population	Growth Rate	U.S. Rate	Ratio
1900	428,556	--	--	--
1910	542,610	26.6%	21.0%	1.27
1920	604,397	11.4%	15.0%	0.76
1930	687,497	13.7%	16.2%	0.85
1940	713,346	3.8%	7.3%	0.52
1950	791,896	11.0%	14.5%	0.76
1960	859,488	8.5%	18.5%	0.46
1970	949,723	10.5%	13.4%	0.79
1980	947,154	-0.3%	11.4%	-0.02
1990	1,003,464	5.9%	9.8%	0.61
2000	998,000	-0.5%	11.1%	-0.05

Figure 3-41 shows population growth in South Carolina compared to the nation from 1900 through 2000. The format is explained on pages 2 and 18. South Carolina grew more slowly than the nation up to 1930 (ratios less than 1.00), partly due to blacks migrating to the industrial cities of the North and West regions. South Carolina beat the nation's low growth rate in the 1930s, but returned to slower growth again in the next three decades. The massive outflow of population from the Northeast and Central regions after 1970, as described in the Introduction, led to good growth in South Carolina. It had been primarily an agricultural state, but even as its main crop shifted from cotton to tobacco as the century progressed, the manufacturing of textile and chemical products became the largest source of job creation after 1950. This helped to make South Carolina a target for the population shift to the Sunbelt that became a flood in the 1970s.

South Carolina's actual population line trailed the normalized line through the century, but the gap shrank after 1970. In 1950 the actual line was 20 percent below the normalized line. In 2000 the actual line will be 19 percent below the normalized line, meaning that South Carolina will grow a little more rapidly than the nation from 1950 through 2000, after being well behind from 1900 through 1950. South Carolina was 39th on the growth list from 1900 through 1950 (Table 3-3), falling from 24th on the population ranking list in 1900 to 27th in 1950 (Table 3-2). It will be 20th on the growth list from 1950 through 2000 and will be 26th on the population ranking list in 2000. South Carolina will grow at the same rate as the nation after 2000 and will be in 26th place on the population ranking list in 2050 (Table 5-1).

South Carolina is a Sunbelt state that barely makes the high growth list because it will grow only slightly more rapidly than the nation from 1950 through 2000. It is not a target for immigrants, and it tends to be overshadowed by its larger neighbors, North Carolina and Georgia. Columbia was South Carolina's largest city in 1990 with 103,477 people. Charleston, perhaps the best known city, had a population of only 79,925, but with North Charleston the total was 150,229. The Charleston metropolitan area had 506,875 people, compared to only 453,331 for the Columbia area. But the largest metropolitan area in the state was the Greenville-Spartanberg-Anderson area with 830,563, which was 24 percent of the state's population. With Charleston on the coast, Columbia in the center of the state, and Greenville in the northwest corner, the three areas are well distributed across the state. In total, they had 51 percent of the state's population.

Figure 3-41. South Carolina Population (in Millions)

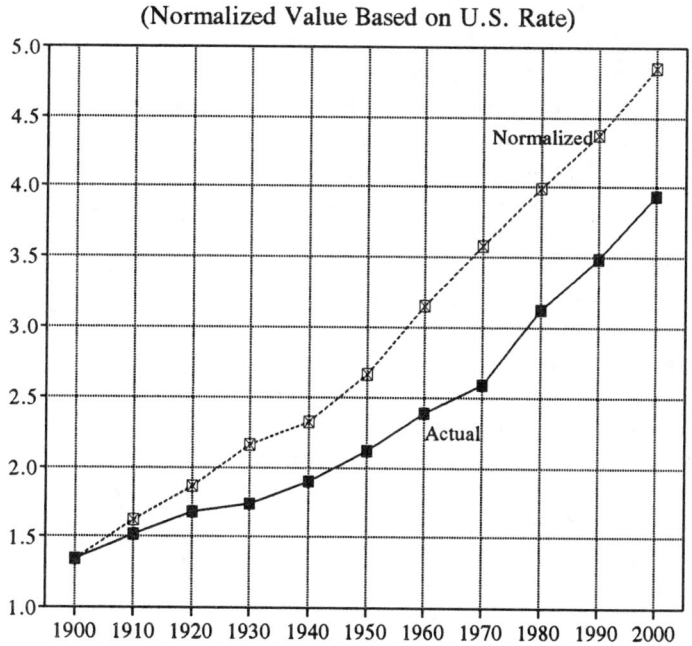

Year	Population	Growth Rate	U.S. Rate	Ratio
1900	1,340,316	--	--	--
1910	1,515,400	13.1%	21.0%	0.62
1920	1,683,724	11.1%	15.0%	0.74
1930	1,738,765	3.3%	16.2%	0.20
1940	1,899,804	9.3%	7.3%	1.27
1950	2,117,027	11.4%	14.5%	0.79
1960	2,382,594	12.5%	18.5%	0.68
1970	2,590,713	8.7%	13.4%	0.65
1980	3,120,729	20.5%	11.4%	1.79
1990	3,486,703	11.7%	9.8%	1.20
2000	3,932,000	12.8%	11.1%	1.15

Figure 3-42 shows population growth in South Dakota compared to the nation from 1900 through 2000. The format is explained on pages 2 and 18. South Dakota grew more rapidly than the nation only in the 1900-1910 decade. In every decade afterward, it grew more slowly than the nation (ratios less than 1.00). The initial high growth was due to the surge of homesteading that took place in the central part of the nation from late in the nineteenth century into the beginning of the 1900s. Growth slowed immediately after the 1910-1911 drought, and the population fell in the 1930s in the depression (as shown by the negative ratio). South Dakota also lost population in the 1960s, and it was not until 1990 that the population exceeded the level reached in 1930. Although South Dakota has been a leading supplier of gold, its major products are corn and cattle, and relatively few people are attracted to the tough lifestyle involved with producing these commodities in the climate of South Dakota.

The surge of growth in the 1900-1910 decade kept South Dakota's actual population line above the normalized line up to 1930, but the population loss in the 1930s drove the actual line below the normalized line by 1940. It fell further behind in each subsequent decade. By 2000 the actual line will be about 50 percent below the normalized line, even if the optimistic forecast of the Bureau of the Census for the 1990s takes place. This means that South Dakota's growth ratio from 1900 through 2000 will be about 50 percent below that of the nation.

South Dakota was 38th on the growth list from 1900 through 1950 (Table 3-3), and it fell from 38th on the population ranking list in 1900 (Table 3-2) to 41st in 1950. It will be 46th on the growth list from 1950 through 2000, and it will fall to 45th on the population ranking list by 2000. South Dakota is projected to continue to grow slowly after 2000, and it will be passed by Delaware and Alaska, the two states just behind it on the 2000 rankings list. South Dakota will fall to 47th on the population ranking list by 2050 (Table 5-1).

South Dakota's largest city is Sioux Falls. It had 100,836 people in 1990, 14 percent of the state's population. Rapid City, at the other end of the state, is South Dakota's second largest city with 54,523 people. No metropolitan area in South Dakota is big enough to make the top eighty-five list (400,000 minimum), and there will not be one for many years to come. Sioux Falls and Rapid City had only 22 percent of the state's population between them, and the next thirteen largest cities in the state do not have as many people together as do Sioux Falls and Rapid City. Congestion is not a problem in the state.

South Dakota

Figure 3-42. South Dakota Population (in Millions)

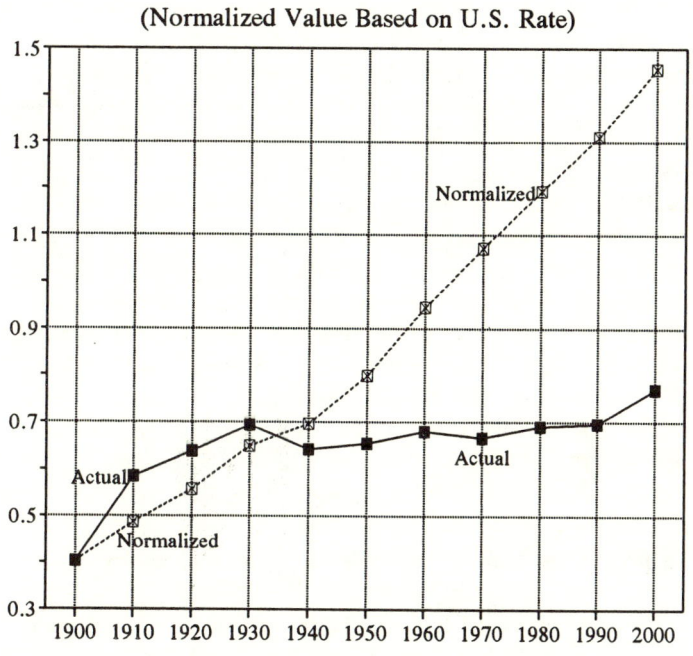

Year	Population	Growth Rate	U.S. Rate	Ratio
1900	401,570	--	--	--
1910	583,888	45.4%	21.0%	2.16
1920	636,547	9.0%	15.0%	0.60
1930	692,849	8.8%	16.2%	0.55
1940	642,961	-7.2%	7.3%	-0.99
1950	652,740	1.5%	14.5%	0.10
1960	680,514	4.3%	18.5%	0.23
1970	666,257	-2.1%	13.4%	-0.16
1980	690,768	3.7%	11.4%	0.32
1990	696,004	0.8%	9.8%	0.08
2000	770,000	10.6%	11.1%	0.96

Figure 3-43 shows population growth in Tennessee compared to the nation from 1900 through 2000. The format is explained on pages 2 and 18. Except for the 1930s, Tennessee grew slowly (ratios less than 1.00) up to 1970. Tennessee's edge in the 1930s was helped by the nation's having its lowest growth rate of the century and by the start of the Tennessee Valley Authority. The outflow of population from the Northeast and Central regions that began in 1970, as described in the Introduction, gave Tennessee a boost in the 1970s. Growth fell again in the 1980s, but a rebound is projected for the 1990s. Tennessee's move from an agricultural to an industrial state, with a focus on cities rather than farms, and its development as the center for the country music industry, helped to improve growth later in the century.

Tennessee's actual population line has been below the normalized line since the start of the century, with the gap growing larger as the century progressed. But in the last three decades the difference stabilized. By 2000 the actual line will be about 24 percent below the normalized line, while in 1950 it was about 18 percent below. The additional loss came from 1950 through 1970. Tennessee was 37th on the growth list from 1900 through 1950 (Table 3-3), falling from 14th on the population ranking list in 1900 (Table 3-2) to 16th in 1950. It will be 23rd on the growth list from 1950 through 2000, and it will hold onto 16th place in the population rankings by 2000. Although Tennessee is projected to grow more slowly than the nation after 2000, it will still be 16th on the population ranking list in 2050 (Table 5-1). This will put Tennessee in the unusual position of maintaining the same place on the population ranking list in 1950, 2000, and 2050.

Tennessee is in the northern tier of Sunbelt states, but it is a landlocked state in the low-growth category. Memphis (610,337) was its largest city in 1990, with Nashville (510,784) catching up fast after mergers. The Memphis lead of 326,650 in 1960 was down to 99,463 in 1990. If metropolitan areas within the state borders are considered, Nashville went ahead in 1990. The Nashville area was 985,026, an increase of 16 percent from 1980. Although the Memphis area includes parts of Arkansas and Mississippi, it had only 1,007,306 people. This was 22,280 ahead of Nashville in total, but behind within state borders. Both areas had about 20 percent of the state's population, with the third largest area, Knoxville, having 12 percent. With Memphis in the southwest corner of the state, Nashville in the middle, and Knoxville in the east, the population centers in Tennessee are well distributed (and growing more rapidly than the state).

Figure 3-43. Tennessee Population (in Millions)

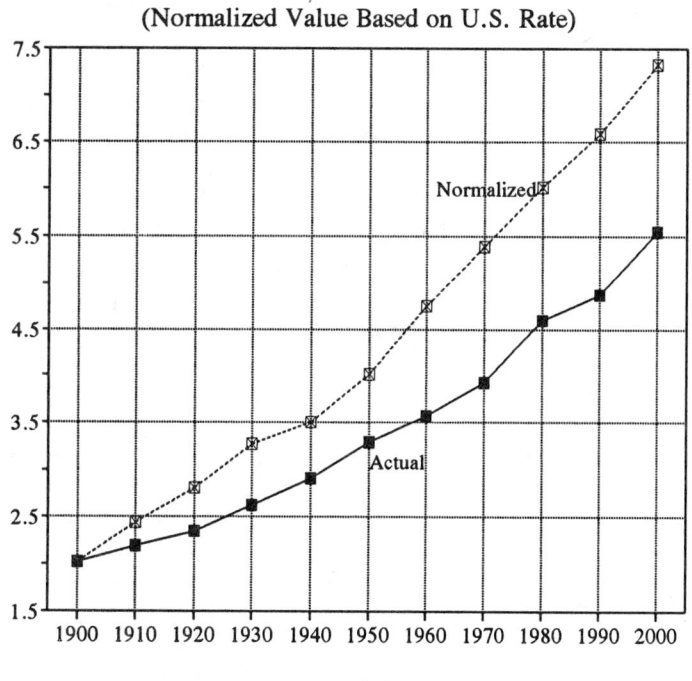

(Normalized Value Based on U.S. Rate)

Year	Population	Growth Rate	U.S. Rate	Ratio
1900	2,020,616	--	--	--
1910	2,184,789	8.1%	21.0%	0.39
1920	2,337,885	7.0%	15.0%	0.47
1930	2,616,556	11.9%	16.2%	0.74
1940	2,915,841	11.4%	7.3%	1.57
1950	3,291,718	12.9%	14.5%	0.89
1960	3,567,089	8.4%	18.5%	0.45
1970	3,926,018	10.1%	13.4%	0.75
1980	4,591,023	16.9%	11.4%	1.48
1990	4,877,185	6.2%	9.8%	0.64
2000	5,538,000	13.5%	11.1%	1.22

Figure 3-44 shows population growth in Texas compared to the nation from 1900 through 2000. The format is explained on pages 2 and 18. Texas was a high-growth state (ratios greater than 1.00) through the century. It was already the nation's sixth most populous state in 1900, and its diversified combination of cotton, cattle, and oil (the famous Spindletop strike came in 1901) kept people coming in every decade. Texas became a major manufacturing state after World War II, with aircraft and electronics adding to its chemical and oil industries. This diversification played a big role in the state's most recent growth cycle. The varied jobs available made Texas a target for the population outflow from the Northeast and Central regions that began in 1970, as described in the Introduction. The population of Texas soared in the 1970s, and growth stayed high afterwards.

The actual population line for Texas stayed above the normalized line at every point, meaning that the state's growth ratio since 1900 was above that of the nation throughout the century. The gap grew larger as the century progressed, with the largest increase taking place in the last three decades. By 2000 the actual line will be 80 percent above the normalized line, meaning that Texas's growth ratio from 1900 through 2000 will be 80 percent higher than that of the nation.

Texas was 15th on the growth list from 1900 through 1950 (Table 3-3), but this was only good enough to keep it in 6th place on the population ranking list in both 1900 and 1950 (Table 3-2). Texas will improve to 10th on the growth list from 1950 through 2000, and it will move up to 2nd on the population ranking list by 2000, passing Ohio, Illinois, Pennsylvania, and New York. Texas is projected to continue to grow much more rapidly than the nation after 2000. It will stay in 2nd place behind California on the population ranking list in 2050 (Table 5-1), passing 33 million in population on the way.

Texas is a model high-growth Sunbelt state. It has a diversified economy, capital investment flows like water (or oil), and it is a target for immigrants. It should grow indefinitely. The growth of the three major cities in Texas is shown in Figure 4-26. Houston, Dallas, and San Antonio were close in size in 1900, but oil drove Houston into the lead and to a population of 1,629,902 in 1990. However, Dallas led in metropolitan area with 4.0 million, compared to 3.7 million for Houston and 1.3 million for San Antonio. Dallas and Houston had almost equal shares of 46 percent of the state's population. As growth continues during the 1990s, Texas will become the first state to have three cities over 1 million in population.

Texas

Figure 3-44. Texas Population (in Millions)

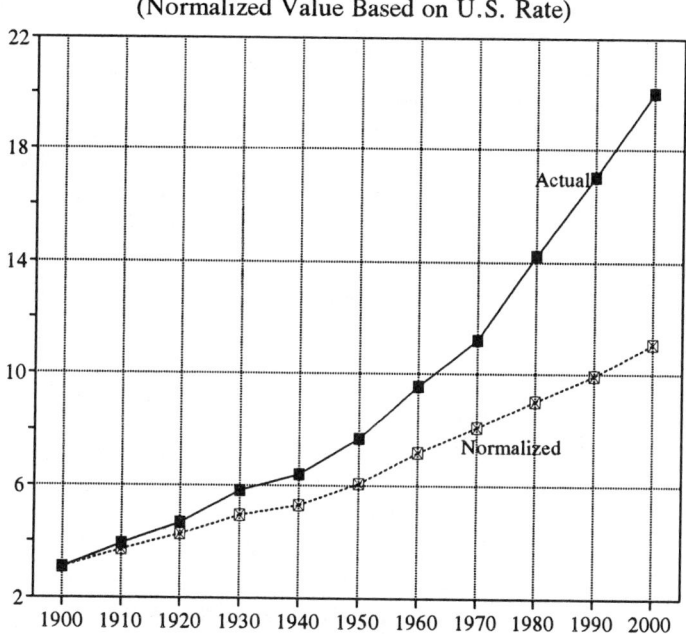

(Normalized Value Based on U.S. Rate)

····⊠···· Normalized   ─■─ Actual

Year	Population	Growth Rate	U.S. Rate	Ratio
1900	3,048,710	--	--	--
1910	3,896,542	27.8%	21.0%	1.32
1920	4,663,228	19.7%	15.0%	1.32
1930	5,824,715	24.9%	16.2%	1.54
1940	6,414,824	10.1%	7.3%	1.39
1950	7,711,194	20.2%	14.5%	1.39
1960	9,579,677	24.2%	18.5%	1.31
1970	11,198,655	16.9%	13.4%	1.26
1980	14,225,513	27.0%	11.4%	2.36
1990	16,986,510	19.4%	9.8%	1.98
2000	20,038,000	18.0%	11.1%	1.62

Figure 3-45 shows population growth in Utah compared to the nation from 1900 through 2000. The format is explained on pages 2 and 18. Utah grew more rapidly than the nation (ratios greater than 1.00) in every decade but the 1920s. The mining of minerals (especially copper) and the use of irrigation to raise crops, following the lead of the Mormons, kept Utah growing early in the century. There was a surge in growth in the 1940s, due to army installations associated with World War II, but the highest growth period was the 1970s. This was due to the population outflow from the Northeast and Central regions that began in 1970, as described in the Introduction. Utah was seen as a well organized, low crime state due to its heavy Mormon influence. The diversification of the economy led by electronics firms coming to the state from higher-cost areas made Utah an attractive relocation target. Growth has stayed strong since 1970.

Like that of Texas, the actual population line for Utah was always above the normalized line, meaning that Utah's growth ratio since 1900 was always above that of the nation. Also like Texas, the gap grew larger as the century progressed, with the largest increase taking place in the last three decades. By 2000 the actual line will be 115 percent above the normalized line, meaning that Utah's growth ratio from 1900 through 2000 will be 115 percent higher than that of the nation.

Utah was 16th on the growth list from 1900 through 1950 (Table 3-3), moving up three places from 42nd on the population ranking list in 1900 to 39th in 1950 (Table 3-2). Utah will be 6th on the growth list from 1950 through 2000, and it will move up to 34th on the population ranking list by 2000. Utah is projected to continue to grow much more rapidly than the nation in the first half of the next century, and it will move up to 31st on the population ranking list in 2050 (Table 5-1).

Utah is too cold to be a Sunbelt state, and it is not a target for immigrants. But it has enjoyed good capital investment because of its reputation as a good place to live. Salt Lake City, the headquarters of the Mormon Church, is by far Utah's largest city. But at 159,928 people in 1990 it was 12 percent smaller that it was in 1950, and the 9 percent of the state's population it held in 1990 was down from 26 percent in 1950. However, the metropolitan area of Salt Lake City (which includes Ogden) had almost 1.1 million people in 1990. This represented over 62 percent of the state's population, and is a much truer picture of how the population is concentrated in the Salt Lake City area. The area grew by 17.8 percent in the 1980s, almost exactly the same rate at which the state grew.

Utah

Figure 3-45. Utah Population (in Millions)

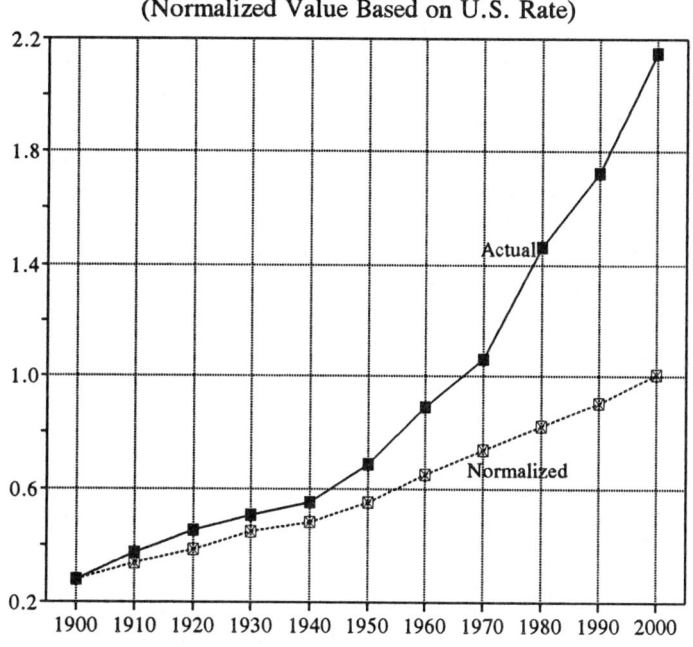

Year	Population	Growth Rate	U.S. Rate	Ratio
1900	276,749	--	--	--
1910	373,351	34.9%	21.0%	1.66
1920	449,396	20.4%	15.0%	1.36
1930	507,847	13.0%	16.2%	0.80
1940	550,310	8.4%	7.3%	1.15
1950	688,862	25.2%	14.5%	1.74
1960	890,627	29.3%	18.5%	1.58
1970	1,059,273	18.9%	13.4%	1.42
1980	1,461,037	37.9%	11.4%	3.32
1990	1,722,850	17.9%	9.8%	1.83
2000	2,148,000	24.7%	11.1%	2.23

Figure 3-46 shows population growth in Vermont compared to the nation from 1900 through 2000. The format is explained on pages 2 and 18. Vermont grew more slowly than the nation (ratios well below 1.00) in every decade up to 1960. Vermont lost population in the 1910-1920 decade and in the 1930s. It grew so slowly in the other decades that by 1940 its population was only 5 percent higher than it had been in 1900. This continued a trend that started late in the previous century. Between the census of 1870 and that of 1940, Vermont added only 28,680 people, a gain of less than 9 percent in seven decades.

Vermont had few natural resources, no land suitable for large-scale agriculture, no industrial base, and it was outside the main population centers. The result was little migration into the state and a very small population increase. Growth improved slightly in the 1940s and 1950s, and then, from 1960 through 1990, Vermont benefited from the population outflow from the large industrial states of the Northeast region that peaked in the 1970s, as described in the Introduction. Vermont was an alternative for those who wanted to stay in the region and found a lifestyle centered on dairy farming to be satisfactory. However, the improved growth was just a little higher than the national rate, and in the 1990s Vermont will be a low-growth state again.

The actual population line for Vermont stayed well below the normalized line from 1900 onward, with the actual line being practically flat up to 1940. Even with the improved growth later in the century, by 2000 the actual line will be more than 50 percent below the normalized line, meaning that the growth ratio for Vermont from 1900 through 2000 will be less than half that of the nation.

Vermont was last in growth from 1900 through 1950 (Table 3-3), and it fell eight places from 39th on the population ranking list in 1900 to 47th in 1950 (Table 3-2). Only Kansas and Iowa fell further during that period (Table 3-4). Vermont will be 27th on the growth list from 1950 through 2000 but will fall to 49th on the population ranking list by 2000 because the states behind it in 1950 have grown more rapidly since then. Vermont will grow more slowly than the nation after 2000, and it will be last on the population ranking list in 2050 (Table 5-1).

Vermont's largest city is Burlington (39,127 in 1990), the smallest city in the nation to be a state's largest. With South Burlington it had 51,936, just ahead of Cheyenne, Wyoming. With only 7 percent of the state's population, Burlington is still twice as big as the next largest city and is the major metropolitan area in the state. By this measure, Vermont is the most rural state in the nation.

Vermont

Figure 3-46. Vermont Population (in Millions)

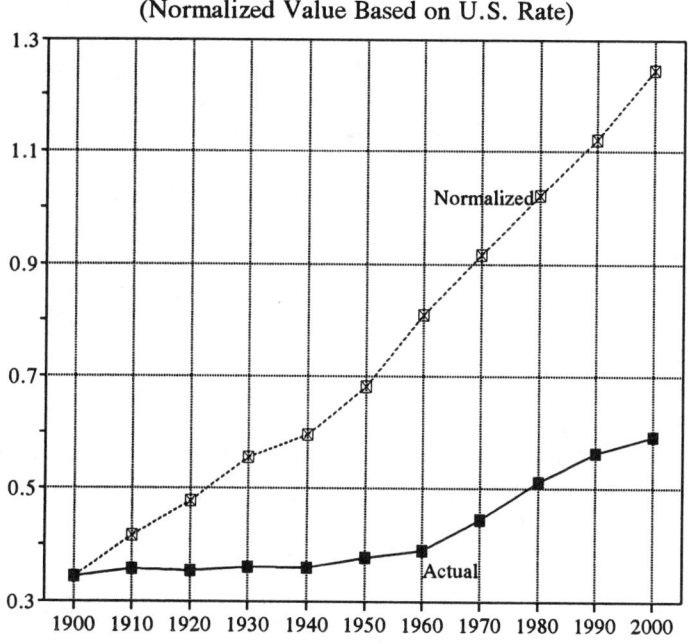

Year	Population	Growth Rate	U.S. Rate	Ratio
1900	343,641	--	--	--
1910	355,956	3.6%	21.0%	0.17
1920	352,428	-1.0%	15.0%	-0.07
1930	359,611	2.0%	16.2%	0.13
1940	359,231	-0.1%	7.3%	-0.01
1950	377,747	5.2%	14.5%	0.36
1960	389,881	3.2%	18.5%	0.17
1970	444,732	14.1%	13.4%	1.05
1980	511,456	15.0%	11.4%	1.31
1990	562,758	10.0%	9.8%	1.02
2000	592,000	5.2%	11.1%	0.47

Figure 3-47 shows population growth in Virginia compared to the nation from 1900 through 2000. The format is explained on pages 2 and 18. Virginia grew more slowly than the nation (ratios below 1.00) up to 1930, but it grew more rapidly afterwards (ratios greater than 1.00). Virginia was mainly an agricultural state early in the century, with tobacco the main crop. But the growth of the federal government from the 1930s onward greatly benefited Virginia. The state was a prime location for government workers living outside the District of Columbia and for buildings like the Pentagon. Virginia also benefited from government growth in terms of the naval base at Norfolk and the shipyards and shipbuilding activities in Hampton Roads and Newport News. Virginia developed a diversified economy as the century progressed, with chemical manufacturing becoming the leading industrial activity. Thus, when the population outflow from the Northeast and Central regions began in the 1970s, as described in the Introduction, Virginia became a target for people leaving these regions.

The actual population line trailed the normalized line from 1900 onward, due to the slow growth before 1930. But as Virginia grew more rapidly than the nation after 1930, the gap between the lines kept shrinking until the actual line moved ahead in 1990. This meant that Virginia's growth ratio since the 1900 baseline exceeded that of the nation for the first time. Continued good growth in the 1990s will put the actual line above the normalized line by about 5 percent in 2000.

Virginia was 30th on the growth list from 1900 through 1950 (Table 3-3), going from 17th on the population ranking list in 1900 to 15th in 1950 (Table 3-2). It will be 18th on the growth list from 1950 through 2000, and move to 12th on the population ranking list by 2000. Virginia will grow at the same rate as the nation after 2000 and will stay in 12th place on the population ranking list in 2050 (Table 5-1).

Up to 1950 Richmond was the largest city in Virginia, but it was passed by Norfolk at 304,869 people in 1960. Norfolk was passed in 1990 by a former suburb, Virginia Beach, which merged its way to 393,089, a 50 percent jump from 1980. Each city held less than 7 percent of state population at its peak. The Virginia Beach-Norfolk metropolitan area (which includes part of North Carolina) had 1.4 million people in 1990. The Richmond area, seventy-five miles away, had 0.9 million, giving the southeast corner of the state a third of the population. The northeast corner, 100 miles north of Richmond, also had a sizable share of the state as part of the 6.7 million people in the Baltimore-Washington metropolitan area.

Figure 3-47. Virginia Population (in Millions)

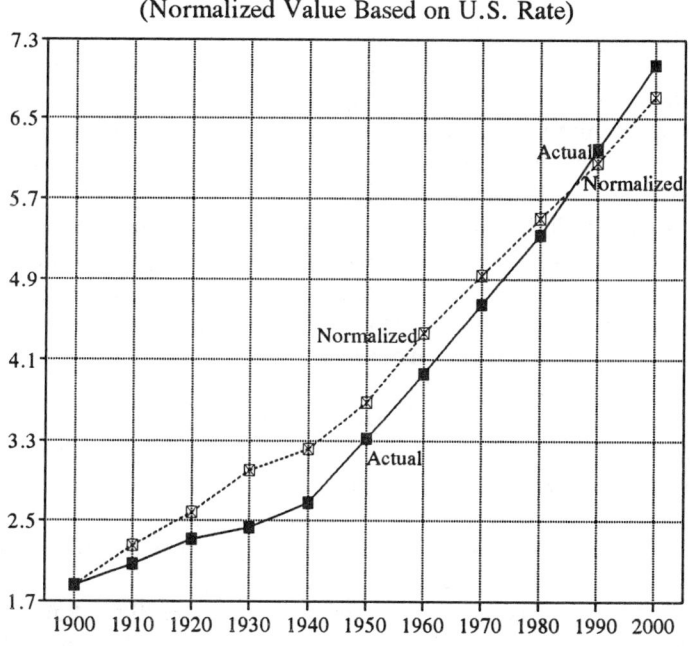

(Normalized Value Based on U.S. Rate)

Year	Population	Growth Rate	U.S. Rate	Ratio
1900	1,854,184	--	--	--
1910	2,061,612	11.2%	21.0%	0.53
1920	2,309,187	12.0%	15.0%	0.80
1930	2,421,851	4.9%	16.2%	0.30
1940	2,677,773	10.6%	7.3%	1.45
1950	3,318,680	23.9%	14.5%	1.65
1960	3,966,949	19.5%	18.5%	1.06
1970	4,651,448	17.3%	13.4%	1.29
1980	5,346,797	14.9%	11.4%	1.31
1990	6,187,358	15.7%	9.8%	1.61
2000	7,048,000	13.9%	11.1%	1.26

Figure 3-48 shows population growth in Washington compared to the nation from 1900 through 2000. The format is explained on pages 2 and 18. Washington grew more slowly than the nation only in the 1920s. It grew six times as fast as the nation in the 1900-1910 decade, more than doubling its population. This was a carryover of tremendous growth in the 1890s, when the completion of transcontinental railroads to the state brought a huge influx of settlers. The discovery of gold in Alaska in 1897 produced a boom in the Seattle area, the point of departure for the Klondike. Washington's lumber industry in its coastal forests and its shipping and fishing industries kept growth going up to 1940. World War II, the related aircraft industry in Seattle, and plutonium production for the atomic bomb at the Hanford Works (Richland), led another spurt of growth in the 1940s. Its key position on the Pacific Rim and its aircraft and lumber industries kept Washington growing after the war. It was growing even more rapidly recently as a haven from the crowds flowing into California.

The actual population line for Washington soared above the normalized line throughout the century. By 2000 the actual line will be more than three times as high as the normalized line, meaning that Washington's growth ratio from 1900 through 2000 will be more than three times as high as that of the nation.

Washington was 4th on the growth list from 1900 through 1950, behind only California, Arizona, and Florida (Table 3-3). It moved up from 34th on the population ranking list in 1900 to 23rd in 1950 (Table 3-2). Only California and Florida moved up more places in the same period (Table 3-4). Washington will be 11th on the growth list from 1950 through 2000, and it will be 13th on the population ranking list by 2000. Its gain of twenty-one places in population ranking from 1900 through 2000 leads all states except Florida and Arizona. Washington will continue to grow more rapidly than the nation after 2000, and it will be the 9th largest state in the nation in 2050 (Table 5-1).

As was the case for Oregon, the coastal area of Washington, where most people live, is like a Sunbelt state in terms of temperature, growth, resources, and capital investment. Washington's major city, Seattle (516,259 in 1990), had three times as many people as Spokane or Tacoma, the next largest cities. Seattle fell from a peak of 557,087 in 1960, and its 11 percent of the state's population in 1990 was down from 20 percent in 1950. But the Seattle-Tacoma metropolitan area had just under 3.0 million people in 1990, 61 percent of the population in the state. The area grew by an impressive 23 percent in the 1980s.

Figure 3-48. Washington Population (in Millions)

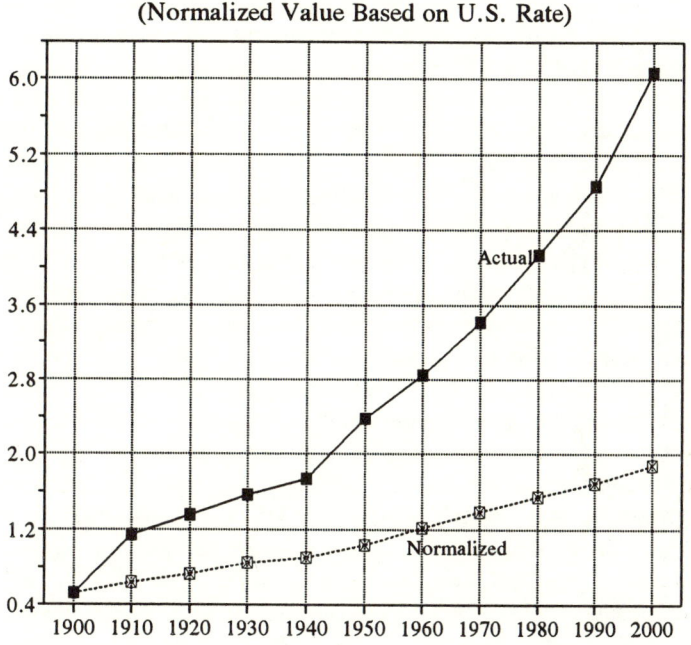

Year	Population	Growth Rate	U.S. Rate	Ratio
1900	518,103	--	--	--
1910	1,141,990	120.4%	21.0%	5.73
1920	1,356,621	18.8%	15.0%	1.26
1930	1,563,396	15.2%	16.2%	0.94
1940	1,736,191	11.1%	7.3%	1.52
1950	2,378,963	37.0%	14.5%	2.55
1960	2,853,214	19.9%	18.5%	1.08
1970	3,413,244	19.6%	13.4%	1.47
1980	4,132,353	21.1%	11.4%	1.84
1990	4,866,692	17.8%	9.8%	1.82
2000	6,070,000	24.7%	11.1%	2.23

Figure 3-49 shows population growth in West Virginia compared to the nation from 1900 through 2000. The format is explained on pages 2 and 18. West Virginia was a high-growth state up to 1940. But after 1940 it became the slowest growing state in the nation. It reached its peak population in 1950, and even its 1940 population was higher than either its 1990 level or its projected level in 2000. West Virginia grew (and declined) because of its huge coal reserves. Early in the century miners came to work the mines and drove population growth above the national rate. But improved mining technology cut the number of miners required, and the declining use of coal due to pollution and alternative fuels brought economic and population growth to a halt. West Virginia lost population for the first time in the 1950s, but it also lost population in the 1960s and 1980s (negative ratios).

The actual population line for West Virginia was above the normalized line until 1950. The actual line fell below the normalized line when the population fell in the 1950s, and it has moved essentially sideways ever since, falling farther and farther below the normalized line. By 2000 the actual line will be 50 percent below the normalized line, meaning that West Virginia's growth ratio from 1900 through 2000 will be 50 percent lower than that of the nation.

West Virginia was a respectable 21st on the growth list from 1900 through 1950 (Table 3-3), falling from 28th on the population ranking list in 1900 to 29th in 1950 (Table 3-2). But West Virginia will be next to last on the growth list from 1950 through 2000, and it is the only state with a growth ratio below 1.00 in that period, meaning that it will lose population from 1950 through 2000. (The District of Columbia was in last place on the growth list, so West Virginia had the worst record for a state.) West Virginia will be 35th on the population ranking list by 2000. It is projected to lose population after 2000, falling to 40th on the population ranking list in 2050 (Table 5-1). Its population will be nearly the same in 2050 as it was in 1930.

West Virginia is a landlocked state with no significant natural resources other than coal. It is mountainous and heavily forested and has few prospects for capital investment and growth. Its largest city, Charleston, had only 57,287 people in 1990, 10 percent fewer than in 1980. Huntington (54,844), the next largest city, is only fifty miles away, but even together their metropolitan area is under 150,000. West Virginia, Vermont, and Wyoming are the only states with no city over 60,000. But the other two states have less than one-third the population of West Virginia. West Virginia is thus a highly rural state.

Figure 3-49. West Virginia Population (in Millions)

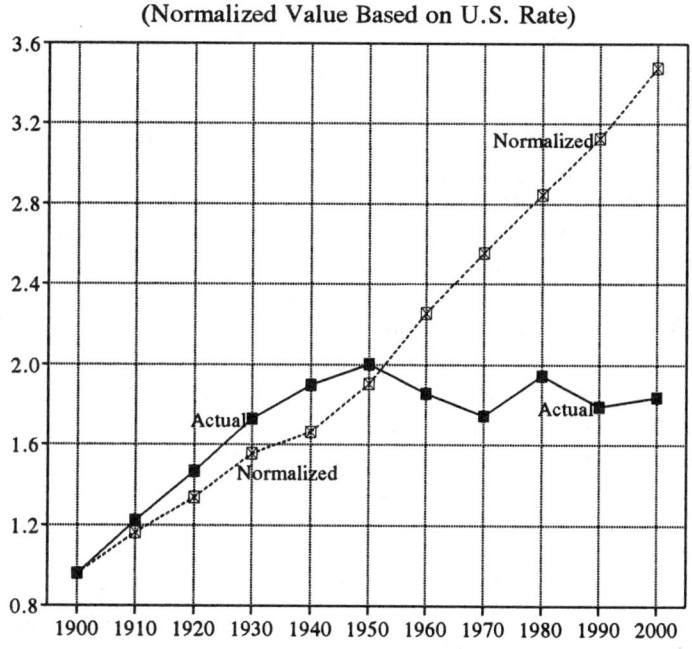

Year	Population	Growth Rate	U.S. Rate	Ratio
1900	958,800	--	--	--
1910	1,221,119	27.4%	21.0%	1.30
1920	1,463,701	19.9%	15.0%	1.33
1930	1,729,205	18.1%	16.2%	1.12
1940	1,901,974	10.0%	7.3%	1.37
1950	2,005,552	5.4%	14.5%	0.38
1960	1,860,421	-7.2%	18.5%	-0.39
1970	1,744,237	-6.2%	13.4%	-0.47
1980	1,950,186	11.8%	11.4%	1.03
1990	1,793,477	-8.0%	9.8%	-0.82
2000	1,840,000	2.6%	11.1%	0.23

Figure 3-50 shows population growth in Wisconsin compared to the nation from 1900 through 2000. The format is explained on pages 2 and 18. Wisconsin was below the national growth rate in every decade (all ratios less than 1.00). The worst period was after 1970, when the population outflow from the Central region took place, as described in the Introduction. But Wisconsin grew steadily even if at a rate below that of the nation. Wisconsin had a diversified economy, ranging from lumber and paper products earlier in the century to the manufacturing of machinery and the brewing of beer later, but the dairy industry was always a key part of the state. Wisconsin led the nation in dairy products for many years. The relatively steady nature of this industry was a key to the slow but steady growth of the state.

The actual population line for Wisconsin trailed the normalized line at every point in the century. The gap widened in the 1970s and 1980s, when Wisconsin had its periods of slowest growth, and by 2000 the actual line will be about 30 percent below the normalized line. This means Wisconsin's growth ratio from 1900 through 2000 will be 30 percent lower than that of the nation.

Wisconsin was 36th on the growth list from 1900 through 1950 (Table 3-3), falling from 13th in 1900 to 14th in 1950 on the population ranking list (Table 3-2). Wisconsin will move up to 28th on the growth list from 1950 through 2000, but it will fall to 18th on the ranking list by 2000, mostly because Florida, Washington, and Virginia, states with much faster growth, will pass it easily. Wisconsin is projected to grow more slowly than the nation after 2000, and it will fall to 20th on the population ranking list in 2050 (Table 5-1).

Wisconsin is far from the Sunbelt and is not an immigrant target. Its major city, Milwaukee, grew much more rapidly than the state (and the nation) from 1900 through 1960. But like most other large industrial cities in the Northeast and Central regions of the nation, Milwaukee lost population from its peak. It went from 14 percent of state population in 1900 to 19 percent in 1950, then fell to less than 13 percent in 1990. Milwaukee had 628,088 people in 1990, 15 percent below its 1960 peak. The Milwaukee-Racine metropolitan area had 1.6 million people in 1990, 33 percent of state population. The next largest city, Madison (190,766) is seventy-five miles due west, and the area south of Milwaukee-Racine along Lake Michigan is part of the huge Chicago metropolitan area (8.2 million in 1990). Thus the majority of the state's population lives in the southeast corner of the state, below a line from Milwaukee to Madison.

Figure 3-50. Wisconsin Population (in Millions)

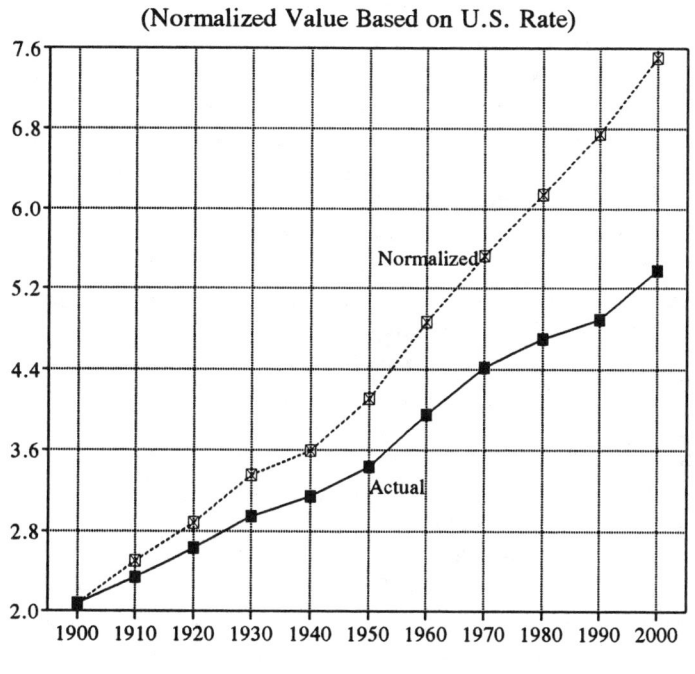

(Normalized Value Based on U.S. Rate)

Year	Population	Growth Rate	U.S. Rate	Ratio
1900	2,069,042	--	--	--
1910	2,333,860	12.8%	21.0%	0.61
1920	2,632,067	12.8%	15.0%	0.85
1930	2,939,006	11.7%	16.2%	0.72
1940	3,137,587	6.8%	7.3%	0.93
1950	3,434,575	9.5%	14.5%	0.65
1960	3,951,777	15.1%	18.5%	0.81
1970	4,417,821	11.8%	13.4%	0.88
1980	4,705,642	6.5%	11.4%	0.57
1990	4,891,769	4.0%	9.8%	0.40
2000	5,381,000	10.0%	11.1%	0.90

Figure 3-51 shows population growth in Wyoming compared to the nation from 1900 through 2000. The format is explained on pages 2 and 18. Wyoming grew more rapidly than the nation during the century, but its growth was very uneven. In the first two decades, it grew more than twice as rapidly as the nation (ratios greater than 2.00) as people moved in under favorable settlement laws and the development of the oil industry. Growth slowed but stayed near national levels from 1920 through 1960, as cattle and petroleum products supported the economy. Growth stopped completely in the 1960s, but the state hit its highest growth level of the century in the 1970s, when the population outflow from the Northeast and Central regions, as described in the Introduction, gave rise to people looking for a new lifestyle in places like Wyoming. Reality set in during the 1980s, and Wyoming lost population for the first time in the century. A new spurt in growth is projected for the 1990s.

The actual population line for Wyoming led the normalized line at every point in the century. This means that since 1900, the growth ratio for Wyoming has always been greater than the growth ratio for the nation. The gap closed when Wyoming had no growth in the 1960s and lost population in the 1980s, but it jumped again with the next spurt in growth. By 2000 the actual line will be about 56 percent ahead of the normalized line, meaning that Wyoming's growth ratio from 1900 through 2000 will be 56 percent higher than that of the nation.

Wyoming was 10th on the growth list from 1900 through 1950 (Table 3-3), but because of its small population base it stayed in 49th place on the population ranking list in both 1900 and 1950 (Table 3-2). Wyoming will be 21st on the growth list from 1950 through 2000, but it will fall to last on the population ranking list in 2000 because the two states behind it in 1950 (Nevada and Alaska) grew more rapidly from 1950 through 2000. Wyoming is projected to grow faster than the nation after 2000, and by 2050 it will have a large enough population to move up to 48th on the population ranking list (Table 5-1).

Wyoming is far from the Sunbelt and is not a target for immigrants. Its growth depends on attracting people who like a rugged lifestyle. Its major city, Cheyenne (50,008), took over the top spot in 1990 from Casper, which fell 10 percent to 46,756. Only Vermont has a smaller city with the title of the largest in the state. Cheyenne and Casper between them have 21 percent of the state's population, but they are 175 miles apart and each is nearly twice as big as the third largest city. There are no large metropolitan areas in Wyoming.

Figure 3-51. Wyoming Population (in Millions)

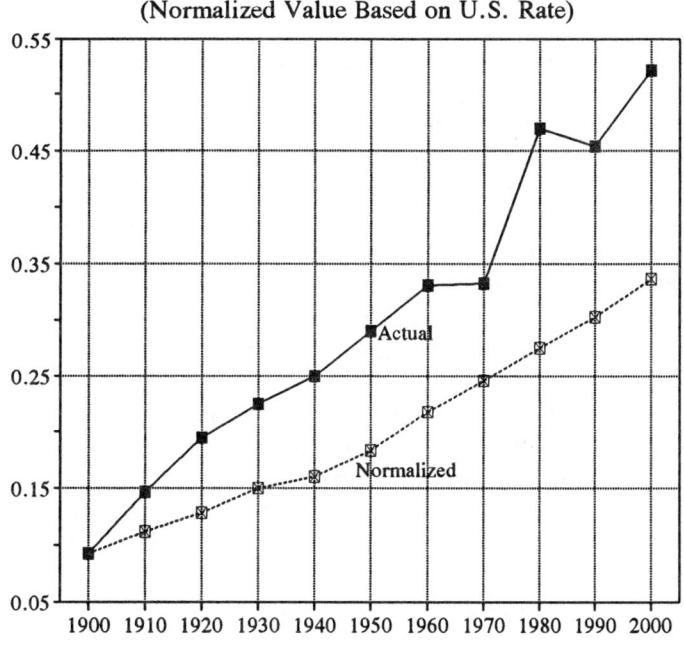

Year	Population	Growth Rate	U.S. Rate	Ratio
1900	92,531	--	--	--
1910	145,965	57.7%	21.0%	2.75
1920	194,402	33.2%	15.0%	2.22
1930	225,565	16.0%	16.2%	0.99
1940	250,742	11.2%	7.3%	1.54
1950	290,529	15.9%	14.5%	1.09
1960	330,066	13.6%	18.5%	0.74
1970	332,416	0.7%	13.4%	0.05
1980	469,557	41.3%	11.4%	3.61
1990	453,588	-3.4%	9.8%	-0.35
2000	522,000	15.1%	11.1%	1.36

Table 3-2 shows the states and the District of Columbia ranked by population for 1900, 1950, and 2000. Due to population momentum, the top ten and top fifteen states change slowly. The top states are much larger than those farther down, and even if the top states grow slowly they still add more people than smaller states with higher growth rates. California and Florida moved into the top ten because they maintained high growth rates even with large populations. California jumped from 21st place in 1900 to 2nd place in 1950, and it will be in 1st place in 2000, with a big lead over second-place Texas. Florida jumped from 33rd in 1900 to 20th in 1950, and it will move up to 4th in 2000. But California and Florida are very unusual states.

Other ranking changes were more typical. Six of the top ten states in 1900 will still be in the top ten in 2000 (New York, Pennsylvania, Illinois, Ohio, Texas, and Michigan). Four other states (Massachusetts, Indiana, Georgia, and North Carolina) will be in the top fifteen in both 1900 and 2000. This means that ten of the top fifteen states in 1900 will still be in the top fifteen in 2000. In a similar way, only Missouri and Wisconsin will fall from the top fifteen states between the census of 1950 and that of 2000, meaning that thirteen of the top fifteen states in 1950 will still be in the top fifteen in 2000. Growth rates can vary widely, but it takes a very long time for a smaller state to add enough people to displace a large state from the top of the rankings.

The top ten states (20 percent of the number of states) held 51 percent of the population of the nation in 1900 and 53 percent in 1950. They will hold 54 percent in 2000. The top fifteen states (30 percent of the number of states) held 64 percent of the population of the nation in 1900 and 65 percent in 1950. They will hold 66 percent in 2000. The top ten states in the 2000 census will have an average population of 15 million. The average population of the other forty states and the District of Columbia will be just over 3 million. The top fifteen states will average 12 million each, and the remaining states only 2.6 million.

Comparisons of this type emphasize how difficult it is to move up in the rankings. For example, the states in 11th through 15th place in 2000 will average 6.5 million in population. If the top ten did not grow at all and stayed at their 15 million average, the next five states would have to more than double in size to match the top ten average. Even at a great growth rate of 15 percent per decade, it takes almost fifty years for a state to double in population. Ranking data is always interesting to review, but separating the states in terms of growth requires an analysis of growth rates. This is done in the succeeding table.

States Summary

Table 3-2. States Population Rankings 1900-2000

1900 Census		1950 Census		2000 Census (est)	
1. New York	7,268,894	1. New York	14,830,192	1. California	34,888,000
2. Penn.	6,302,115	2. California	10,586,223	2. Texas	20,038,000
3. Illinois	4,821,550	3. Penn.	10,498,012	3. New York	18,237,000
4. Ohio	4,157,545	4. Illinois	8,712,176	4. Florida	15,313,000
5. Missouri	3,106,665	5. Ohio	7,946,627	5. Penn.	12,296,000
6. Texas	3,048,710	6. Texas	7,711,194	6. Illinois	12,168,000
7. Mass.	2,805,346	7. Michigan	6,371,766	7. Ohio	11,453,000
8. Indiana	2,516,462	8. New Jer.	4,835,329	8. Michigan	9,759,000
9. Michigan	2,420,982	9. Mass.	4,690,514	9. New Jer.	8,135,000
10. Iowa	2,231,853	10. N.Carolina	4,061,929	10. Georgia	7,637,000
11. Georgia	2,216,331	11. Missouri	3,954,653	11. N.Carolina	7,617,000
12. Kentucky	2,147,174	12. Indiana	3,934,224	12. Virginia	7,048,000
13. Wisconsin	2,069,042	13. Georgia	3,444,578	13. Washington	6,070,000
14. Tennessee	2,020,616	14. Wisconsin	3,434,575	14. Indiana	6,045,000
15. N.Carolina	1,893,810	15. Virginia	3,318,680	15. Mass.	5,950,000
16. New Jer.	1,883,669	16. Tennessee	3,291,718	16. Tennessee	5,538,000
17. Virginia	1,854,184	17. Alabama	3,061,743	17. Missouri	5,437,000
18. Alabama	1,828,697	18. Minnesota	2,982,483	18. Wisconsin	5,381,000
19. Minnesota	1,751,394	19. Kentucky	2,944,806	19. Maryland	5,322,000
20. Mississippi	1,551,270	20. Florida	2,771,305	20. Minnesota	4,824,000
21. California	1,485,053	21. Louisiana	2,683,516	21. Alabama	4,485,000
22. Kansas	1,470,495	22. Iowa	2,621,073	22. Louisiana	4,478,000
23. Louisiana	1,381,625	23. Washington	2,378,963	23. Arizona	4,437,000
24. S.Carolina	1,340,316	24. Maryland	2,343,001	24. Colorado	4,059,000
25. Arkansas	1,311,564	25. Oklahoma	2,233,351	25. Kentucky	3,989,000
26. Maryland	1,188,044	26. Mississippi	2,178,914	26. S.Carolina	3,932,000
27. Nebraska	1,066,300	27. S.Carolina	2,117,027	27. Oregon	3,404,000
28. W.Virginia	958,800	28. Connecticut	2,007,280	28. Oklahoma	3,382,000
29. Connecticut	908,420	29. W.Virginia	2,005,552	29. Connecticut	3,271,000
30. Oklahoma	790,391	30. Arkansas	1,909,511	30. Iowa	2,930,000
31. Maine	694,466	31. Kansas	1,905,299	31. Mississippi	2,750,000
32. Colorado	539,700	32. Oregon	1,521,341	32. Kansas	2,722,000
33. Florida	528,542	33. Nebraska	1,325,510	33. Arkansas	2,578,000
34. Washington	518,103	34. Colorado	1,325,089	34. Utah	2,148,000
35. Rhode Isl.	428,556	35. Maine	913,774	35. W.Virginia	1,840,000
36. Oregon	413,536	36. D.C.	802,178	36. New Mex.	1,823,000
37. New Hamp.	411,588	37. Rhode Isl.	791,896	37. Nebraska	1,704,000
38. S.Dakota	401,570	38. Arizona	749,587	38. Nevada	1,691,000
39. Vermont	343,641	39. Utah	688,862	39. Hawaii	1,327,000
40. N.Dakota	319,146	40. New Mex.	681,187	40. Idaho	1,290,000
41. D.C.	278,718	41. S.Dakota	652,740	41. Maine	1,240,000
42. Utah	276,749	42. N.Dakota	619,636	42. New Hamp.	1,165,000
43. Montana	243,329	43. Montana	591,024	43. Rhode Isl.	998,000
44. New Mex.	195,310	44. Idaho	588,637	44. Montana	920,000
45. Delaware	184,735	45. New Hamp.	533,242	45. S.Dakota	770,000
46. Idaho	161,772	46. Hawaii	499,794	46. Delaware	759,000
47. Hawaii	154,001	47. Vermont	377,747	47. Alaska	699,000
48. Arizona	122,931	48. Delaware	318,085	48. N.Dakota	643,000
49. Wyoming	92,531	49. Wyoming	290,529	49. Vermont	592,000
50. Alaska	63,592	50. Nevada	160,083	50. D.C.	537,000
51. Nevada	42,335	51. Alaska	128,643	51. Wyoming	522,000

134   The States

Table 3-3 shows the states and the District of Columbia ranked by growth ratio from 1900 through 1950, 1950 through 2000, and 1900 through 2000. The ratios are based on the population values in Table 3-2. Growth ratios compare population at 50- and 100-year intervals. They are expressed as numbers showing whether the population grew by a ratio of 1.3 or 2.4 or 3.5, etc. The growth rates shown in the figures in the book are ratios of population at the beginning of each decade. They are expressed as percentages, the standard way for rates to be shown. Population changes over longer periods are more easily understood as ratios, and thus Table 3-3 uses ratios. Growth ratios for the nation based on the population data shown in Figure 1-1 are:

Year	Population	Growth Ratio
1900	76,212,168	From 1900 through 1950: 1.99
1950	151,325,798	From 1950 through 2000: 1.83
2000	276,241,000	From 1900 through 2000: 3.62

The growth ratio for the century was 3.62 (the population in 2000 was 3.62 times higher than in 1900). The growth ratio in the first fifty years was 1.99 compared to 1.83 for the second fifty years. Only twenty-three states in Table 3-3 grew more rapidly than the nation from 1900 through 1950. Alaska ranked 23rd among the states with a ratio of 2.02, just over the national ratio of 1.99. Maryland was 24th with a ratio of 1.97, just under the national ratio. From 1950 through 2000, South Carolina in 20th place marks the dividing point, and from 1900 through 2000, Montana in 22nd place marks the dividing point.

The top states grew much more rapidly than the nation. From 1900 through 2000, Nevada grew more than ten times as fast as the nation and Arizona grew nearly ten times as fast. But these states had very small populations in 1900 (Table 3-2). The overall growth champion is California. It grew by a ratio of 23.5 from 1900 through 2000 (6.5 times as fast as the nation), even though it had 1.5 million people in 1900 and ranked 21st in population. Iowa ranks last, its ratio of 1.31 being just over a third of that of the nation from 1900 through 2000. Only West Virginia and the District of Columbia lost population in a period, both having ratios of less than 1.00 from 1950 through 2000.

Growth ratios are discussed in detail in the text accompanying the figure for each state, and the text explains why the ratio rose or fell. Table 3-4 shows how the population rankings for the states changed as their growth ratios changed.

States Summary

Table 3-3. States Growth Ratio Rankings 1900-2000

1900-1950 Ratio		1950-2000 Ratio		1900-2000 Ratio	
1. California	7.13	1. Nevada	10.6	1. Nevada	39.9
2. Arizona	6.10	2. Arizona	5.92	2. Arizona	36.1
3. Florida	5.24	3. Florida	5.53	3. Florida	29.0
4. Washington	4.59	4. Alaska	5.43	4. California	23.5
5. Nevada	3.78	5. California	3.30	5. Washington	11.7
6. Oregon	3.68	6. Utah	3.12	6. Alaska	11.0
7. Idaho	3.64	7. Colorado	3.06	7. New Mex.	9.33
8. New Mex.	3.49	8. New Mex.	2.68	8. Hawaii	8.62
9. Hawaii	3.25	9. Hawaii	2.66	9. Oregon	8.23
10. Wyoming	3.14	10. Texas	2.60	10. Idaho	7.97
11. D.C.	2.88	11. Washington	2.55	11. Utah	7.76
12. Oklahoma	2.83	12. Delaware	2.39	12. Colorado	7.52
13. Michigan	2.63	13. Maryland	2.27	13. Texas	6.57
14. New Jer.	2.57	14. Oregon	2.24	14. Wyoming	5.64
15. Texas	2.53	15. Georgia	2.22	15. Maryland	4.48
16. Utah	2.49	16. Idaho	2.19	16. New Jer.	4.32
17. Colorado	2.46	17. New Hamp.	2.18	17. Oklahoma	4.28
18. Montana	2.43	18. Virginia	2.12	18. Delaware	4.11
19. Connecticut	2.21	19. N.Carolina	1.88	19. Michigan	4.03
20. N.Carolina	2.14	20. S.Carolina	1.86	20. N.Carolina	4.02
21. W.Virginia	2.09	21. Wyoming	1.80	21. Virginia	3.80
22. New York	2.04	22. New Jer.	1.68	22. Montana	3.78
23. Alaska	2.02	23. Tennessee	1.68	23. Connecticut	3.60
24. Maryland	1.97	24. Louisiana	1.67	24. Georgia	3.45
25. Louisiana	1.94	25. Connecticut	1.63	25. Louisiana	3.24
26. N.Dakota	1.94	26. Minnesota	1.62	26. S.Carolina	2.93
27. Ohio	1.91	27. Vermont	1.57	27. New Hamp.	2.83
28. Rhode Isl.	1.85	28. Wisconsin	1.57	28. Ohio	2.75
29. Illinois	1.81	29. Montana	1.56	29. Minnesota	2.75
30. Virginia	1.79	30. Indiana	1.54	30. Tennessee	2.74
31. Delaware	1.72	31. Michigan	1.53	31. Wisconsin	2.60
32. Minnesota	1.70	32. Oklahoma	1.51	32. Illinois	2.52
33. Alabama	1.67	33. Alabama	1.46	33. New York	2.51
34. Mass.	1.67	34. Ohio	1.44	34. Alabama	2.45
35. Penn.	1.67	35. Kansas	1.43	35. Indiana	2.40
36. Wisconsin	1.66	36. Illinois	1.40	36. Rhode Isl.	2.33
37. Tennessee	1.63	37. Missouri	1.37	37. Mass.	2.12
38. S.Dakota	1.63	38. Maine	1.36	38. N.Dakota	2.01
39. S.Carolina	1.58	39. Kentucky	1.35	39. Arkansas	1.97
40. Indiana	1.56	40. Arkansas	1.35	40. Penn.	1.95
41. Georgia	1.55	41. Nebraska	1.29	41. D.C.	1.93
42. Arkansas	1.46	42. Mass.	1.27	42. W.Virginia	1.92
43. Mississippi	1.40	43. Mississippi	1.26	43. S.Dakota	1.92
44. Kentucky	1.37	44. Rhode Isl.	1.26	44. Kentucky	1.86
45. Maine	1.32	45. New York	1.23	45. Kansas	1.85
46. Kansas	1.30	46. S.Dakota	1.18	46. Maine	1.79
47. New Hamp.	1.30	47. Penn.	1.17	47. Mississippi	1.77
48. Missouri	1.27	48. Iowa	1.12	48. Missouri	1.75
49. Nebraska	1.24	49. N.Dakota	1.04	49. Vermont	1.72
50. Iowa	1.17	50. W.Virginia	0.92	50. Nebraska	1.60
51. Vermont	1.10	51. D.C.	0.67	51. Iowa	1.31

Table 3-4 shows population ranking changes for the states and the District of Columbia. The first four columns list the states alphabetically to make it easy to find the ranking for each census. The remaining columns show the number of places the state moved up or down in the rankings from 1900 through 1950, 1950 through 2000, and 1900 through 2000. The ranking data are taken from Table 3-2.

Large ranking changes require the proper combination of growth ratio, base population, and ranking position. For example, Pennsylvania had low growth ratios throughout the century, as shown in Table 3-3. But its huge initial population in 1900 kept it from moving very far down the ranking list. This demonstrates the population momentum effect shown in Table 3-2. Most large states that were ranked high in 1900 but had subsequent low growth changed in a similar way.

California had high growth ratios through the century. But once it soared nineteen positions to lead the list from 1900 through 1950, it could only move up one position from 2nd to 1st place thereafter. Texas was a high-growth state with very little movement because it had a high ranking (6th) in 1900. Florida was a very high growth state that had a low ranking in 1900. Thus it was able to move up many places in the rankings, both from 1900 through 1950 and from 1950 through 2000. Florida led in ranking improvements from 1900 through 2000, as it moved up twenty-nine places from 33rd in 1900 to 4th in 2000.

Arizona and Nevada were high-growth states with small initial populations in 1900. Arizona moved sharply up the rankings list in both parts of the century, putting it just behind Florida for the overall lead. Nevada barely budged from 1900 through 1950 because its population was so low in 1900, but it jumped twelve places from 1950 through 2000. Washington was much larger than both states in 1900, but its high growth ratios in each part of the century kept it near the top in ranking changes. This made it third overall from 1900 through 2000.

Iowa is the unchallenged "leader" at the other end of the list. It was the 10th largest state in 1900, but, as shown in Table 3-3, it had the lowest growth ratio of any state. It fell the most places from 1900 through 1950, and the only reason it did not fall the most from 1950 through 2000 was because the District of Columbia collapsed after 1950. Iowa is in 51st place from 1900 through 2000, and the state in 50th place, Kentucky, is as close to 36th place as it is to Iowa.

The ranking changes in Table 3-4 are discussed in detail in the text accompanying the figure for each state, and the discussion explains why the state moved up or down the ranking list.

States Summary

Table 3-4. States Population Ranking Changes

State	Rank Position 1900	Rank Position 1950	Rank Position 2000	Change in Rank Position 1900-1950		Change in Rank Position 1950-2000		Change in Rank Position 1900-2000	
Alabama	18	17	21	1. California	19	1. Florida	16	1. Florida	29
Alaska	50	51	47	2. Florida	13	2. Arizona	15	2. Arizona	25
Arizona	48	38	23	3. Wash.	11	3. Nevada	12	3. Wash.	21
Arkansas	25	30	33	4. Arizona	10	4. Colorado	10	4. California	20
California	21	2	1	5. New Jer.	8	5. Wash.	10	5. Nevada	13
Colorado	32	34	24	6. D.C.	5	6. Hawaii	7	6. Oregon	9
Connecticut	29	28	29	7. N.Carolina	5	7. Maryland	5	7. Colorado	8
Delaware	45	48	46	8. Oklahoma	5	8. Oregon	5	8. Hawaii	8
D.C.	41	36	50	9. New Mex.	4	9. Utah	5	9. New Mex.	8
Florida	33	20	4	10. Oregon	4	10. Alaska	4	10. Utah	8
Georgia	11	13	10	11. Utah	3	11. Idaho	4	11. Maryland	7
Hawaii	47	46	39	12. Idaho	2	12. New Mex.	4	12. New Jer.	7
Idaho	46	44	40	13. Louisiana	2	13. Texas	4	13. Idaho	6
Illinois	3	4	6	14. Maryland	2	14. Georgia	3	14. Virginia	5
Indiana	8	12	14	15. Michigan	2	15. NewHamp.	3	15. N.Carolina	4
Iowa	10	22	30	16. Virginia	2	16. Virginia	3	16. Texas	4
Kansas	22	31	32	17. Alabama	1	17. Delaware	2	17. Alaska	3
Kentucky	12	19	25	18. Conn.	1	18. California	1	18. Oklahoma	2
Louisiana	23	21	22	19. Hawaii	1	19. S.Carolina	1	19. Georgia	1
Maine	31	35	41	20. Minnesota	1	20. Tennessee	0	20. Louisiana	1
Maryland	26	24	19	21. Nevada	1	21. Conn.	-1	21. Michigan	1
Mass.	7	9	15	22. Montana	0	22. Kansas	-1	22. Conn.	0
Michigan	9	7	8	23. New York	0	23. Louisiana	-1	23. Delaware	-1
Minnesota	19	18	20	24. Texas	0	24. Michigan	-1	24. Minnesota	-1
Mississippi	20	26	31	25. Wyoming	0	25. Montana	-1	25. Montana	-1
Missouri	5	11	17	26. Alaska	-1	26. N.Carolina	-1	26. New York	-2
Montana	43	43	44	27. Illinois	-1	27. New Jer.	-1	27. S.Carolina	-2
Nebraska	27	33	37	28. Ohio	-1	28. Illinois	-2	28. Tennessee	-2
Nevada	51	50	38	29. Penn.	-1	29. Indiana	-2	29. Wyoming	-2
New Hamp.	37	45	42	30. W.Virginia	-1	30. Minnesota	-2	30. Alabama	-3
New Jer.	16	8	9	31. Wisconsin	-1	31. New York	-2	31. Illinois	-3
New Mex.	44	40	36	32. Colorado	-2	32. Ohio	-2	32. Ohio	-3
New York	1	1	3	33. Georgia	-2	33. Penn.	-2	33. Penn.	-3
N.Carolina	15	10	11	34. Mass.	-2	34. Vermont	-2	34. NewHamp.	-5
N.Dakota	40	42	48	35. N.Dakota	-2	35. Wyoming	-2	35. Wisconsin	-5
Ohio	4	5	7	36. Rhode Isl.	-2	36. Arkansas	-3	36. Indiana	-6
Oklahoma	30	25	28	37. Tennessee	-2	37. Oklahoma	-3	37. S.Dakota	-7
Oregon	36	32	27	38. Delaware	-3	38. Alabama	-4	38. W.Virginia	-7
Penn.	2	3	5	39. S.Carolina	-3	39. Nebraska	-4	39. Arkansas	-8
Rhode Isl.	35	37	43	40. S.Dakota	-3	40. S.Dakota	-4	40. Mass.	-8
S.Carolina	24	27	26	41. Indiana	-4	41. Wisconsin	-4	41. N.Dakota	-8
S.Dakota	38	41	45	42. Maine	-4	42. Miss.	-5	42. Rhode Isl.	-8
Tennessee	14	16	16	43. Arkansas	-5	43. Kentucky	-6	43. D.C.	-9
Texas	6	6	2	44. Miss.	-6	44. Maine	-6	44. Kansas	-10
Utah	42	39	34	45. Missouri	-6	45. Mass.	-6	45. Maine	-10
Vermont	39	47	49	46. Nebraska	-6	46. Missouri	-6	46. Nebraska	-10
Virginia	17	15	12	47. Kentucky	-7	47. N.Dakota	-6	47. Vermont	-10
Washington	34	23	13	48. NewHmp.	-8	48. Rhode Isl.	-6	48. Miss.	-11
W.Virginia	28	29	35	49. Vermont	-8	49. W.Virginia	-6	49. Missouri	-12
Wisconsin	13	14	18	50. Kansas	-9	50. Iowa	-8	50. Kentucky	-13
Wyoming	49	49	51	51. Iowa	-12	51. D.C.	-14	51. Iowa	-20

Part IV
The Cities

Cities Profile

Table 4-1 shows population and growth rates for twenty-four cities as of the 1990 census. They are listed alphabetically in the first set of columns, ranked by population in the second set, and ranked by growth rate in the set at the bottom of the page. The twenty-four cities were derived by initially selecting the fifteen largest cities in the nation in 1900. Then the top fifteen were selected from the 1990 census, and because only six of the original cities remained on the top fifteen list in 1990 (New York, Chicago, Philadelphia, Detroit, Baltimore, and San Francisco) nine new cities were added from the 1990 list.

The population ranking shows the rank of the twenty-four cities compared to all other cities in the nation. This results in gaps in the ranking numbers after position fifteen. For example, Buffalo is 24th among the twenty-four cities, but it is 50th in the nation overall. The growth rate rankings are for the twenty-four cities only. Other cities in the nation have higher (or lower) growth ratios than the twenty-four shown here, but, for this part of the book, only the growth rates of the cities under discussion are considered. The growth rates listed in Table 4-1 are for the 1980-1990 decade.

Population momentum applies to very large cities as well as states, and this is why New York, Chicago, and Philadelphia still rank in the top five even though they lost population from 1950 through 1990. This effect will probably keep New York first and Chicago third for a long time. However, Philadelphia is now small enough that it can be expected to drop out of the top ten in the first half of the next century.

The growth rates show that except for Phoenix, cities in California, Florida, and Texas lead the high growth list. Los Angeles maintained high growth after passing 2 million in population, but Houston, which grew rapidly through 1980, appears to be leveling off after passing 1.5 million. The census of 2000 will show which of these two examples the other high-growth cities will follow. In addition to the growth prospects of the state in which they are located, the growth of cities depends on the land area they have available for expansion, their ability to merge with adjacent suburbs, and their attractiveness to immigrants. All of these factors will be discussed for each city in this part of the book.

Cities Profile

Table 4-1. Cities Population Profile (1990 Census)

City	Population	Growth Rate	Overall Population Ranking City	Population
Baltimore	736,014	-6.4%	1. New York City	7,322,564
Boston	574,283	2.0%	2. Los Angeles	3,485,557
Buffalo	328,175	-8.3%	3. Chicago	2,783,726
Chicago	2,783,726	-7.4%	4. Houston	1,629,902
Cincinnati	364,114	-5.5%	5. Philadelphia	1,585,577
Cleveland	505,616	-11.9%	6. San Diego	1,110,623
Dallas	1,007,618	11.5%	7. Detroit	1,027,974
Detroit	1,027,974	-14.6%	8. Dallas	1,007,618
Houston	1,629,902	2.2%	9. Phoenix	983,403
Indianapolis	741,952	5.9%	10. San Antonio	935,393
Jacksonville	672,971	24.4%	11. San Jose	782,224
Los Angeles	3,485,557	17.5%	12. Indianapolis	741,952
Milwaukee	628,088	-1.3%	13. Baltimore	736,014
New Orleans	496,938	-10.9%	14. San Francisco	723,959
New York City	7,322,564	3.5%	15. Jacksonville	672,971
Philadelphia	1,585,577	-6.1%	17. Milwaukee	628,088
Phoenix	983,403	24.5%	19. Washington, D.C.	606,900
Pittsburgh	369,879	-12.8%	20. Boston	574,283
St. Louis	396,685	-12.4%	24. Cleveland	505,616
San Antonio	935,393	19.0%	25. New Orleans	496,938
San Diego	1,110,623	26.9%	34. St. Louis	396,685
San Francisco	723,959	6.6%	40. Pittsburgh	369,879
San Jose	782,224	24.3%	45. Cincinnati	364,114
Washington, D.C.	606,900	-4.9%	50. Buffalo	328,175

Growth Rate Rankings for the 24 Selected Cities Only

City	Growth Rate	City	Growth Rate
1. San Diego	26.9%	13. Milwaukee	-1.3%
2. Phoenix	24.5%	14. Washington, D.C.	-4.9%
3. Jacksonville	24.4%	15. Cincinnati	-5.5%
4. San Jose	24.3%	16. Philadelphia	-6.1%
5. San Antonio	19.0%	17. Baltimore	-6.4%
6. Los Angeles	17.5%	18. Chicago	-7.4%
7. Dallas	11.5%	19. Buffalo	-8.3%
8. San Francisco	6.6%	20. New Orleans	-10.9%
9. Indianapolis	5.9%	21. Cleveland	-11.9%
10. New York City	3.5%	22. St. Louis	-12.4%
11. Houston	2.2%	23. Pittsburgh	-12.8%
12. Boston	2.0%	24. Detroit	-14.6%

Figure 4-1 shows population growth for Baltimore compared to the nation from 1900 through 1990. With the exception that 1990 is the last year for cities, the format is as explained on pages 2 and 18. The cities' ratio of growth since 1900 is also added on the bottom line of the graph. Baltimore grew more slowly than the nation in the first decade (ratio below 1.00), but grew by 31.4 percent in the next decade, more than twice the national rate. It was Baltimore's growth peak. It has been below the national rate since the 1920s. The population peak for Baltimore was 1950 at 949,708 people. By then the actual line was 6 percent below the normalized line, meaning that from 1900 through 1950 Baltimore's growth ratio was 6 percent below that of the nation.

The national rush from the major cities of the Northeast and Central regions, as described in the Introduction, began in the 1950s. The ease of movement to the suburbs and the problems of integrated schools emptied the cities rapidly. The percentage of minorities in cities climbed as the total population fell, and the taxes necessary to support them drove even more people from the cities. Baltimore lost population slowly in the 1950s and 1960s, but in the 1970s there was a sharp loss of 13.1 percent, meaning that Baltimore lost 119,046 people in the decade. The losses slowed in the 1980s, but it was still the second worst decade in the century. More losses can be expected in the 1990s.

Baltimore's decline did not hurt growth in Maryland because most people just moved to the suburbs. The Baltimore-Washington metropolitan area grew by 16.2 percent to 6.7 million people in the 1980s. Baltimore's percentage of state population declined, however, going from 43 percent in 1900 to 41 percent in 1950, and then to 15 percent in 1990. The percentage will continue to fall as Maryland continues to grow and Baltimore proper continues to shrink. The Baltimore-Washington metropolitan area will continue to grow because the combined population of government workers and lobbyists is still growing and because the area is a target for immigrants.

Baltimore was the 6th largest city in the nation in 1900 (Table 4-2), and it was still 6th in 1950. But it was 13th by 1990. If Baltimore had grown at the same rate as the nation, in 1990 it would have had almost 1.7 million people, as shown by the normalized line. That would have made it the 4th largest city in the nation. Instead, Baltimore in 1990 was only 0.3 percent larger than it was in 1920, and by 2000 it should be well below the 1920 level. The growth phase of cities like Baltimore ended in 1950, and the main question for future years is how long it will take the population to stabilize at the new lower levels.

Baltimore

Figure 4-1. Baltimore Population (in Millions)

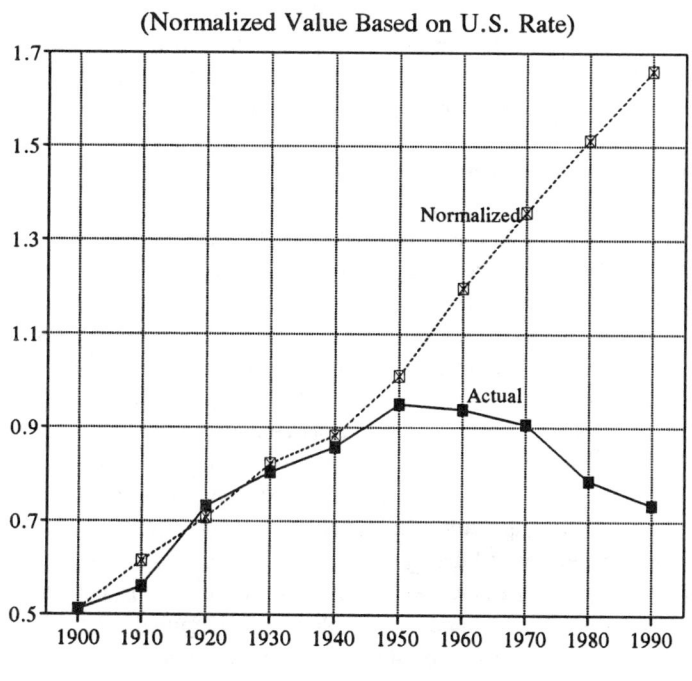

(Normalized Value Based on U.S. Rate)

Year	Population	Growth Rate	U.S. Rate	Ratio
1900	508,957	--	--	--
1910	558,485	9.7%	21.0%	0.46
1920	733,826	31.4%	15.0%	2.10
1930	804,874	9.7%	16.2%	0.60
1940	859,100	6.7%	7.3%	0.93
1950	949,708	10.5%	14.5%	0.73
1960	939,024	-1.1%	18.5%	-0.06
1970	905,787	-3.5%	13.4%	-0.26
1980	786,741	-13.1%	11.4%	-1.15
1990	736,014	-6.4%	9.8%	-0.66

Ratio of population in 1990 to population in 1900: 1.45

Figure 4-2 shows population growth for Boston compared to the nation from 1900 through 1990. The format for cities is explained on page 142. Boston grew more slowly than the nation in every decade from 1900 through 1990 (ratios less than 1.00). It lost population as early as the 1930s (negative ratio), the first of four decades in which it lost population. Boston managed to stay close to the national growth rate only until 1920, and by 1950, when Boston reached its peak population of 801,444, the actual line was about 28 percent below the normalized line. This meant that from 1900 through 1950 Boston's growth ratio was 28 percent lower than that of the nation.

Boston lost 13 percent of its population in the 1950s, when the national exodus from the major cities of the Northeast and Central regions began, as described in the Introduction. Boston lost 30 percent of its population from 1950 through 1980, a loss of 238,450 people. Boston then gained 11,289 in the 1980s. But even in its best days Boston did not have nearly as large a percentage of state population as most large Northeast region cities. Boston went from 20 percent of state population in 1900 to 17 percent in 1950, and then to less than 10 percent in 1990. It appears to be stabilizing at the new lower level.

Massachusetts was hurt by the loss in Boston's population. Many people moved over the state border to nearby New Hampshire to escape high city and state taxes and the problems of integrated schools. They stayed in the Boston metropolitan area (which stretches over Maine, Hew Hampshire, and Connecticut), but they left Massachusetts. The Boston metropolitan area increased by 6.5 percent in the 1980s, reaching 5.4 million in 1990. But the state grew by only 4.9 percent and is projected to lose population in the 1990s. Boston may have started the process of stabilizing its population, but the state has not.

Boston was the 5th largest city in the nation in 1900 (Table 4-2), but its slow growth after 1920 made it 10th in 1950. Boston grew so slowly from 1900 through 1950 that it had the lowest growth ratio of the twenty-four cities covered in this part of the book. By 1990 Boston was 20th on the ranking list, a fall of ten places since 1950 and fifteen since 1900. If Boston had grown at the same rate as the nation, in 1990 it would have had over 1.8 million people, as shown by the normalized line. That would have made it the 4th largest city in the nation. Instead, Boston in 1990 was only 2 percent larger than it was in 1900 (ratio of 1.02 from 1900 to 1990), and it almost fell below the 1900 level in 1980. Boston had 448,477 people in 1890, so even if it falls below the 1900 level it should stay ahead of its 1890 level for a long time.

Boston

Figure 4-2. Boston Population (in Millions)

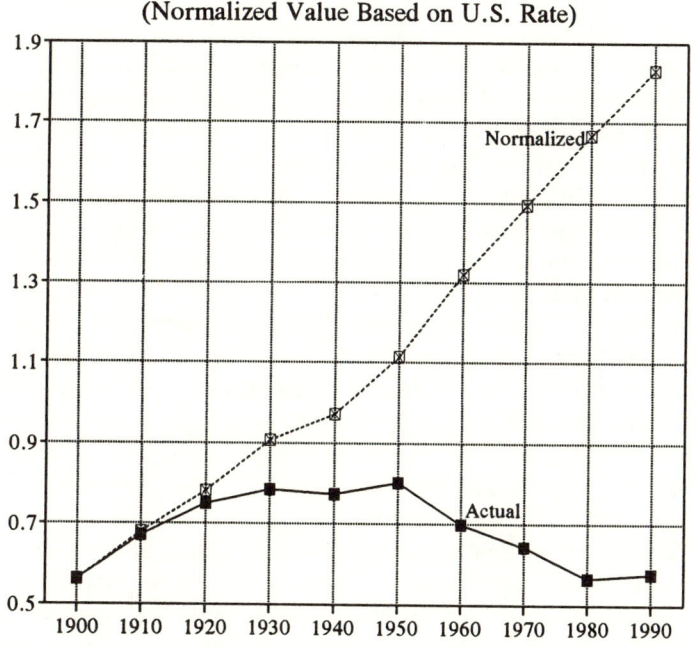

Year	Population	Growth Rate	U.S. Rate	Ratio
1900	560,892	--	--	--
1910	670,585	19.6%	21.0%	0.93
1920	748,060	11.6%	15.0%	0.77
1930	781,188	4.4%	16.2%	0.27
1940	770,816	-1.3%	7.3%	-0.18
1950	801,444	4.0%	14.5%	0.27
1960	697,197	-13.0%	18.5%	-0.70
1970	641,071	-8.1%	13.4%	-0.60
1980	562,994	-12.2%	11.4%	-1.07
1990	574,283	2.0%	9.8%	0.20

Ratio of population in 1990 to population in 1900: 1.02

Figure 4-3 shows population growth for Buffalo compared to the nation from 1900 through 1990. The format for cities is explained on page 142. Buffalo grew at nearly the same rate as the nation in the 1900-1910 decade, and it exceeded the national rate in the 1910-1920 decade (ratio greater than 1.00). It was still reasonably close in the 1920s, and thus by 1930 the actual line for Buffalo was a little above the normalized line. This means that Buffalo grew a little more rapidly than the nation from 1900 through 1930. Then the growth switch was turned off in Buffalo. The city barely grew in the 1930s and 1940s, and it peaked in population at 580,132 in 1950. It was downhill from there.

Buffalo lost 8.2 percent of its population in the 1950s, when the national exodus from the major cities of the Northeast and Central regions began, as described in the Introduction. Buffalo lost 43 percent of its population from 1950 through 1990, a loss of 251,957 people. Its population in 1990 was 7 percent less than it had been when the century started in 1900 (ratio of 0.93 from 1900 through 1990). Buffalo had 255,646 people in 1890, 22 percent below its 1990 level. If present trends continue, Buffalo could fall below its 1890 population level in the first half of the next century.

New York state grew much more rapidly than Buffalo. The state nearly matched the national rate up to 1970, then changed little in the next three decades. With New York City making up half the population of the state for a long time, Buffalo had only a small fraction. Buffalo had 4.8 percent of the state's population in 1900, declining to 3.9 percent in 1950, and then to 1.8 percent in 1990. Many people leaving Buffalo left the area as well. Buffalo lost 29,695 people in the 1980s, but the Buffalo metropolitan area lost 53,538, which was 4.3 percent of the area's population. With 1.2 million people in 1990, the area had 6.6 percent of the state's population.

Buffalo was the 9th largest city in the nation in 1900 (Table 4-2), but it fell to 15th place in 1950, and plummeted to 50th in 1990. It will fall again in the next census. Located in the middle of the "Snow Belt" on the shores of Lake Erie, Buffalo is not a target for immigrants, and capital investment is going to other, higher growth areas in the nation. Even if Buffalo stabilizes its population losses, there are many faster growing cities coming up to pass it on the population ranking list. Buffalo is still the 2nd largest city in the state of New York, but it appears in this book only because it was one of the top fifteen cities in 1900 (actually one of the top ten), a fact that may be hard for present and future generations to believe.

Buffalo

Figure 4-3. Buffalo Population (in Millions)

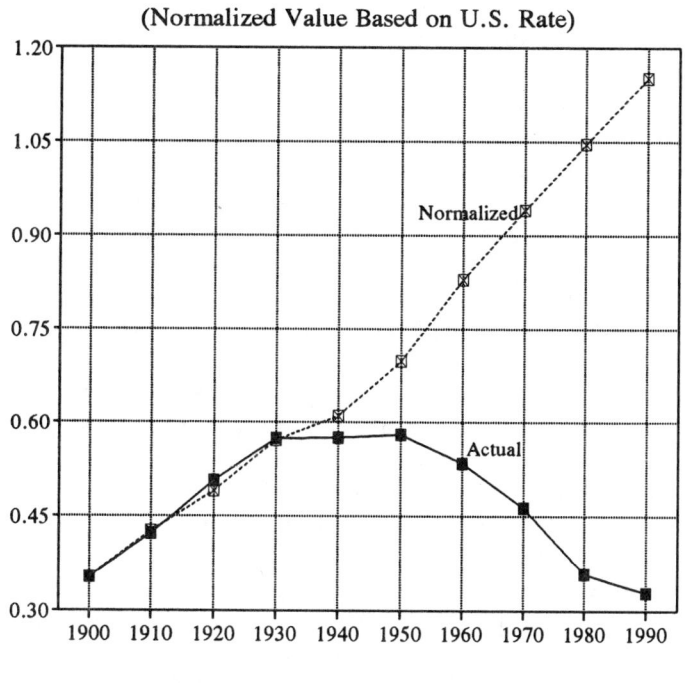

Year	Population	Growth Rate	U.S. Rate	Ratio
1900	352,387	--	--	--
1910	423,715	20.2%	21.0%	0.96
1920	506,775	19.6%	15.0%	1.31
1930	573,076	13.1%	16.2%	0.81
1940	575,901	0.5%	7.3%	0.07
1950	580,132	0.7%	14.5%	0.05
1960	532,759	-8.2%	18.5%	-0.44
1970	462,768	-13.1%	13.4%	-0.98
1980	357,870	-22.7%	11.4%	-1.98
1990	328,175	-8.3%	9.8%	-0.85

Ratio of population in 1990 to population in 1900: 0.93

Figure 4-4 shows population growth for Chicago compared to the nation from 1900 through 1990. The format for cities is explained on page 142. Chicago grew much more rapidly than the nation from 1900 through 1930. By 1930 the actual line was about 23 percent above the normalized line, meaning that the growth ratio for the city was 23 percent higher than that for the nation for that period. Growth slowed in the next two decades, but by 1950 the actual line was still more than 7 percent above the normalized line. As was the case for twelve of the cities in the top fifteen in the 1900 census, Chicago reached its peak in 1950. It lost population at an increasing rate after that.

Chicago lost 1.9 percent of its population in the 1950s, when the national exodus from the major cities of the Northeast and Central regions, as described in the Introduction, began in earnest. The rate of loss increased sharply after 1960, and Chicago lost 23 percent of its population from 1950 through 1990. This was a loss of 837,236 people, 7 percent more than the population of San Jose in 1990, when San Jose was the nation's 11th largest city. Ironically, San Jose may have been the destination of some of the people leaving Chicago.

Chicago had 35 percent of the state's population in 1900 and 42 percent in 1950. But in 1990 Chicago had only 24 percent of the state's population, even though the state hardly grew after 1970. Many of the people leaving Chicago in the 1980s may have ended up in the suburbs. The Chicago metropolitan area grew by 1.5 percent in the 1980s, adding 124,976 people while Chicago was losing 221,346. The area is the nation's third largest, and it had 8.2 million people in 1990. It stretches along the shore of Lake Michigan from Indiana in the east to Wisconsin in the north. How many people leaving Chicago remained in Illinois is hard to tell, but the part of the metropolitan area outside the city proper gained 346,322 people in the 1980s.

Chicago was the 2nd largest city in the nation in 1900 (Table 4-2), and it was still 2nd in 1950, 75 percent larger than Philadelphia in 3rd place. By 1990 Chicago fell to 3rd place behind Los Angeles, and Los Angeles was then 25 percent larger than Chicago. But Chicago in turn was still 71 percent larger than the next city, Houston. Its immense size and diversification makes Chicago a target for immigration in spite of its cold-weather location. Population momentum means that it will be a long time before any city catches up to Chicago on the population ranking list. But Chicago is still losing population, and in 1990 it was about the same size it was in 1920. There are not enough immigrants arriving to reverse that trend.

Chicago

Figure 4-4. Chicago Population (in Millions)

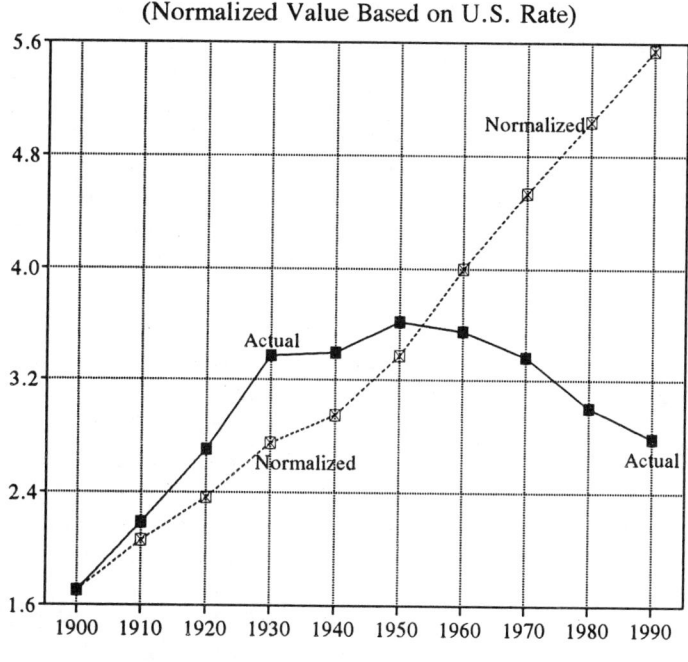

(Normalized Value Based on U.S. Rate)

Year	Population	Growth Rate	U.S. Rate	Ratio
1900	1,698,575	--	--	--
1910	2,185,283	28.7%	21.0%	1.36
1920	2,701,705	23.6%	15.0%	1.58
1930	3,376,438	25.0%	16.2%	1.54
1940	3,396,808	0.6%	7.3%	0.08
1950	3,620,962	6.6%	14.5%	0.46
1960	3,550,404	-1.9%	18.5%	-0.11
1970	3,369,357	-5.1%	13.4%	-0.38
1980	3,005,072	-10.8%	11.4%	-0.95
1990	2,783,726	-7.4%	9.8%	-0.75

Ratio of population in 1990 to population in 1900: 1.64

Figure 4-5 shows population growth for Cincinnati compared to the nation from 1900 through 1990. The format for cities is explained on page 142. Cincinnati grew more slowly than the nation in every decade from 1900 through 1990 (ratios less than 1.00), losing population in every decade from 1950 through 1990 (negative ratios). By 1990 the actual line was 66 percent below the normalized line, meaning that Cincinnati's growth ratio was 66 below the nation's from 1900 through 1990. But most people leaving Cincinnati did not leave the state. Ohio grew well until 1970, and the Cincinnati metropolitan area grew by 5.3 percent in the 1980s, reaching 1.8 million in 1990. Columbus, only 100 miles away and the largest city in Ohio in 1990, is still gaining population. This is a rarity among large eastern industrial cities.

Cincinnati lost population for the first time in the 1950s, when the national exodus from the major cities of the Northeast and Central regions, as described in the Introduction, began in earnest. Cincinnati lost 28 percent of its population from 1950 through 1990, a loss of 139,884 people. It returned to its 1910 level of population in 1990, and it was only 12 percent larger than it was in 1900 (1900 through 1990 ratio of 1.12). At its present rate of loss, Cincinnati will be back to its 1900 population level by the census of 2010. It had 296,908 people in 1890, and even that level is not out of reach.

Being overshadowed first by Cleveland, then by Columbus after 1970, and with Toledo getting close in recent decades, Cincinnati has never held a large percentage of state population. It held about 8 percent of state population in 1900, 6 percent in 1950, and 3 percent in 1990. The metropolitan area had 17 percent of state population in 1990, but the area includes part of Kentucky across the Ohio River. Even without the Kentucky contribution, the Cincinnati metropolitan area is the state's second largest behind the Cleveland area.

Cincinnati, the 11th largest city in the nation in 1900 (Table 4-2), was 18th in 1950 and 45th in 1990. It should fall further down the list in the future. The normalized line shows that if Cincinnati had grown at the same rate as the nation, it would have had nearly 1.1 million people in 1990, which would have made it the 7th largest city in the nation. But Cincinnati did not match the national rate at any time in the century. With its location outside the Sunbelt and the immigrant stream, and with local capital investment going up the Interstate to Columbus, there's no reason to believe that Cincinnati can match the national growth rate. Like St. Louis, Pittsburgh, and Buffalo, Cincinnati's once high position on the population ranking list is a distant memory.

Cincinnati

Figure 4-5. Cincinnati Population (in Millions)

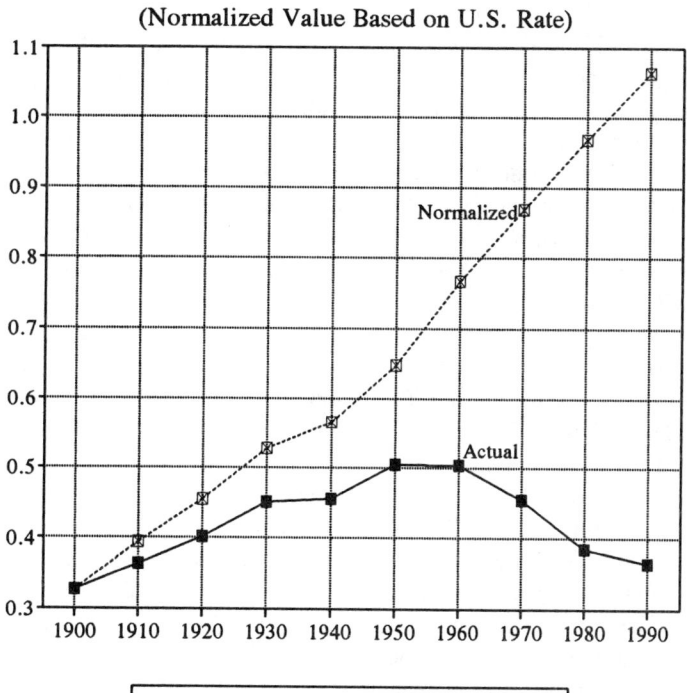

(Normalized Value Based on U.S. Rate)

Year	Population	Growth Rate	U.S. Rate	Ratio
1900	325,902	--	--	--
1910	363,591	11.6%	21.0%	0.55
1920	401,247	10.4%	15.0%	0.69
1930	451,160	12.4%	16.2%	0.77
1940	455,610	1.0%	7.3%	0.14
1950	503,998	10.6%	14.5%	0.73
1960	502,550	-0.3%	18.5%	-0.02
1970	453,514	-9.8%	13.4%	-0.73
1980	385,410	-15.0%	11.4%	-1.31
1990	364,114	-5.5%	9.8%	-0.56

Ratio of population in 1990 to population in 1900: 1.12

Figure 4-6 shows population growth for Cleveland compared to the nation from 1900 through 1990. The format for cities is explained on page 142. Cleveland grew more rapidly than the nation from 1900 through 1920, and nearly as rapidly in the 1920s. By 1930 the actual line was 46 percent above the normalized line, meaning that the growth ratio for the city was 46 percent higher than that of the nation from 1900 through 1930. Cleveland lost population (negative ratio) in the 1930s, and grew only a little in the 1940s. But the actual line was still more than 21 percent above the normalized line in 1950, and Cleveland was still a success story. The story ended in 1950 as Cleveland's population peaked and then fell at a steadily increasing rate afterwards.

Cleveland lost 4.2 percent of its population in the 1950s, when the national exodus from the major cities of the Northeast and Central regions began, as described in the Introduction. The rate of population loss increased sharply after 1960, and Cleveland lost 45 percent of its population from 1950 through 1990. This was a loss of 409,192 people, more than the population of Tucson, Arizona, in 1990. The Cleveland metropolitan area lost 2.7 percent of its population in the 1980s, falling to 2.9 million in 1990. This was a loss of 78,633 people compared to Cleveland's loss of 68,206 people in the same decade. But the Columbus area gained 131,159 in the 1980s and could have absorbed most of the loss. The state of Ohio grew by only 0.5 percent or 49,512 people in the decade. At best the net result of the exodus from Cleveland was very slow growth in the state.

Cleveland had 9.2 percent of state population in 1900 and 11.5 percent in 1950 (the city grew more rapidly than the state). In 1990 Cleveland had only 4.7 percent of state population, but its metropolitan area held 26 percent. Even though Columbus took over the top city ranking in the state in 1990, its metropolitan area had only 1.3 million people, less than half the size of the Cleveland metropolitan area.

Cleveland was the 8th largest city in the nation in 1900 (Table 4-2), and it moved up to 7th place in 1950. But it lived up to its designation as the "Mistake by the Lake" after 1950, and it fell to 24th place on the ranking list by 1990. Cleveland in 1990 was 10 percent smaller than it was in 1910, although it was well ahead of its 1900 level, thanks to its great growth early in the century. In 1990 Cleveland was 6th on the list of highest percentage loss in population for cities over 100,000. It is not in the Sunbelt and not an immigrant target, and there is a growing city not far away (Columbus) that could get preference for capital investment. This is a prime recipe for continued population loss.

Figure 4-6. Cleveland Population (in Millions)

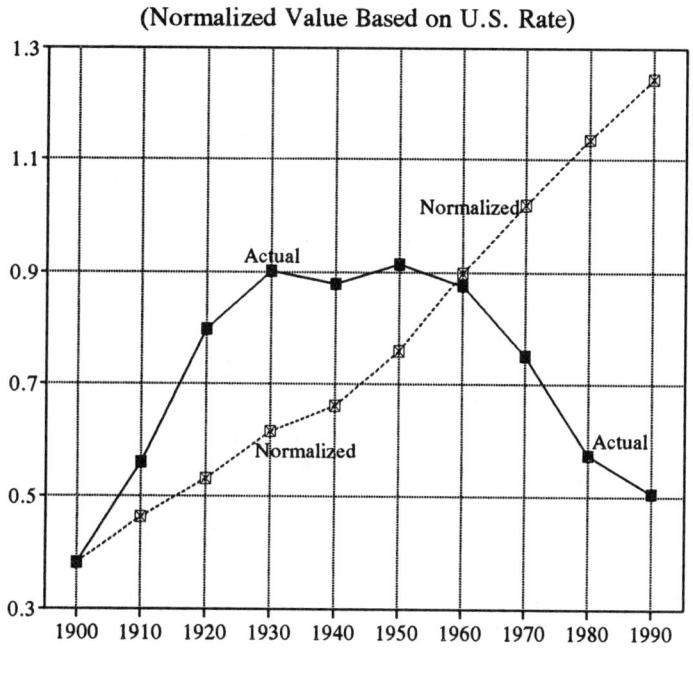

Year	Population	Growth Rate	U.S. Rate	Ratio
1900	381,768	--	--	--
1910	560,663	46.9%	21.0%	2.23
1920	796,841	42.1%	15.0%	2.82
1930	900,429	13.0%	16.2%	0.80
1940	878,336	-2.5%	7.3%	-0.34
1950	914,808	4.2%	14.5%	0.29
1960	876,050	-4.2%	18.5%	-0.23
1970	750,879	-14.3%	13.4%	-1.07
1980	573,822	-23.6%	11.4%	-2.06
1990	505,616	-11.9%	9.8%	-1.21

Ratio of population in 1990 to population in 1900: 1.32

Figure 4-7 shows population growth for Dallas compared to the nation from 1900 through 1990. The format for cities is explained on page 142. Dallas grew more rapidly than the nation in every decade from 1900 through 1970, as people flowed into Texas as part of industries ranging from oil to cattle to high-technology electronics. By 1970 the actual line was 7.5 times as high as the normalized line, meaning that the growth ratio for Dallas was 7.5 times higher than that of the nation from 1900 through 1970. Dallas grew more slowly than the nation in the 1970s (ratio less than 1.00), but more rapidly again in the 1980s. Dallas went over 1 million in population in 1990, becoming one of only eight cities to reach that level in the nation's history.

Because of the dip in the 1970s, Dallas grew a little more slowly than the nation from 1970 through 1990, a sign that its growth rate may be stabilizing. In the case of high-growth cities like Dallas, stabilization means that its growth rate slows to the national growth rate. There is no sign of the population decrease that has been typical of older cities in the nation. Dallas benefited from the exodus of people from the cities of the Northeast and Central regions that began in the 1950s, as described in the Introduction and in the text accompanying the figures for those cities. But this exodus reached a peak after 1970, just when Dallas had a slowdown in growth. So there is reason to believe that the immensely high growth period for Dallas is coming to an end.

As shown in Figure 4-26, Dallas, Houston, and San Antonio grew rapidly from 1900 onward, with no one city having a high percentage of state population. Dallas went from 1.4 percent of state population in 1900 to 5.9 percent in 1990. But the Dallas-Fort Worth metropolitan area in 1990 had 4.0 million people and 24 percent of state population. The Houston metropolitan area had only 22 percent, even though Houston was 60 percent larger than Dallas as a city. The Dallas-Fort Worth area also grew by 32.5 percent in the 1980s, 66 percent more than the 19.6 percent growth for the Houston area.

Dallas was 88th on the population ranking list in 1900 (Table 4-2), but by 1950 it was 22nd. In 1990 Dallas was the 8th largest city in the nation, and it passed Detroit early in the 1990s to take over 7th place. There is plenty of capital investment available to fund the growth of Dallas, and it is a key city in a dynamic state that is a target for immigrants. This promises continuing growth, but San Diego is ahead of Dallas in population and is growing more rapidly. Both cities will take a long time to catch Philadelphia, a city losing population but still a giant. Thus Dallas may stay in 7th place for several decades.

Dallas

Figure 4-7. Dallas Population (in Millions)

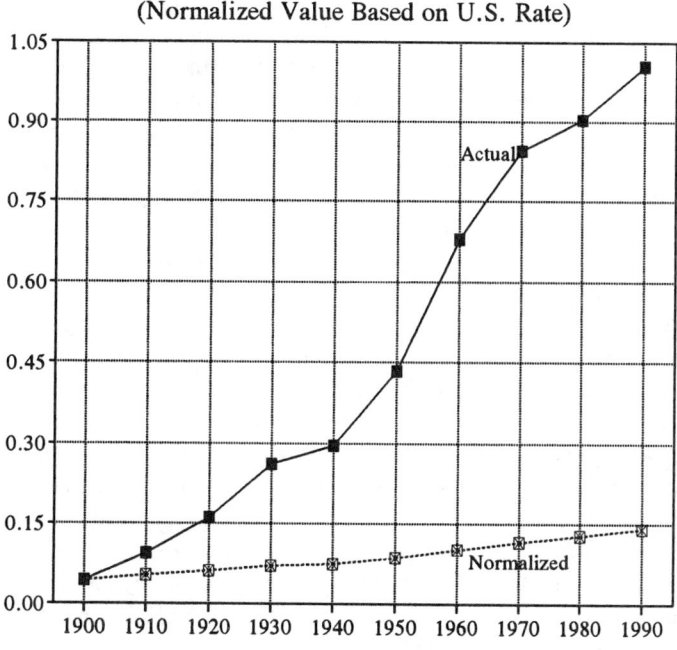

Year	Population	Growth Rate	U.S. Rate	Ratio
1900	42,638	--	--	--
1910	92,104	116.0%	21.0%	5.52
1920	158,976	72.6%	15.0%	4.85
1930	260,475	63.8%	16.2%	3.94
1940	294,734	13.2%	7.3%	1.81
1950	434,462	47.4%	14.5%	3.27
1960	679,684	56.4%	18.5%	3.05
1970	844,401	24.2%	13.4%	1.81
1980	904,078	7.1%	11.4%	0.62
1990	1,007,618	11.5%	9.8%	1.17

Ratio of population in 1990 to population in 1900: 23.6

Figure 4-8 shows population growth for Detroit compared to the nation from 1900 through 1990. The format for cities is explained on page 142. Detroit was a star from 1900 through 1930, growing dramatically after Henry Ford launched the automobile industry in its suburbs. By 1930 the actual line was 3.4 times as high as the normalized line, meaning that the growth ratio for the city was 3.4 times that of the nation from 1900 through 1930. Growth slowed in the 1930s, then was near the national rate in the 1940s. The city peaked in 1950, together with most Northeastern and Central region cities.

Detroit lost 9.7 percent of its population in the 1950s, when the national exodus from the major cities of the Northeast and Central regions began, as described in the Introduction. It lost another 9.3 percent in the 1960s, then the loss jumped to 20.5 percent in the 1970s as the car business crashed at the end of the 1970s and into the early 1980s. Detroit lost 14.6 percent more in the 1980s, bringing its overall loss from 1950 through 1990 to 44 percent of the 1950 level. This was 821,594 people, about the same number lost by Chicago over the same period, even though Chicago was twice as big as Detroit in 1950.

Ironically, because of its great growth early in the century, Detroit in 1990 was almost exactly the size it would have been if it had grown at the national rate through the century. This is shown by the actual and normalized lines nearly touching in 1990. Detroit had 12 percent of the state's population in 1900 when it started its rapid growth. It grew to hold 29 percent at its peak in 1950, but by 1990 it was back down to 11 percent. However, the Detroit metropolitan area had 56 percent of state population with 5.2 million people in 1990.

Detroit was 13th on the population ranking list in 1900 (Table 4-2), but it jumped to 5th in 1950. Detroit was only 6 percent smaller than Los Angeles in 1950, and Los Angeles had jumped to 3rd in the nation. But Detroit was back down to 7th place in 1990, and it is expected to fall out of the top ten by 2000, dropping below 1 million people for the first time since the 1920 census.

The Detroit metropolitan area shrank by 2.0 percent in the 1980s, a loss of 105,990 people. With a loss of 175,394 people in Detroit, the part of the metropolitan area outside the city proper gained 69,404 people. This was not enough to prevent Michigan from having slow growth in the 1980s. As a cold-weather city outside the main immigrant stream, and one that has been dependent on large industry for job creation, Detroit can do little to stop its slide in population. The only question is how far it will fall before it stabilizes at a new level.

Figure 4-8. Detroit Population (in Millions)

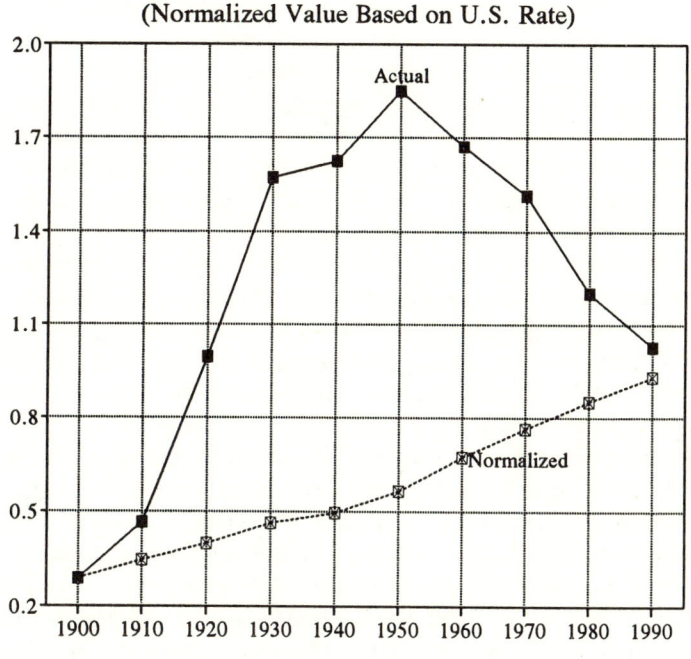

Year	Population	Growth Rate	U.S. Rate	Ratio
1900	285,704	--	--	--
1910	465,766	63.0%	21.0%	3.00
1920	993,678	113.3%	15.0%	7.58
1930	1,568,662	57.9%	16.2%	3.57
1940	1,623,452	3.5%	7.3%	0.48
1950	1,849,568	13.9%	14.5%	0.96
1960	1,670,144	-9.7%	18.5%	-0.52
1970	1,514,063	-9.3%	13.4%	-0.70
1980	1,203,368	-20.5%	11.4%	-1.80
1990	1,027,974	-14.6%	9.8%	-1.49

Ratio of population in 1990 to population in 1900: 3.60

Figure 4-9 shows population growth for Houston compared to the nation from 1900 through 1990. The format for cities is explained on page 142. Houston went from small town to stable metropolis in the twentieth century. It barely made the 100 biggest cities list in 1900, but was in a mature stabilization phase by 1990 as it became the fourth largest city in the nation. Houston grew much more rapidly than the nation in every decade from 1900 through 1980, with its lowest decades the 1960s and 1970s when it grew "only" about 2.5 times as fast as the nation (ratios near 2.5). It was part of the Texas boom in industries ranging from oil to cattle to high-technology electronics, all in a low-tax environment. By 1980 the actual line for Houston was twelve times as high as the normalized line, meaning that Houston's growth ratio was twelve times as high as the nation's from 1900 through 1980. But Houston grew by only 2.2 percent in the 1980s, while its metropolitan area grew by 20 percent. This is a sign that, as the core city of the area, Houston is close to the end of its very high growth period.

Houston grew from holding 1.5 percent of the state's population in 1900 to 9.6 percent in 1990. Its metropolitan area reached 3.7 million in 1990, corresponding to 22 percent of state population. This put Houston just behind the 24 percent of the Dallas-Fort Worth area, which had 4.0 million people in 1990. Houston's growth as a city was much more rapid than that of its competing cities, Dallas and San Antonio. It grew to be nearly twice as big as Dallas and San Antonio by 1980, after starting out nearly equal with Dallas and almost 16 percent behind San Antonio in 1900, as is shown in Figure 4-26. Houston's 1980 edge had shrunk by 1990, however, as Houston entered what appears to be its stabilization phase, while Dallas and especially San Antonio were still in a high-growth phase.

Houston was only 85th on the population ranking list in 1900 (Table 4-2), but by 1950 it had moved up to 14th place. In 1990 Houston passed Philadelphia to take over 4th place on the ranking list. It is a position Houston should hold for a long time. Third-place Chicago is a million people ahead of Houston, and San Diego, on its way to catching Philadelphia in a few decades, is a half million behind Houston. There is no shortage of investment capital to help Houston maintain its position, and its location in a dynamic Sunbelt state that is a target for immigrants (Houston is the top target in Texas for legal immigrants) will also add to its potential for continued growth. The only question is how much of that growth will be in Houston proper versus in its metropolitan area.

Figure 4-9. Houston Population (in Millions)

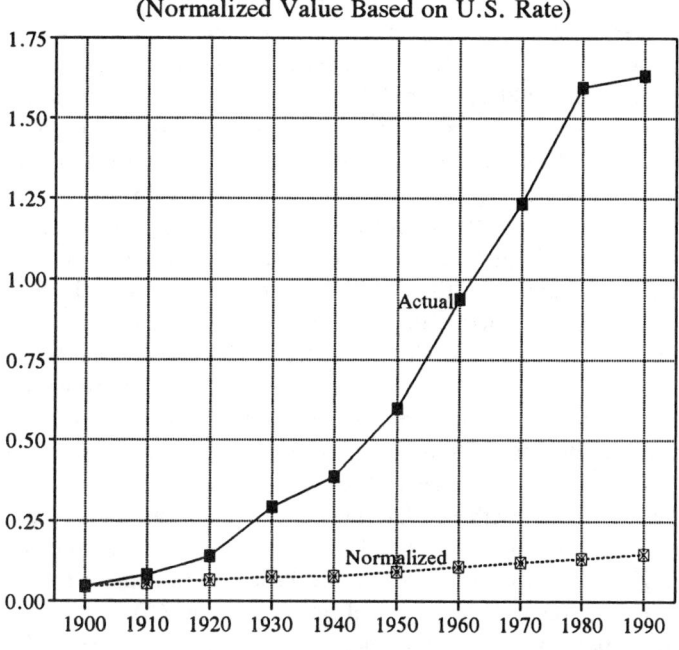

Year	Population	Growth Rate	U.S. Rate	Ratio
1900	44,633	--	--	--
1910	78,800	76.6%	21.0%	3.64
1920	138,276	75.5%	15.0%	5.05
1930	292,352	111.4%	16.2%	6.87
1940	384,514	31.5%	7.3%	4.34
1950	596,163	55.0%	14.5%	3.80
1960	938,219	57.4%	18.5%	3.10
1970	1,233,535	31.5%	13.4%	2.35
1980	1,595,138	29.3%	11.4%	2.56
1990	1,629,902	2.2%	9.8%	0.22

Ratio of population in 1990 to population in 1900: 36.5

Figure 4-10 shows population growth for Indianapolis compared to the nation from 1900 through 1990. The format for cities is explained on page 142. Indianapolis appears to have avoided the fate of most Northeastern and Central region cities by continuing high growth after 1950. But the story is not quite as unusual as it seems. Indianapolis did very well from 1900 through 1930, growing more rapidly than the nation (as did other Central region cities like Chicago, Cleveland, and Detroit). By 1930 the actual line was 33 percent above the normalized line, meaning that the growth ratio for the city was 33 percent above that of the nation from 1900 through 1930, even though growth slowed to almost exactly the national rate in the 1920s. Indianapolis grew more slowly than the nation in the next three decades, each decade being a little worse than the one before. But it did avoid losing population, and by 1960 the actual line was still 20 percent above the normalized line.

A national exodus from the major cities of the Northeast and Central regions had begun in earnest in the 1950s, as described in the Introduction. Indianapolis was on the verge of a similar fate in the 1960s, when it did what many cities had done earlier in the century, which was to merge with an adjacent county. That produced a "growth" of over 50 percent in the 1960s. The new Indianapolis lost population in the 1970s, but it gained again in the 1980s, even if the growth rate was only 60 percent of the national rate (ratio of 0.60).

Indianapolis was 21st on the population ranking list in 1900 (Table 4-2), and it fell to 23rd in 1950, in spite of growing much faster than the nation from 1900 through 1950. This was because many Sunbelt cities previously behind it were growing more rapidly. Indianapolis jumped to 12th place in 1990. Its merger kept it just ahead of the national growth rate from 1950 through 1990, and it passed many of the older Northeastern and Central region cities on their way down.

Indianapolis is hampered by being in a slow-growth state out of both the Sunbelt and the immigrant stream. But the city constantly grew more rapidly than the state during the century. Indianapolis went from holding 6.7 percent of the state's population in 1900 to 10.9 percent in 1950, before the merger helped it to jump to 13.4 percent in 1990. The Indianapolis metropolitan area had 1.4 million people in 1990, corresponding to 25 percent of state population. In the 1980s, the metropolitan area gained 74,580 people while the city gained 41,145. Their percentage increases were similar (5.7 percent for the area and 5.9 percent for the city), and both rates were higher than the 1.0 percent for the state. This means that the city is still in a growth mode.

Figure 4-10. Indianapolis Population (in Millions)

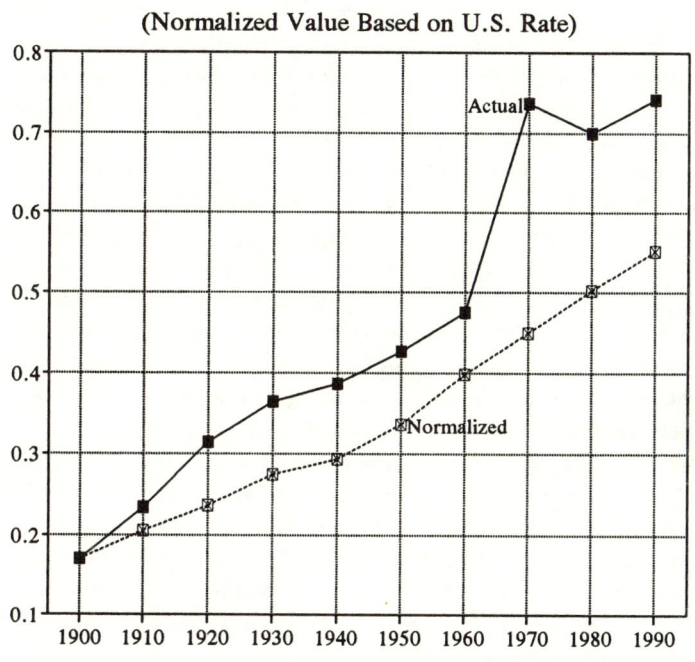

Year	Population	Growth Rate	U.S. Rate	Ratio
1900	169,164	--	--	--
1910	233,650	38.1%	21.0%	1.81
1920	314,194	34.5%	15.0%	2.30
1930	364,161	15.9%	16.2%	0.98
1940	386,972	6.3%	7.3%	0.86
1950	427,173	10.4%	14.5%	0.72
1960	476,258	11.5%	18.5%	0.62
1970	736,856	54.7%	13.4%	4.09
1980	700,807	-4.9%	11.4%	-0.43
1990	741,952	5.9%	9.8%	0.60

Ratio of population in 1990 to population in 1900: 4.39

Figure 4-11 shows population growth for Jacksonville compared to the nation from 1900 through 1990. The format for cities is explained on page 142. Jacksonville is similar to Indianapolis in having a huge surge in "growth" in the 1960s by merging with an adjacent area. But Jacksonville's location in Florida, one of the fastest growing states in the nation, gave Jacksonville an extra boost upward, especially after the merger. Jacksonville grew much more rapidly than the nation from 1900 through 1950, exceeding the national rate in every decade (ratios greater than 1.00), and usually by a big margin. By 1950 the actual line was 3.6 times as high as the normalized line, meaning that the growth ratio for the city was 3.6 times higher than that of the nation from 1900 through 1950. But because Jacksonville was very small in 1900, it had only 204,517 people in 1950 in spite of its dramatic growth rate.

Jacksonville lost population in the 1950s, making it appear that it might fall victim to the same kind of exodus from the major cities in the Northeast and Central regions that began in the 1950s, as described in the Introduction. This seemed especially so considering that Florida had its biggest single decade for growth in the 1950s. But the city proper only lost 1.7 percent of its population, and the area was growing together with Florida. The 1960s merger produced a "growth" of over 150 percent for the new Jacksonville, and although growth slowed in the 1970s, the new combination grew by 24.4 percent in the 1980s.

Jacksonville had a population of 672,971 in 1990. Its actual line was seven times as high as the normalized line, meaning that its growth ratio was seven times greater than that of the nation from 1900 through 1990. Jacksonville was almost twenty-four times larger in 1990 than in 1900 (1900 through 1990 ratio of 23.7). It did not even appear on the list of the 100 biggest cities in 1900, and it was only 49th in 1950 (Table 4-2). In 1990 Jacksonville was the 15th largest city in the nation, making it the last city to qualify for inclusion in this book.

Jacksonville is 88 percent larger than Miami, the next largest city in Florida. But Jacksonville's metropolitan area is only 0.9 million, or 7 percent of state population. The Miami area has 3.2 million, the Tampa-St. Petersburg area 2.1 million, and even the Orlando area is bigger at 1.2 million. Jacksonville has incorporated most of its metropolitan area in the city proper. But Jacksonville should continue to benefit from the solid growth of Florida, a Sunbelt state high on the immigration target list and a state that is well on its way to becoming the 3rd largest state in the nation. This should keep Jacksonville in the top fifteen list of cities for several decades.

Figure 4-11. Jacksonville Population (in Millions)

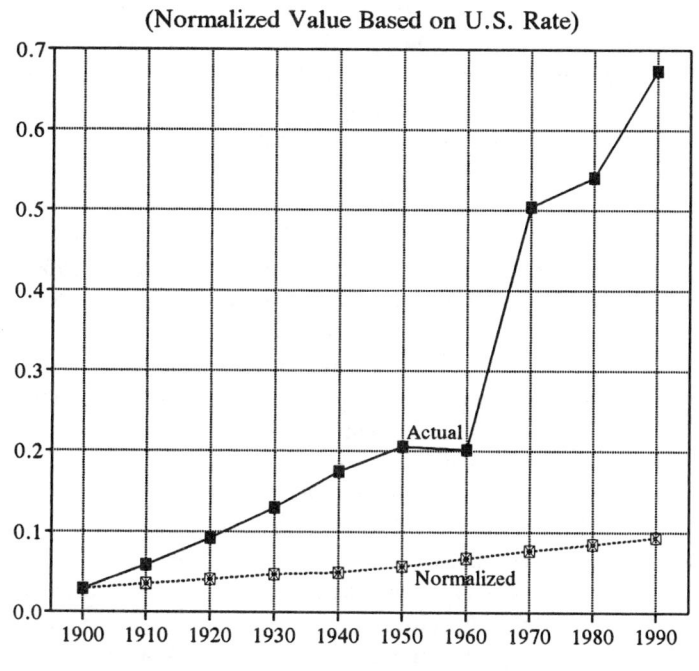

Year	Population	Growth Rate	U.S. Rate	Ratio
1900	28,429	--	--	--
1910	57,699	103.0%	21.0%	4.90
1920	91,558	58.7%	15.0%	3.92
1930	129,549	41.5%	16.2%	2.56
1940	173,065	33.6%	7.3%	4.62
1950	204,517	18.2%	14.5%	1.25
1960	201,030	-1.7%	18.5%	-0.09
1970	504,265	150.8%	13.4%	11.28
1980	540,920	7.3%	11.4%	0.64
1990	672,971	24.4%	9.8%	2.49

Ratio of population in 1990 to population in 1900: 23.7

Figure 4-12 shows population growth for Los Angeles compared to the nation from 1900 through 1990. The format for cities is explained on page 142. Los Angeles and California grew in the same phenomenal way. With 102,479 people in 1900, Los Angeles was only 36th in the nation (Table 4-2) and 2nd in the state behind San Francisco, which had 342,782 people. But from 1900 through 1950, Los Angeles grew more rapidly than all of the twenty-four cities in this book except Phoenix, which was so small in 1900 that by 1950 it was just barely larger than Los Angeles had been in 1900. The growth ratio for Los Angeles was ten times as high as that of the nation (and eight times as high as that of San Francisco) from 1900 through 1950. Los Angeles passed San Francisco in population by 1920, and in 1950 Los Angeles was the 4th largest city in the nation.

Los Angeles grew partly by absorbing its neighbors, especially after bringing water from the Owens Valley (over 200 miles away) in the 1920s. Adjacent areas were annexed as part of the bargain to gain access to water. Water was later brought from the Colorado River and from northern California to support the growth of Los Angeles and southern California. In 1960 Los Angeles was rated as the nation's largest city in area at 455 square miles. But even with 465 square miles in 1990, Los Angeles has been passed by other cities learning the annexation game. Of the cities in this book, both Jacksonville and Houston were much larger in area in 1990 than Los Angeles.

Los Angeles was the nation's 2nd most populous city in 1990 in spite of being only 8th on the growth ratio list from 1950 to 1990. But Los Angeles was 5th on the growth list from 1980 to 1990. It no longer grows by annexation, but its metropolitan area and that of New York are the nation's top targets for immigrants (legal and illegal), and this will continue to fuel growth for many years.

Los Angeles grew from having 7 percent of California's population in 1900 to 19 percent in 1950. It fell to 12 percent in 1990 because, as shown in Figure 4-25, cities like San Diego and San Jose led the state in growth rate after 1950. But the Los Angeles metropolitan area had 14.5 million people in 1990, or 49 percent of the state's population. The Los Angeles metropolitan area is the nation's 2nd largest behind New York, and it grew by 26.4 percent in the 1980s. The New York area grew by only 3.4 percent. This means that although the city of Los Angeles will remain second in population to New York City for the indefinite future, the Los Angeles metropolitan area probably will become the nation's largest in the first half of the next century.

Figure 4-12. Los Angeles Population (in Millions)

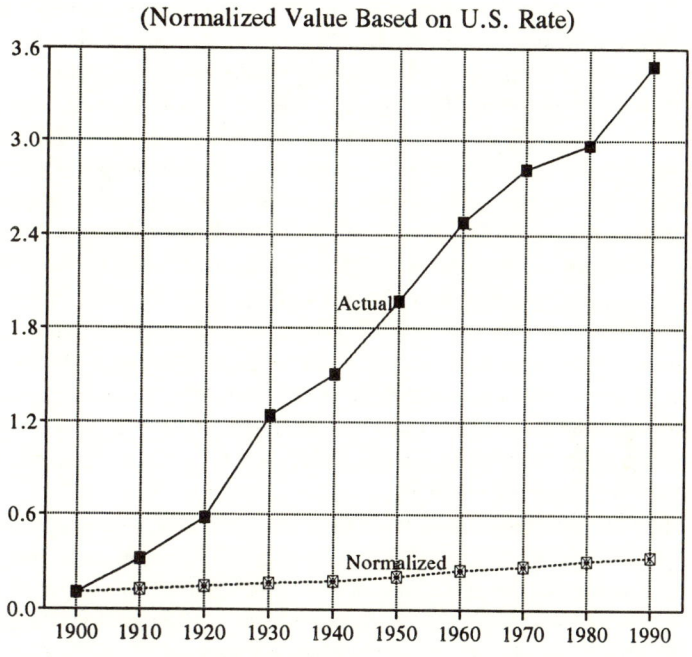

Year	Population	Growth Rate	U.S. Rate	Ratio
1900	102,479	--	--	--
1910	319,198	211.5%	21.0%	10.1
1920	576,673	80.7%	15.0%	5.39
1930	1,238,048	114.7%	16.2%	7.08
1940	1,504,277	21.5%	7.3%	2.96
1950	1,970,358	31.0%	14.5%	2.14
1960	2,479,015	25.8%	18.5%	1.40
1970	2,811,801	13.4%	13.4%	1.00
1980	2,966,850	5.5%	11.4%	0.48
1990	3,485,557	17.5%	9.8%	1.79

Ratio of population in 1990 to population in 1900: 34.0

Figure 4-13 shows population growth for Milwaukee compared to the nation from 1900 through 1990. The format for cities is explained on page 142. From 1900 through 1960 Milwaukee grew more rapidly than Wisconsin and the nation with a diverse economy ranging from beer brewing, meat packing, and machinery manufacturing. But its best growth took place from 1900 through 1930 (ratios well over 1.00). It grew more slowly than the nation from 1930 through 1960, but grew more rapidly (actual line staying above the normalized line) from 1900 through 1960 overall. Milwaukee's share of state population increased from 14 percent in 1900 to 19 percent in 1950, showing that it grew more rapidly than the state from 1900 through 1950.

Milwaukee lost population from 1960 through 1990, declining like the other industrial cities of the Northeast and Central regions, as explained in the Introduction. By 1990 the actual line was 33 percent below the normalized line, meaning that Milwaukee's growth ratio was 33 percent lower than that of the nation from 1900 through 1990. Milwaukee's percentage of Wisconsin's population fell from 19 percent in 1950 to 13 percent in 1990.

Milwaukee improved from 14th on the population ranking list in 1900 to 13th in 1950 (Table 4-2). But it fell to 17th in the nation in 1990. Its peak population came in 1960 after a spurt in growth in the 1950s, making Milwaukee one of the few major cities in the Northeast and Central regions to have a population increase in the 1950s. However, by 1990 Milwaukee's population was 15 percent below its 1960 peak, and it had fewer people in 1990 than it had in 1950. The rate of loss did at least slow in the 1980s.

The Milwaukee-Racine metropolitan area had 1.6 million people in 1990. This was 33 percent of state population, but the area grew by only 2.4 percent in the 1980s. The area added 37,031 people in the decade, while the central city was losing 8,124. The net increase in area population would be a good sign if it were not for the very low growth rate. The state grew very slowly at 4.0 percent, but that was still higher than the metropolitan area. This indicates slow growth in the future for the Milwaukee area.

Milwaukee is far away from the Sunbelt, but only 100 miles from Chicago. As a result, the immigration that does take place in the Lake Michigan area ends up in the Chicago area and not in Milwaukee. The state of Wisconsin is projected to grow much more slowly than the nation after 2000, and this is the final confirmation that Milwaukee can expect little (if any) growth in the future.

Milwaukee

Figure 4-13. Milwaukee Population (in Millions)

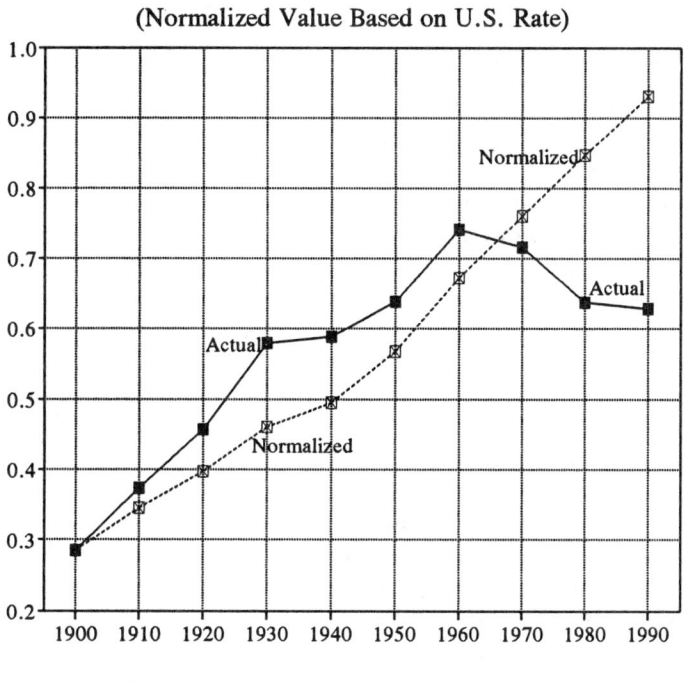

Year	Population	Growth Rate	U.S. Rate	Ratio
1900	285,315	--	--	--
1910	373,857	31.0%	21.0%	1.48
1920	457,147	22.3%	15.0%	1.49
1930	578,249	26.5%	16.2%	1.63
1940	587,472	1.6%	7.3%	0.22
1950	637,392	8.5%	14.5%	0.59
1960	741,324	16.3%	18.5%	0.88
1970	717,372	-3.2%	13.4%	-0.24
1980	636,212	-11.3%	11.4%	-0.99
1990	628,088	-1.3%	9.8%	-0.13

Ratio of population in 1990 to population in 1900: 2.20

Figure 4-14 shows population growth for New Orleans compared to the nation from 1900 through 1990. The format for cities is explained on page 142. New Orleans tracked the national growth rate from 1900 through 1950, as the actual population line and the normalized line were nearly superimposed (all ratios were close to 1.00). This duplicates the growth of Louisiana, and New Orleans held 21 percent of the population of the state in both 1900 and 1950. But although the state continued to track the national growth rate after 1950, New Orleans slowed in the 1950s and lost population in every decade from 1960 onward. This followed the trend of the older cities of the Northeast and Central regions, as explained in the Introduction, but it was not common in the Sunbelt, of which Louisiana is a part.

New Orleans's share of the state's population fell to only 12 percent in 1990, and the rate at which New Orleans lost population increased in each decade from 1960 onward. The loss reached 10.9 percent in the 1980s, making New Orleans one of only ten cities in the nation of more than 100,000 people to lose 10 percent or more of its population in the 1980s. Five of the ten were cities in this part of the book (Table 4-1), and the other four (Detroit, Pittsburgh, St. Louis, and Cleveland) did even worse than New Orleans.

New Orleans was a thriving port city on the Mississippi River (although 100 miles from the ocean), with a reputation for gaudy living. But as energy became more important in the state's economy, New Orleans became less important. The city also became less important in the South, as the cities of boom states like Florida and Texas moved to the top. New Orleans has little industry of its own, and tourists interested in Jazz, the French Quarter, and the Superdome are not enough to keep the population from continuing to fall.

New Orleans was 12th on the population ranking list in 1900 and 16th in 1950 (Table 4-2), even though it matched the nation's growth rate over that period. Other cities grew faster. New Orleans was 25th in the nation in 1990, and its population then was just ahead of its 1940 level. New Orleans lost 21 percent of its population between 1990 and its 1960 peak, and it should continue to lose population in the 1990s.

The New Orleans metropolitan area had 1.3 million people in 1990, 30 percent of state population. The area lost 1.5 percent (189,420 people) in the 1980s, far more than the 60,989 people who left New Orleans. Areas such as Baton Rouge will continue to pull population away from the New Orleans area, while the city itself falls farther down the population ranking list.

Figure 4-14. New Orleans Population (in Millions)

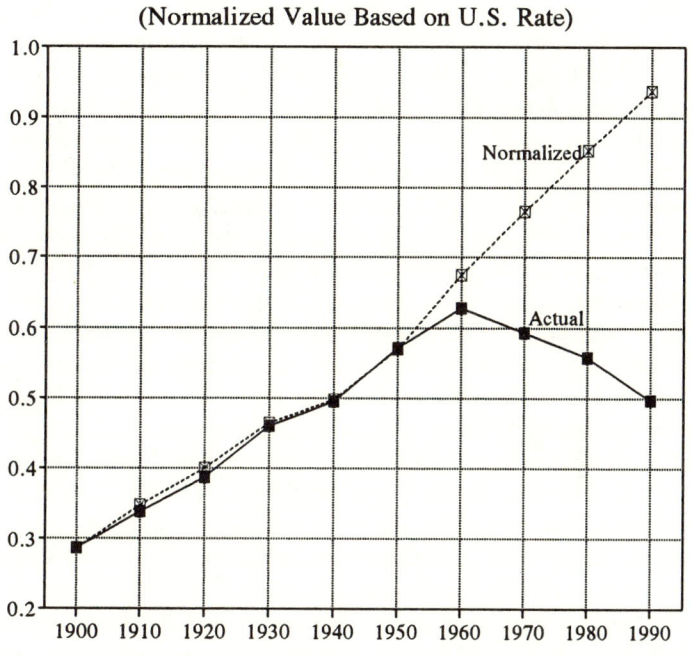

Year	Population	Growth Rate	U.S. Rate	Ratio
1900	287,104	--	--	--
1910	339,075	18.1%	21.0%	0.86
1920	387,219	14.2%	15.0%	0.95
1930	458,762	18.5%	16.2%	1.14
1940	494,537	7.8%	7.3%	1.07
1950	570,445	15.3%	14.5%	1.06
1960	627,525	10.0%	18.5%	0.54
1970	593,471	-5.4%	13.4%	-0.41
1980	557,927	-6.0%	11.4%	-0.52
1990	496,938	-10.9%	9.8%	-1.12

Ratio of population in 1990 to population in 1900: 1.73

Figure 4-15 shows population growth for New York City compared to the nation from 1900 through 1990. The format for cities is explained on page 142. Up to 1950, New York City was as strong a force in the development and growth of the nation as any state. In fact, if it had been listed as a state, New York City would have ranked fifth in the nation in both 1900 and 1950. (In 1950 it would have ranked ahead of the rest of New York State.) Buoyed by the flow of immigrants, New York City grew more rapidly than the nation from 1900 through 1930, continuing its trend from the previous century. Even in the 1930s depression it grew more rapidly than the nation. But the growth of the city slowed in the 1940s. World War II started a redistribution of population that would produce great changes in the nation. As explained in the Introduction, people poured out of the old industrial cities of the Northeast and Central regions after 1950.

New York City had 47 percent of the state's population in 1900, and it held more than 53 percent in 1950. This means that the city grew more rapidly than the state from 1900 through 1950. It also grew more rapidly than the nation during that period, as shown by the actual line's staying above the normalized line. But the city lost population for the first time in the 1950s, and after recovering a little in the 1960s, it lost over 10.4 percent of its population in the 1970s. This was a loss of 823,924 people, more than the 1970 population of New Hampshire.

In spite of its huge loss in the 1970s, New York City gained population in the 1980s, and in 1990 it held 41 percent of the state's population. It was still 10th in the nation if ranked as a state, and it remained attractive to immigrants. The New York and Los Angeles areas have been the favorite targets for immigrants for many years, and both are far ahead of the Chicago area in third place. This should keep New York City above 7 million in population for a long time.

New York City has been first on the city population ranking list for over 200 years. It was the nation's financial and cultural center for most of that time, and it still has a diversified economy as a port and manufacturing center. The shift to the Sunbelt reduced the importance of the city, and it has many problems with its huge minority population and welfare costs. The New York metropolitan area, which includes parts of four states, was the nation's largest with 19.3 million people in 1990. However, although New York City will remain the largest city in the nation indefinitely, the Los Angeles metropolitan area should take the lead as the largest metropolitan area during the first half of the next century.

Figure 4-15. New York City Population (in Millions)

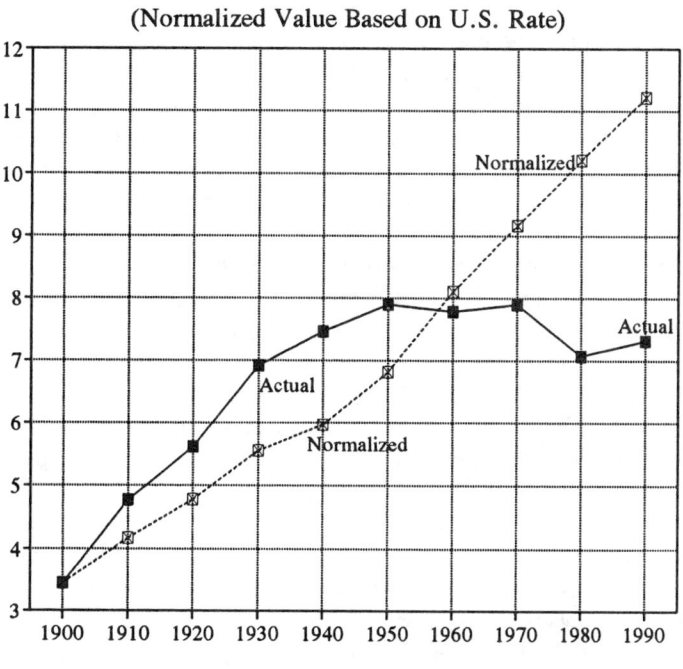

Year	Population	Growth Rate	U.S. Rate	Ratio
1900	3,437,202	--	--	--
1910	4,766,883	38.7%	21.0%	1.84
1920	5,620,048	17.9%	15.0%	1.20
1930	6,930,446	23.3%	16.2%	1.44
1940	7,454,995	7.6%	7.3%	1.04
1950	7,891,957	5.9%	14.5%	0.40
1960	7,781,984	-1.4%	18.5%	-0.08
1970	7,895,563	1.5%	13.4%	0.11
1980	7,071,639	-10.4%	11.4%	-0.91
1990	7,322,564	3.5%	9.8%	0.36

Ratio of population in 1990 to population in 1900: 2.13

Figure 4-16 shows population growth for Philadelphia compared to the nation from 1900 through 1990. The format for cities is explained on page 142. Philadelphia was similar to Boston in giving an early indication that the period of growth for the old cities of the Northeast was coming to an end. It grew at the same rate as the nation only from 1900 through 1920, slowed in the 1920s, and then lost population for the first time in the depression of the 1930s. It grew at half the national rate during the 1940s, then lost population in every decade after 1950 (negative ratios). Philadelphia was ripe for the population outflow from the cities of the Northeast and Central regions that started in 1950, as explained in the Introduction.

Philadelphia stayed at 20 percent of the population of Pennsylvania in 1900 and 1950 because the state grew as slowly as the city. But Philadelphia's share of the state's population fell to only 13 percent in 1990, as the city lost over 23 percent of its population from 1950 through 1990. This loss of 486,028 people meant that the population of Philadelphia in 1990 was almost exactly the same as it had been in 1910. As shown by the normalized line, if Philadelphia had matched the growth of the nation since 1900, it would have had almost 4.3 million people in 1990, making it the 2nd largest city in the nation.

In spite of its slow growth in the first half of the century, Philadelphia stayed in 3rd place on the city population ranking list in 1900 and 1950 (Table 4-2). This shows the power of population momentum. In 1990 Philadelphia fell to 5th, after being passed by both Los Angeles and Houston. It can be expected to fall farther down the list because there are rapidly growing cities behind and Philadelphia will continue to lose population. Philadelphia will probably fall out of the top ten list during the first half of the next century, and, when it does, it might have a smaller population by then than it had in 1900.

Philadelphia was hurt by its location. People moved to New Jersey, Delaware, and Maryland, while still staying in commuting distance of Philadelphia. This enabled them to avoid the taxes of Philadelphia, which grew higher as the minority population of the city grew and its welfare burden increased. Also, with New York City only ninety miles away, capital investment was easily diverted away from Philadelphia. The Philadelphia metropolitan area had 5.9 million people in 1990, and it grew by 4.3 percent in the 1980s. This was much better growth than that of either the city or the state. But the area includes portions of the three states to which people fled from Philadelphia. So the strength of the metropolitan area is of no help to the city of Philadelphia.

Philadelphia

Figure 4-16. Philadelphia Population (in Millions)

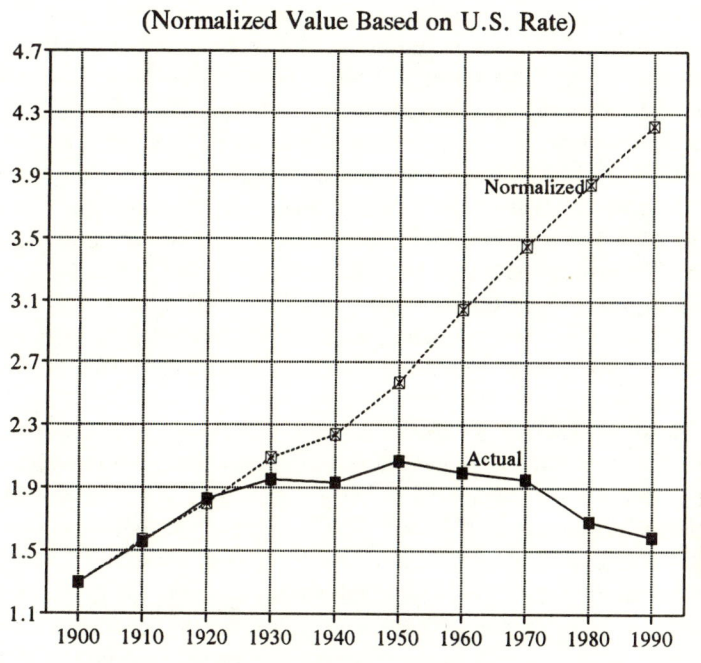

Year	Population	Growth Rate	U.S. Rate	Ratio
1900	1,293,697	--	--	--
1910	1,549,008	19.7%	21.0%	0.94
1920	1,823,779	17.7%	15.0%	1.19
1930	1,950,961	7.0%	16.2%	0.43
1940	1,931,334	-1.0%	7.3%	-0.14
1950	2,071,605	7.3%	14.5%	0.50
1960	2,002,512	-3.3%	18.5%	-0.18
1970	1,949,996	-2.6%	13.4%	-0.20
1980	1,688,210	-13.4%	11.4%	-1.17
1990	1,585,577	-6.1%	9.8%	-0.62

Ratio of population in 1990 to population in 1900: 1.23

Figure 4-17 shows population growth for Phoenix compared to the nation from 1900 through 1990. The format for cities is explained on page 142. Phoenix is the king of growth among the major cities of the nation. It leads the growth ratio list (Table 4-2) from 1900 through 1950 and from 1950 through 1990, giving it the lead from 1900 through 1990 by default. Phoenix was helped by being located in a very high growth state, but its growth ratio was six times as high as that of Arizona from 1900 through 1990, even though Arizona was the second fastest growing state in the nation (Table 3-3). Phoenix was a small village of 5,544 people in 1900. Even after a great growth ratio of 19.3 from 1900 through 1950, its population was only 106,818 in 1950, and it ranked just 98th on the largest city list (Table 4-2). But in spite of its higher population base, Phoenix had a growth ratio of 9.21 from 1950 through 1990, giving it 983,403 people in 1990, and putting it in 9th place on the population ranking list.

Phoenix grew (as do many cities) by absorbing neighboring areas as well as by attracting more people to the area. By 1990 Phoenix had a city area of 324 square miles, larger than all but six of the cities discussed in this part of the book. For example, Phoenix is seven times as large in area as San Francisco. With room to grow and a low-tax business environment, combined with weather suitable for a resort area, Phoenix went far beyond the good growth expected of a Sunbelt state city. To put its growth in perspective, if Phoenix had grown at the same rate as the nation from 1900 through 1990, it would have had only 18,000 people in 1990 (the normalized line value on the graph).

Phoenix held 4.5 percent of the population of the state in 1900. It grew to hold 14 percent by 1950, and then to 27 percent in 1990. The Phoenix metropolitan area, which includes Mesa, had over 2.2 million people in 1990, which was 61 percent of the population of the state. In the 1980s, the metropolitan area grew by 40 percent, the state grew by 35 percent, and the city grew by 25 percent. All three grew much more rapidly than the 9.8 percent growth rate of the nation in the 1980s.

These relative rates of growth suggest that Phoenix may be entering a mature growth phase, in which the city does not grow as fast as the state. But Arizona is projected to continue to be a high-growth state after 2000 as it moves up to become the 14th largest state in the nation (Table 5-2). Thus Phoenix can be expected to continue to climb up the city population ranking list, even if it does not match the state in growth. Both the state and the city are a target for immigrants (legal and illegal), and this will continue to fuel the growth of both.

Figure 4-17. Phoenix Population (in Millions)

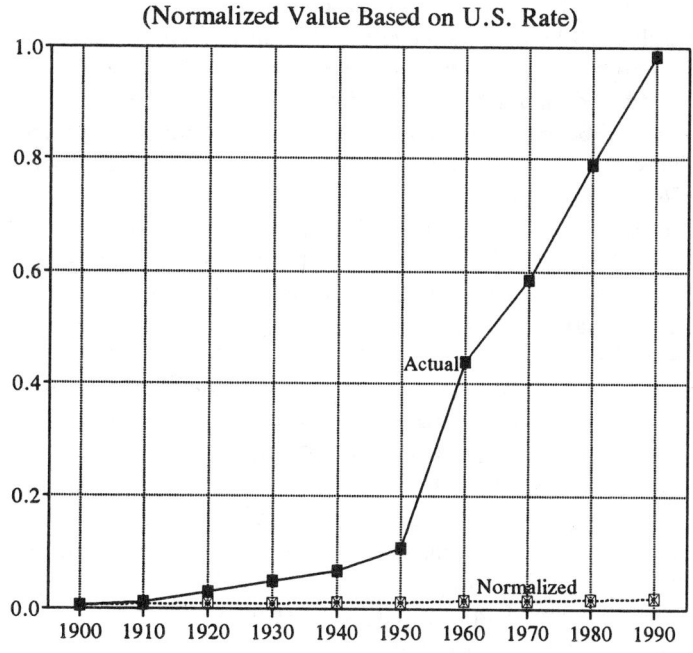

Year	Population	Growth Rate	U.S. Rate	Ratio
1900	5,544	--	--	--
1910	11,134	100.8%	21.0%	4.80
1920	29,053	160.9%	15.0%	10.8
1930	48,118	65.6%	16.2%	4.05
1940	65,414	35.9%	7.3%	4.94
1950	106,818	63.3%	14.5%	4.37
1960	439,170	311.1%	18.5%	16.8
1970	584,303	33.0%	13.4%	2.47
1980	789,704	35.2%	11.4%	3.08
1990	983,403	24.5%	9.8%	2.51

Ratio of population in 1990 to population in 1900: 177

Figure 4-18 shows population growth for Pittsburgh compared to the nation from 1900 through 1990. The format for cities is explained on page 142. It should be noted that the population shown for Pittsburgh in 1900 includes the city of Allegheny, which was absorbed by Pittsburgh after the census of 1900. In the rest of the book such mergers are shown in the census following the merger. But this merger affects the 1900 baseline, and its size was so significant (the city of Allegheny had 129,896 people in 1900), that it would be misleading to show Pittsburgh separately in 1900.

The steel and coal industries dominated Pittsburgh early in the century. The city grew slowly in the 1910-1920 decade, but a surge in growth in the 1920s kept it near the national rate (actual line near the normalized line). Pittsburgh grew very little from 1930 through 1950, and after 1950 it lost more than 10 percent of its population in every decade. It had a peak loss of 18.5 percent in the 1970s. Pittsburgh suffered from the same problems that produced the population outflow from the cities of the Northeast and Central regions after 1950, as discussed in the Introduction, but its losses were worse than most.

Pittsburgh had only 7 percent of the state's population in 1900 and 6 percent in 1950. This means that the city grew even more slowly than the state from 1900 through 1950. By 1990 Pittsburgh had only 3 percent of state population. It fell from 7th in 1900 to 12th in 1950 on the population ranking list (Table 4-2), and it plummeted to 40th in 1990. Pittsburgh lost 45 percent of its population from 1950 through 1990 and was 18 percent smaller in 1990 than in 1900 (1900 through 1990 ratio of 0.82). Of the cities in this book, only St. Louis had a worse growth ratio than Pittsburgh from 1950 through 1990 and from 1900 through 1990. St. Louis and Buffalo are the only other cities to have smaller populations in 1990 than they had in 1900.

Both Pittsburgh and its metropolitan area are losing population. The area had 2.4 million people in 1990, 20 percent of the population of the state. The area lost 6.9 percent (176,412 people) in the 1980s, while Pittsburgh lost 12.8 percent (54,081 people). This means that the area lost more than three times as many people as the city. Of the cities in this book, only Detroit had a higher loss in the 1980s than did Pittsburgh (Table 4-1). Of the eighty-five largest metropolitan areas in the nation, only nine had losses in the 1980s, and the Pittsburgh area had the biggest loss of all. Located in a state that is projected to show no growth in the first half of the next century, Pittsburgh and its metropolitan area seem sure to continue to lose population.

Pittsburgh

Figure 4-18. Pittsburgh Population (in Millions)

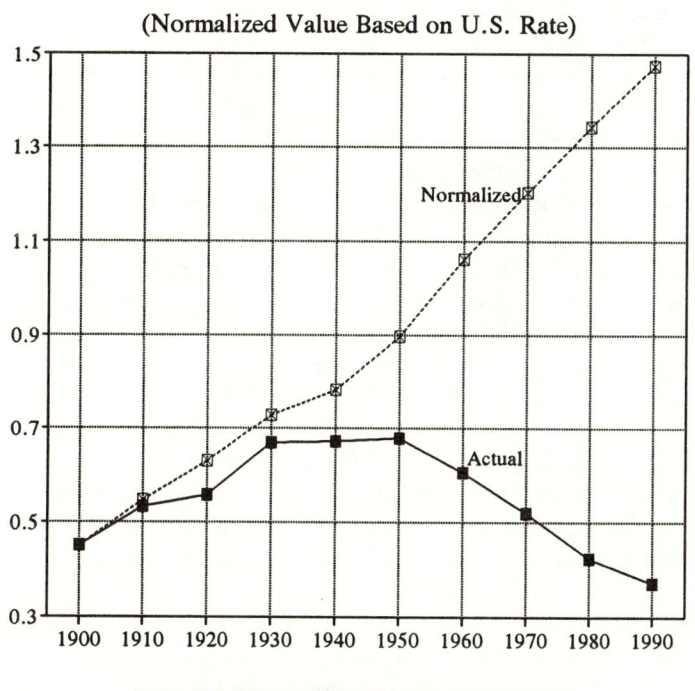

Year	Population	Growth Rate	U.S. Rate	Ratio
1900	451,512	--	--	--
1910	533,905	18.2%	21.0%	0.87
1920	558,343	4.6%	15.0%	0.31
1930	669,817	20.0%	16.2%	1.23
1940	671,659	0.3%	7.3%	0.04
1950	676,806	0.8%	14.5%	0.05
1960	604,332	-10.7%	18.5%	-0.58
1970	520,089	-13.9%	13.4%	-1.04
1980	423,960	-18.5%	11.4%	-1.62
1990	369,879	-12.8%	9.8%	-1.30

Ratio of population in 1990 to population in 1900: 0.82

Figure 4-19 shows population growth for St. Louis compared to the nation from 1900 through 1990. The format for cities is explained on page 142. St. Louis was a very important city in 1900. It was the fourth most populous city in the nation (Table 4-2), and as late as 1870 it was bigger than Chicago. Its strategic location at the junction of the Missouri and Mississippi Rivers made it both the supply center for people heading west and the market for fur traders who operated in the West. It grew from there to become a major industrial city early in this century. But 1900 was in many ways the peak for St. Louis.

The city grew more slowly than the nation in the 1900-1910 decade, and it slowed even more in the next decade. The growth ratio fell sharply to 0.39 in the 1920s, and in the 1930s depression St. Louis lost population for the first time. It gained a little in the 1940s, hit its peak population in 1950, and then lost over 12 percent of its population in every decade afterwards. St. Louis lost 27.2 percent of its population in the 1970s, the highest loss in one decade for any city in this book. Even though it was west of the Mississippi, St. Louis was part of the population outflow that took place in the cities of the Northeast and Central regions after 1950, as explained in the Introduction. Its losses had the same causes, but St. Louis had the biggest losses.

St. Louis went from holding 19 percent of the state's population in 1900 to 22 percent in 1950 (the state grew more slowly than the city). But by 1990 it had only 8 percent of the state's population. St. Louis fell from 4th on the population ranking list in 1900 to 8th in 1950, and it fell to 34th place in 1990. St. Louis lost 54 percent of its population from 1950 to 1990, and, as shown by the ratio of 0.69 at the bottom of the figure, St. Louis was 31 percent smaller in 1990 than it was in 1900. It was even 10 percent smaller in 1990 than it had been 100 years earlier in 1890. Of the cities in this book, only Pittsburgh and Buffalo also lost population from 1900 through 1990. St. Louis had the worst growth ratio from 1950 through 1990 and from 1900 through 1990. Only Boston was worse from 1900 through 1950.

The St. Louis metropolitan area had 2.5 million people in 1990 (49 percent of state population), but the area includes parts of Illinois on the eastern bank of the Mississippi. The area grew by 3.3 percent in the 1980s, while St. Louis lost another 12.4 percent of its population. This trend should continue. Both Missouri and Illinois are projected to grow more slowly than the nation (but at least in a positive direction) while people continue to leave St. Louis. If St. Louis loses another 12 percent of its population, it will be smaller than it was in 1880.

Figure 4-19. St. Louis Population (in Millions)

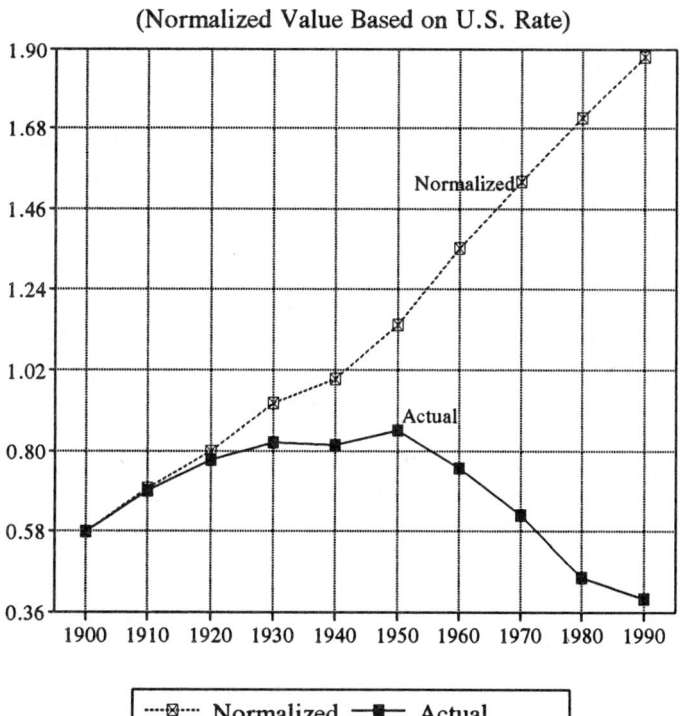

Year	Population	Growth Rate	U.S. Rate	Ratio
1900	575,238	--	--	--
1910	687,029	19.4%	21.0%	0.92
1920	772,897	12.5%	15.0%	0.84
1930	821,960	6.3%	16.2%	0.39
1940	816,048	-0.7%	7.3%	-0.10
1950	856,796	5.0%	14.5%	0.34
1960	750,026	-12.5%	18.5%	-0.67
1970	622,236	-17.0%	13.4%	-1.27
1980	452,801	-27.2%	11.4%	-2.38
1990	396,685	-12.4%	9.8%	-1.27

Ratio of population in 1990 to population in 1900: 0.69

Figure 4-20 shows population growth for San Antonio compared to the nation from 1900 through 1990. The format for cities is explained on page 142. San Antonio grew more rapidly than the nation in every decade from 1900 through 1960 as people flowed into Texas. The state built a diversified economy based on oil, cattle, agriculture, aircraft, and high-technology electronics, all in a low-tax environment. San Antonio focused on cattle and agriculture, and it was the largest city in Texas in 1900. As shown in Figure 4-26, San Antonio, in spite of its high growth, fell to 3rd place in Texas, behind Houston and Dallas, by 1930. The gap widened when San Antonio had its only decade of growth slower than that of the nation in the 1960s (ratio less than 1.00). But San Antonio grew sharply in the 1970s and 1980s, and it led both Dallas and Houston in growth in the 1980s (Table 4-1).

San Antonio moved up from 71st on the population ranking list in 1900 to 25th in 1950 (Table 4-2), and by 1990 it was the 10th largest city in the nation. San Antonio should go over the 1 million mark by 2000, passing Detroit as Detroit falls farther down the ranking list. But the cities just ahead of San Antonio (Phoenix, Dallas, and San Diego) are still growing rapidly, and San Antonio may have to wait a long time to move any farther up the population ranking ladder.

Dallas, Houston, and San Antonio grew rapidly from 1900 onward, and thus none of the three ever had a high percentage of the population of Texas. San Antonio went from having 1.7 percent of the state's population in 1900 to 5.5 percent in 1990. The San Antonio metropolitan area in 1990 had 1.3 million people, but San Antonio itself had 71 percent of them. This is a huge percentage for the core city of a metropolitan area, as anything over 40 percent is considered high. That made the metropolitan area less than 8 percent of the population of Texas in 1990, far behind the 24 percent held by the Dallas area and the 22 percent held by the Houston area. San Antonio is a large city, but its metropolitan area is relatively small because it is the center of a ranching and farm area.

San Antonio, like most Texas cities, is a target for immigrants (both legal and illegal), and this helps to keep it growing. It has plenty of room for growth (its area of 349 square miles is the 5th largest of the cities in this book), and it is located in a high-growth Sunbelt state. This is a recipe for good growth. As shown by the ratio at the bottom of the figure, San Antonio in 1990 was 17.5 times as large as it was in 1900. But this is only the 8th best mark for the cities in this book. Competition is keen among high-growth Sunbelt cities.

San Antonio

Figure 4-20. San Antonio Population (in Millions)

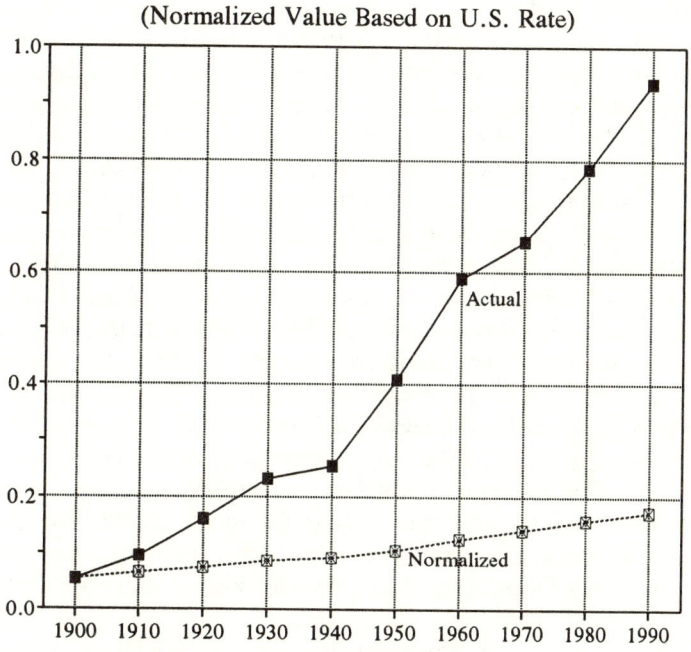

(Normalized Value Based on U.S. Rate)

Year	Population	Growth Rate	U.S. Rate	Ratio
1900	53,321	--	--	--
1910	96,614	81.2%	21.0%	3.86
1920	161,379	67.0%	15.0%	4.48
1930	231,542	43.5%	16.2%	2.68
1940	253,854	9.6%	7.3%	1.33
1950	408,442	60.9%	14.5%	4.20
1960	587,718	43.9%	18.5%	2.37
1970	654,153	11.3%	13.4%	0.85
1980	785,880	20.1%	11.4%	1.76
1990	935,393	19.0%	9.8%	1.94

Ratio of population in 1990 to population in 1900: 17.5

Figure 4-21 shows population growth for San Diego compared to the nation from 1900 through 1990. The format for cities is explained on page 142. Of the cities in this book, San Diego trails only Phoenix in growth ratio from 1900 through 1990 (Table 4-2). Not only did San Diego grow more rapidly than the nation in every decade during the century, but it also grew over five times as fast as the nation in each of the first four decades (ratios greater than 5.00). As shown in Figure 4-25, part of the growth was due to the fact that San Diego was the smallest of the major cities of California in 1900, and a small population base produces very high growth rates in any city with good growth. But the factors that attracted people to California attracted people to San Diego as well. With lots of room (San Diego measured 320 square miles in 1990 and was the 8th largest city in this book), and with ideal weather and a diversified economy, San Diego kept growing.

San Diego was not even ranked in the 100 largest cities in the nation in 1900, but by 1950 it was in 31st place (Table 4-2). It was 3rd in growth ratio from 1900 through 1950 among the twenty-four cities, and from 1950 through 1990 it was also 3rd. This high growth rate made San Diego the 6th largest city in the nation in 1990. San Diego topped the list in growth ratio in the 1980s (Table 4-1), and it will probably catch Philadelphia during the first half of the next century to become the 5th largest city in the nation.

California has four large cities (Los Angeles, San Diego, San Jose, and San Francisco), and none had a large percentage of the state's population in 1990 (Los Angeles led with 12 percent). But the Los Angeles metropolitan area had 49 percent of state population in 1990, and the San Francisco-San Jose area had 21 percent, bringing the total for these two areas to 70 percent. Thus, the 2.5 million people in the San Diego metropolitan area in 1990 represented only 8 percent of state population. Only 100 miles from the Los Angeles metropolitan area, San Diego will continue to grow as one of the nation's largest cities, but its metropolitan area will not be notable by California standards, even though it is the nation's 16th largest area and moving up fast.

San Diego is only thirty miles north of the Mexican border, and it is a key target for immigrants, a large percentage of which are illegal. This will continue to drive its growth and its administrative problems. But its nearly perfect weather will also continue to attract a migration of retirees from all over the United States, many of whom served in the armed forces at airfields and naval bases in the San Diego area. This is another prime factor in San Diego's growth.

San Diego 183

Figure 4-21. San Diego Population (in Millions)

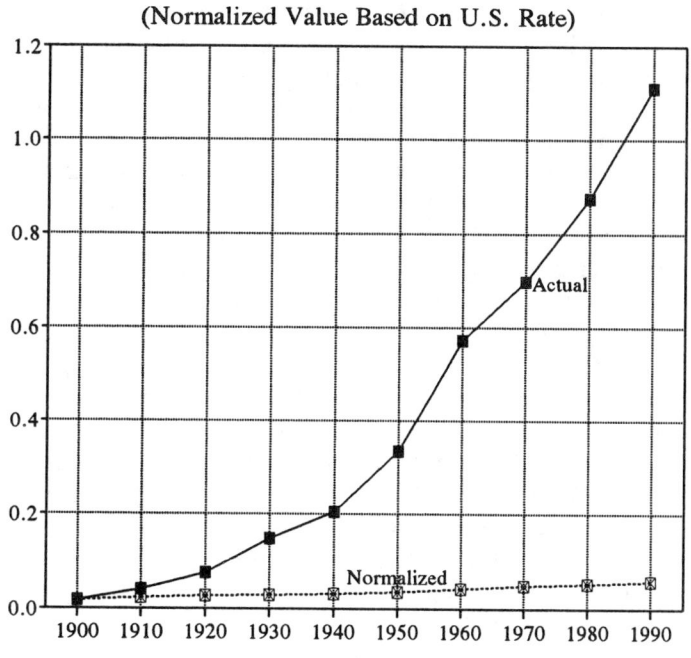

Year	Population	Growth Rate	U.S. Rate	Ratio
1900	17,700	--	--	--
1910	39,578	123.6%	21.0%	5.88
1920	74,361	87.9%	15.0%	5.87
1930	147,995	99.0%	16.2%	6.11
1940	203,341	37.4%	7.3%	5.14
1950	334,387	64.4%	14.5%	4.44
1960	573,224	71.4%	18.5%	3.86
1970	697,471	21.7%	13.4%	1.62
1980	875,538	25.5%	11.4%	2.23
1990	1,110,623	26.9%	9.8%	2.74

Ratio of population in 1990 to population in 1900: 62.7

Figure 4-22 shows population growth for San Francisco compared to the nation from 1900 through 1990. The format for cities is explained on page 142. San Francisco is an example of a city in a high-growth Sunbelt state with a growth pattern very different from that of the state. In spite of California's high growth during the century, San Francisco has a pattern more like that of New York City. This is partly because San Francisco was already well established in 1900, and partly because San Francisco is only forty-seven square miles in area. Most high-growth Sunbelt cities have areas of hundreds of square miles, but of the cities in this book, only Boston and Buffalo are smaller than San Francisco. This severely limits growth in San Francisco.

As by far the biggest city west of St. Louis in 1900, San Francisco had a large population base and did not show the explosive growth of the other cities in California and the West. It grew more rapidly than the nation (actual line above the normalized line and ratios greater than 1.00) from 1900 through 1930. Growth stopped in the depression of the 1930s, then spurted ahead in the 1940s with the arrival of the armed forces and World War II. But San Francisco lost population for the next three decades before growing again in the 1980s.

San Francisco fell from 10th place on the population ranking list in 1900 to 11th place in 1950 (Table 4-2). With a net loss of population from 1950 through 1990, it fell to 14th place in 1990. With little room to expand in the city, people filled the suburbs, including San Jose only forty-five miles down the freeway. As San Jose soared, San Francisco fell. It did not help that the cost of housing in San Francisco was much higher than in San Jose and nearly all other suburbs. As shown in figure 4-25, San Jose passed San Francisco in population soon after 1980, one decade after San Diego had done the same.

The San Francisco metropolitan area includes San Jose or, considering their relative populations, one could say that the San Jose metropolitan area includes San Francisco. The metropolitan area was the nation's 5th largest in 1990, with 6.3 million people. The area grew by 16.5 percent in the 1980s, in spite of the tepid growth in San Francisco. The area held 21 percent of the population of the state, giving San Francisco-San Jose and the Los Angeles metropolitan areas 70 percent of California's population. The San Francisco Bay area and the Los Angeles Basin combined had a larger population than any state (except California) in 1990. The metropolitan area around San Francisco will continue to grow well, but San Francisco, locked in its expensive forty-seven square miles, will not.

Figure 4-22. San Francisco Population (in Millions)

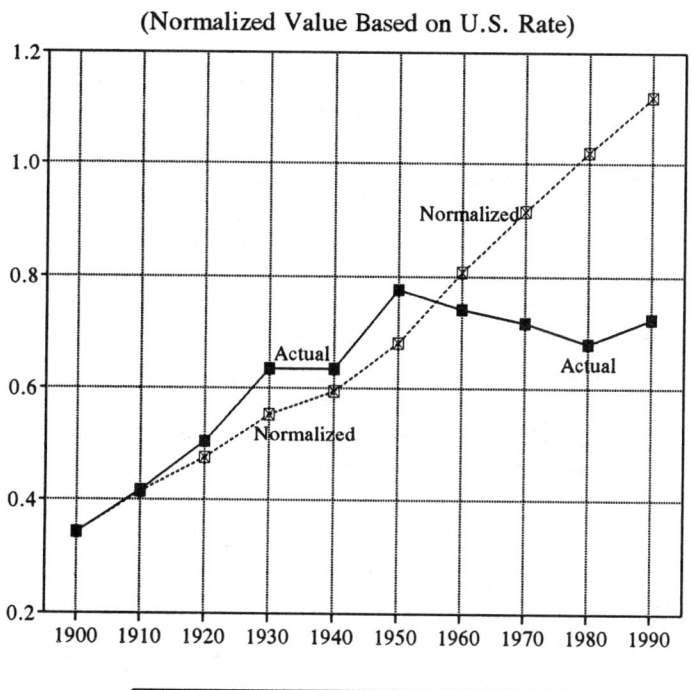

Year	Population	Growth Rate	U.S. Rate	Ratio
1900	342,782	--	--	--
1910	416,912	21.6%	21.0%	1.03
1920	506,676	21.5%	15.0%	1.44
1930	634,394	25.2%	16.2%	1.56
1940	634,536	0.0%	7.3%	0.00
1950	775,357	22.2%	14.5%	1.53
1960	740,316	-4.5%	18.5%	-0.24
1970	715,674	-3.3%	13.4%	-0.25
1980	678,974	-5.1%	11.4%	-0.45
1990	723,959	6.6%	9.8%	0.68

Ratio of population in 1990 to population in 1900: 2.11

Figure 4-23 shows population growth for San Jose compared to the nation from 1900 through 1990. The format for cities is explained on page 142. San Jose grew rapidly from 1900 through 1950, then exploded in growth after 1950. It was second to Phoenix in growth ratio from 1950 through 1990 (Table 4-2), and both Phoenix and San Jose were far ahead of the other twenty-four cities for that period. San Jose grew well for the same reasons that California did but after 1950, the growth of the famous Silicon Valley propelled San Jose to a higher plane. San Jose has a moderate size (158 square miles in 1990) for a high-growth Sunbelt state city, but it absorbed people by the tens of thousands as orange groves were replaced by houses and electronic industrial parks. In the 1980s, San Jose had its lowest growth decade since the depression of the 1930s, but it still ranked fourth among the twenty-four cities with a growth rate of 24.3 percent (Table 4-1).

San Jose was not close to making the list of the 100 largest cities in the nation in 1900, and it still failed to make it in 1950, even though its growth ratio from 1900 through 1950 was 4.43 (it was 4.43 times larger in 1950 than in 1900). In spite of its larger population base in 1950, San Jose had a growth ratio of 8.21 from 1950 through 1990 and was the nation's 11th largest city in 1990 (Table 4-2). San Jose is 153,169 people behind San Antonio, the city just above it on the list, and San Antonio and the next two cities up the list are growing well. Thus the city San Jose is most likely to catch next is Detroit, as Detroit falls from 7th place. This will happen soon after 2000.

With four large cities in California (Los Angeles, San Diego, San Jose, and San Francisco), no city had a large percentage of the state's population in 1990 (Los Angeles led with 12 percent). The San Jose-San Francisco metropolitan area had 6.3 million people in 1990, or 21 percent of the state's population, while the Los Angeles metropolitan area had 49 percent. The designation San Jose-San Francisco metropolitan area is used in this book, even though the census shows San Francisco first, because, as shown in Figure 4-25, San Jose passed San Francisco in population soon after 1980. By 1990 San Jose led San Francisco by 8 percent and was getting further ahead every day.

With more room to grow (San Jose is more than three times as large as San Francisco in area) and much lower cost housing, San Jose should continue to outdistance its former larger neighbor to the north in the coming decades. Both cites are targets for immigrants, but the effect in San Francisco is to keep the population from falling, while in San Jose it fuels higher growth.

Figure 4-23. San Jose Population (in Millions)

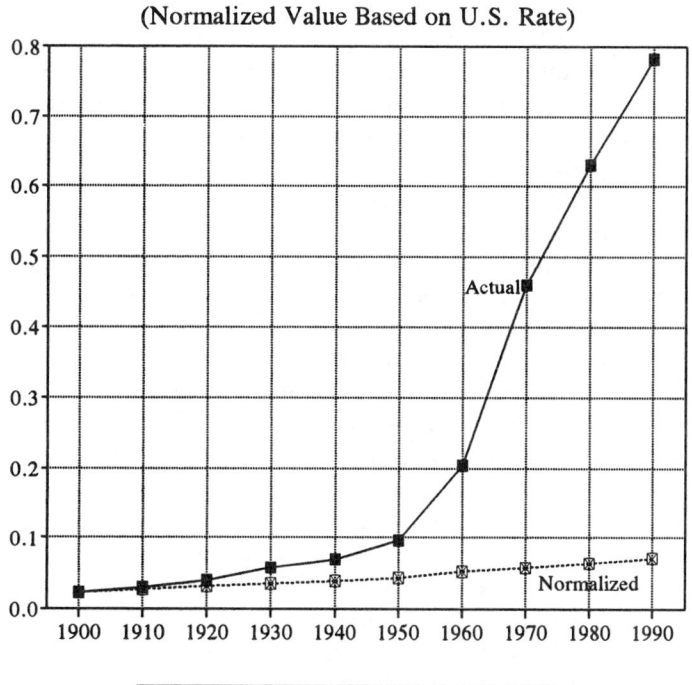

Year	Population	Growth Rate	U.S. Rate	Ratio
1900	21,500	--	--	--
1910	28,946	34.6%	21.0%	1.65
1920	39,642	37.0%	15.0%	2.47
1930	57,651	45.4%	16.2%	2.80
1940	68,457	18.7%	7.3%	2.58
1950	95,280	39.2%	14.5%	2.70
1960	204,196	114.3%	18.5%	6.18
1970	459,913	125.2%	13.4%	9.37
1980	629,442	36.9%	11.4%	3.22
1990	782,224	24.3%	9.8%	2.48

Ratio of population in 1990 to population in 1900: 36.4

Figure 4-24 shows population growth for Washington, D.C., compared to the nation from 1900 through 1990. The format for cities is explained on page 142. Washington was a high-growth city from 1900 through 1950, its population growing in response to the increase in the size of the federal government. But although it was not an industrial city, Washington followed the pattern for the large industrial cities of the Northeast and Central regions, as described in the Introduction, and it lost population in every decade after 1950. Washington lost population for the same reasons as the other cities. The basic difference between those cities and Washington was that in Washington the initial attraction was jobs in the federal government, while in the other cities it was jobs in the factories.

Washington's biggest growth before 1950 was in the depression of the 1930s, when most cities had little or no population growth. Many people came to Washington to work in the government as it grew to fight the depression, and others came to find jobs they believed the government would create for them. This growth was consolidated in the 1940s, as the government grew yet larger to fight World War II. By 1950 Washington's actual population line was 45 percent above the normalized line, meaning that Washington's growth ratio from 1900 through 1950 was 45 percent above than that of the nation.

Washington went from the 15th largest city in 1900 to 9th largest in 1950 (Table 4-2). But growth stopped as the population fell after 1950, and four successive decades of population loss (negative ratios) dropped Washington to 19th place on the population ranking list in 1990. It is difficult to project population changes for cities, but, as shown in Figure 3-9, Washington should lose another 11.5 percent of its population in the 1990s, falling to 537,000 people by 2000. This will drive it farther down the population ranking list as its population loss since 1950 increases to 33 percent of its 1950 population.

Washington did not lose population because the government (and the number of lobbyists who call on it) stopped growing. People moved from the city to the surrounding suburbs in Maryland and Virginia. The Washington-Baltimore metropolitan area was the nation's fourth largest in 1990, with over 6.7 million people, and in the 1980s it grew by a robust 16.2 percent, well ahead of the nation's 9.8 percent. The Washington area is high on the list of preferred destinations for legal immigrants, and it probably attracts illegal immigrants at the same relative rate. The Washington area will continue to grow, but the city itself is not likely to move above the 1990 level for several decades.

Figure 4-24. Washington (D.C.) Pop. (in Millions)

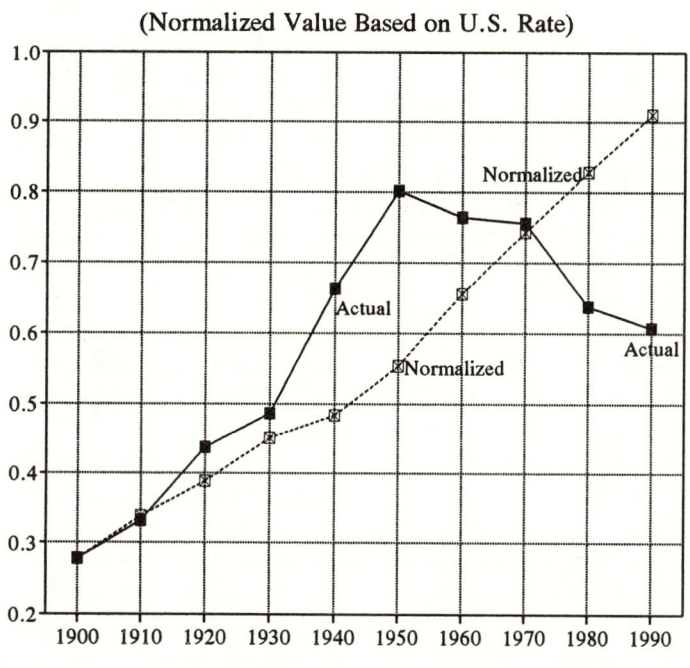

Year	Population	Growth Rate	U.S. Rate	Ratio
1900	278,718	--	--	--
1910	331,069	18.8%	21.0%	0.89
1920	437,571	32.2%	15.0%	2.15
1930	486,869	11.3%	16.2%	0.70
1940	663,091	36.2%	7.3%	4.98
1950	802,178	21.0%	14.5%	1.45
1960	763,956	-4.8%	18.5%	-0.26
1970	756,668	-1.0%	13.4%	-0.07
1980	638,432	-15.6%	11.4%	-1.37
1990	606,900	-4.9%	9.8%	-0.50

Ratio of population in 1990 to population in 1900: 2.18

Figure 4-25 shows population growth for three cities in California from 1900 through 1990. The ratios for San Diego and San Jose compare their populations to that of San Francisco. The "1990/1900" value at the bottom shows the ratio by which the populations increased from 1900 through 1990. Los Angeles is not shown because of its size. Los Angeles had 102,479 people in 1900, but by 1950 it was far off the graph at nearly 2 million, and by 1990 it had 3.5 million.

San Francisco was the largest city in California in 1900 (including Los Angeles), and it was 10th largest in the nation (Table 4-2). San Diego and San Jose were small towns, 5 and 6 percent, respectively, of the size of San Francisco (ratios of 0.05 and 0.06). San Francisco grew well from 1900 through 1950, but San Diego grew eight times as fast as San Francisco, and San Jose grew twice as fast. Due to their low starting populations, San Diego and San Jose were still far behind San Francisco in 1950. But by 1950 San Diego was three times as big as San Jose and was 43 percent of the size of San Francisco.

Changes continued after 1950. The cost of housing and the limited area of San Francisco meant that most growth around the San Francisco Bay area came in the suburbs south of San Francisco where the Silicon Valley was being developed. The result was that the population of San Francisco decreased after 1950 and San Jose grew more rapidly than any of the cities in this book except Phoenix (Table 4-2). There was a continuing boom in southern California, and San Diego was next in line behind San Jose in growth ratio from 1950 through 1990.

San Diego was just behind San Francisco in the census of 1970, and San Diego went ahead soon after. San Jose did the same a decade later, coming within 7 percent of San Francisco in 1980 (ratio of 0.93) and passing it in the middle of the 1980s. By 1990 San Diego was 53 percent larger than San Francisco and the 6th largest city in the nation. San Jose was 8 percent ahead of San Francisco and the 11th largest in the nation. San Francisco fell to 14th on the city ranking list. Both San Diego and San Jose can expect to extend their leads in the next census.

Metropolitan areas are not directly comparable because San Jose and San Francisco are in the same area. The San Jose-San Francisco area had 6.3 million people in 1990, or 21 percent of the state's population. San Diego is 100 miles south of the 14.5 million Los Angeles metropolitan area (49 percent of state population), and the 2.5 million people in the San Diego area were only 8 percent of the state's population. But the San Diego area grew by 34.2 percent in the 1980s, compared to 16.5 percent for the San Jose-San Francisco area.

Cities Summary

Figure 4-25. California Cities Population (in Millions)

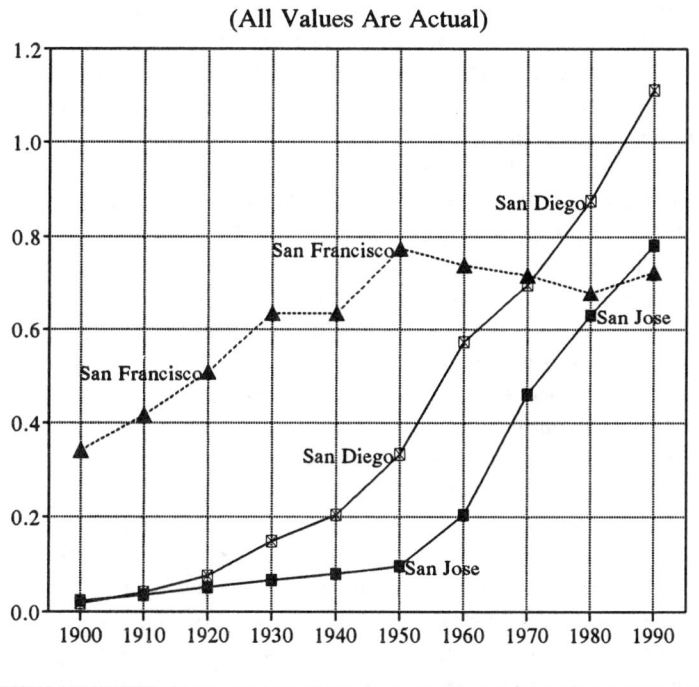

Year	San Francisco	San Diego	Ratio	San Jose	Ratio
1900	342,782	17,700	0.05	21,500	0.06
1910	416,912	39,578	0.09	28,946	0.07
1920	506,676	74,361	0.15	39,642	0.08
1930	634,394	147,995	0.23	57,651	0.09
1940	634,536	203,341	0.32	68,457	0.11
1950	775,357	334,387	0.43	95,280	0.12
1960	740,316	573,224	0.77	204,196	0.28
1970	715,674	697,471	0.97	459,913	0.64
1980	678,974	875,538	1.29	629,442	0.93
1990	723,959	1,110,623	1.53	782,224	1.08
1990/1900:	2.11	1990/1900:	62.7	1990/1900:	36.5

Figure 4-26 shows population growth for the major cities in Texas from 1900 through 1990. The ratios for Dallas and Houston compare their populations to that of San Antonio. The "1990/1900" value at the bottom shows the ratio by which the populations increased from 1900 through 1990. San Antonio ranked only 71st in the nation in 1900 (Table 4-2), but it led in Texas. All three cities grew rapidly after 1900, but Dallas and Houston passed San Antonio by 1930 with Houston in the lead. Fueled by oil and natural gas production, Houston increased its lead after 1930 while the other cities were close together until 1950. In the 1950 census, Houston was 14th in the nation, while Dallas was 22nd and San Antonio 25th.

Texas was a beneficiary of the national population shift that began after 1950, as described in the Introduction. People coming to Texas migrated to Houston and Dallas rather than San Antonio, as these cities had strong industrial bases while San Antonio was the center of a large ranching and farming area. In the next twenty years Houston continued its climb up the national population ladder, while Dallas, although growing more slowly than Houston, pulled farther ahead of San Antonio. As of 1970, Houston was 89 percent larger than San Antonio (ratio of 1.89) and Dallas was 29 percent larger (ratio of 1.29).

After 1970 the relationship between the three cities began to change. Growth in Houston and Dallas focused on their metropolitan areas rather than the cities themselves. In the 1980s, Houston, possibly entering a maturing city phase, grew by only 2.2 percent (Table 4-1). But the Houston metropolitan area grew by 19.6 percent. Dallas grew by 11.5 percent, while its metropolitan area posted an impressive 32.5 percent gain. San Antonio, on the other hand, grew by 19.0 percent, and its metropolitan area had a similar growth rate of 21.7 percent. The result was that Dallas and San Antonio were close together in 1990, with Dallas back to nearly the same edge it had in 1950. Houston stayed far ahead, but its lead shrank in the decade. All three cities grew well compared to the nation. Houston was the nation's 4th largest city in 1990, with Dallas in 8th place and San Antonio in 10th.

The focus on metropolitan area growth gives a different picture of the three cities. The Dallas-Ft. Worth area had 4.0 million people in 1990, the Houston metropolitan area 3.7 million, and the San Antonio area only 1.3 million. The Dallas and Houston areas had 24 percent and 22 percent, respectively, of the population of Texas, and the Dallas area led in growth rate. Thus, although Houston will remain the largest city in Texas for a long time, the Dallas area will be the largest metropolitan area, and the San Antonio area will be far behind.

Cities Summary

Figure 4-26. Texas Cities Population (in Millions)

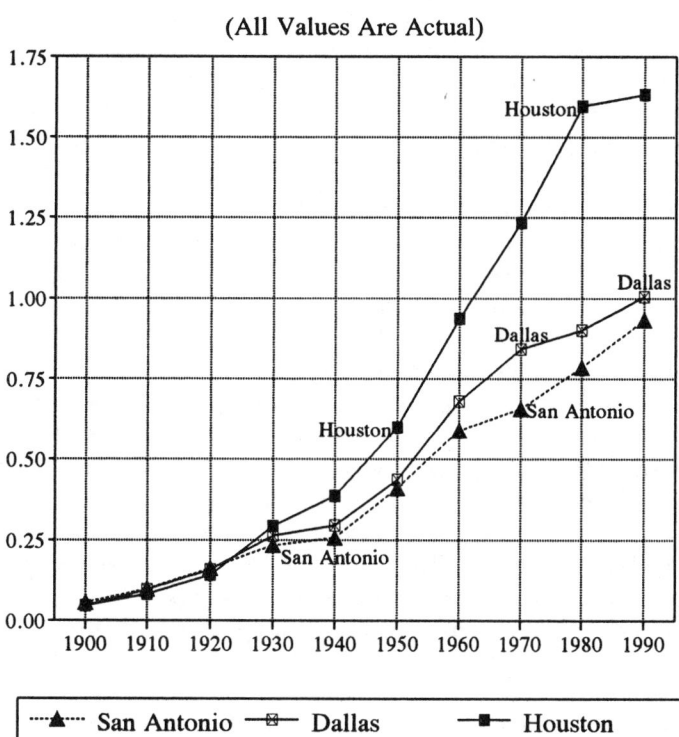

Year	San Antonio	Dallas	Ratio	Houston	Ratio
1900	53,321	42,638	0.80	44,633	0.84
1910	96,614	92,104	0.95	78,800	0.82
1920	161,379	158,976	0.99	138,276	0.86
1930	231,542	260,475	1.12	292,352	1.26
1940	253,854	294,734	1.16	384,514	1.51
1950	408,442	434,462	1.06	596,163	1.46
1960	587,718	679,684	1.16	938,219	1.60
1970	654,153	844,401	1.29	1,233,535	1.89
1980	785,880	904,078	1.15	1,595,138	2.03
1990	935,393	1,007,618	1.08	1,629,902	1.74
	1990/1900: 17.5	1990/1900:	23.6	1990/1900:	36.5

Table 4-2 shows the cities ranked by population and growth ratio for different periods. The percentage of the nation's population living in the top fifteen cities grew from 14.5 percent in 1900 to 16.5 percent in 1950, then fell to 10.3 percent in 1990. The percentage held by the top ten cities increased from 13.0 percent in 1900 to 14.4 percent in 1990, then fell to 8.8 percent in 1990. This is very different from the states (Table 3-1), where the percentage of the population living in the top ten or fifteen states increased steadily from 1900 through 2000.

Thirteen of the top fifteen cities in 1900 were still in the top fifteen in 1950 (New Orleans and Cincinnati were displaced by Los Angeles and Houston). But only seven of the top fifteen in 1950 made the list in 1990, leaving only six of the top fifteen in 1900 still there in 1990 (New York, Chicago, Philadelphia, Detroit, Baltimore, and San Francisco). Only three of the top ten in 1900 were in the top ten in 1990 (New York, Chicago, and Philadelphia). These three cities lost almost 2 million people between 1950 and 1990, a drop of 14 percent.

Growth ratios compare population over long periods. They are expressed as numbers showing whether the population grew by a ratio of 1.5 or 2.5, etc. The growth rates in the figures in the book are ratios of population by decade. They are expressed as percentages, the usual way to show rates. Population changes over long periods are more easily understood as ratios, and thus ratios are used in Table 4-2. Growth ratios for the nation based on Figure 1-1 are:

Year	Population	Growth Ratio
1900	76,212,168	From 1900 through 1950: 1.99
1950	151,325,798	From 1950 through 1990: 1.64
1990	248,709,873	From 1900 through 1990: 3.26

The average growth rate for the nation was 13.7 percent per decade. The growth ratio from 1900 through 1990 was 3.26 (the population in 1990 was 3.26 times higher than in 1900). From 1900 through 1950, seventeen of the twenty-four cities had growth ratios higher than the 1.99 of the nation. But from 1950 through 1990, all of the top fifteen cities in 1900 were not only below the national ratio of 1.64, they were also below 1.00, meaning that they lost population from 1950 through 1990. From 1900 through 1990, only ten of the twenty-four cities had higher growth ratios than the 3.26 of the nation. But the top five cities had ratios that were at least ten times as high as the national ratio, and Phoenix's was more than fifty times higher.

Cities Summary 195

Table 4-2. Cities Population/Growth Ratio Rankings

1900 Census		1950 Census		1990 Census	
1. New York	3,437,202	1. New York	7,891,957	1. New York	7,322,564
2. Chicago	1,698,575	2. Chicago	3,620,962	2. Los Angeles	3,485,557
3. Philadelphia	1,293,697	3. Philadelphia	2,071,605	3. Chicago	2,783,726
4. St. Louis	575,238	4. Los Angeles	1,970,358	4. Houston	1,629,902
5. Boston	560,982	5. Detroit	1,849,568	5. Philadelphia	1,585,577
6. Baltimore	508,957	6. Baltimore	949,708	6. San Diego	1,110,623
7. Pittsburgh	451,512	7. Cleveland	914,808	7. Detroit	1,027,974
8. Cleveland	381,768	8. St. Louis	856,796	8. Dallas	1,007,618
9. Buffalo	352,387	9. Washington	802,178	9. Phoenix	983,403
10. San Francisco	342,782	10. Boston	801,444	10. San Antonio	935,393
11. Cincinnati	325,902	11. San Francisco	775,357	11. San Jose	782,224
12. New Orleans	287,104	12. Pittsburgh	676,806	12. Indianapolis	741,952
13. Detroit	285,704	13. Milwaukee	637,392	13. Baltimore	736,014
14. Milwaukee	285,315	14. Houston	596,163	14. San Francisco	723,959
15. Washington	278,718	15. Buffalo	580,132	15. Jacksonville	672,971
21. Indianapolis	169,164	16. New Orleans	570,445	17. Milwaukee	628,088
36. Los Angeles	102,479	18. Cincinnati	503,998	19. Washington	606,900
71. San Antonio	53,321	22. Dallas	434,462	20. Boston	574,283
85. Houston	44,633	23. Indianapolis	427,173	24. Cleveland	505,616
88. Dallas	42,638	25. San Antonio	408,442	25. New Orleans	496,398
* Jacksonville	28,429	31. San Diego	334,387	34. St. Louis	396,685
* San Jose	21,500	49. Jacksonville	204,517	40. Pittsburgh	369,879
* San Diego	17,700	98. Phoenix	106,818	45. Cincinnati	364,114
* Phoenix	5,544	* San Jose	95,280	50. Buffalo	328,175

* Not ranked in the top 100 cities by the census.

Ratio From 1900 to 1950		Ratio From 1950 to 1990		Ratio From 1900 to 1990	
1. Phoenix	19.3	1. Phoenix	9.21	1. Phoenix	177.4
2. Los Angeles	19.2	2. San Jose	8.21	2. San Diego	62.7
3. San Diego	18.9	3. San Diego	3.32	3. Houston	36.5
4. Houston	13.4	4. Jacksonville	3.29	4. San Jose	36.4
5. Dallas	10.2	5. Houston	2.73	5. Los Angeles	34.0
6. San Antonio	7.67	6. Dallas	2.32	6. Jacksonville	23.7
7. Jacksonville	7.19	7. San Antonio	2.29	7. Dallas	23.6
8. Detroit	6.47	8. Los Angeles	1.77	8. San Antonio	17.5
9. San Jose	4.43	9. Indianapolis	1.74	9. Indianapolis	4.39
10. Washington	2.88	10. Milwaukee	0.99	10. Detroit	3.60
11. Indianapolis	2.53	11. San Francisco	0.93	11. Milwaukee	2.20
12. Cleveland	2.40	12. New York	0.93	12. Washington	2.18
13. New York	2.30	13. New Orleans	0.87	13. New York	2.13
14. San Francisco	2.26	14. Baltimore	0.77	14. San Francisco	2.11
15. Milwaukee	2.23	15. Chicago	0.77	15. New Orleans	1.73
16. Chicago	2.13	16. Philadelphia	0.77	16. Chicago	1.64
17. New Orleans	1.99	17. Washington	0.76	17. Baltimore	1.45
18. Baltimore	1.87	18. Cincinnati	0.72	18. Cleveland	1.32
19. Buffalo	1.65	19. Boston	0.72	19. Philadelphia	1.23
20. Philadelphia	1.60	20. Buffalo	0.57	20. Cincinnati	1.18
21. Cincinnati	1.55	21. Detroit	0.56	21. Boston	1.02
22. Pittsburgh	1.50	22. Cleveland	0.55	22. Buffalo	0.93
23. St. Louis	1.49	23. Pittsburgh	0.55	23. Pittsburgh	0.82
24. Boston	1.43	24. St. Louis	0.46	24. St. Louis	0.69

Part V
The Future

Population Projections

Table 5-1 shows population projections by state and the District of Columbia for 2000, 2020, and 2050. The total population projections for these dates are: 276,241,000 in 2000; 325,942,000 in 2020; and 392,031,000 in 2050 (in this book projected values are rounded to the nearest thousand). Using these projections, the corresponding growth ratios for the nation are: 1.18 from 2000 through 2020; 1.20 from 2020 through 2050; and 1.42 from 2000 through 2050.

The states are listed alphabetically in the first column to make it easy to find the projected population for any state in any year. The states are then ranked by population for the year 2050 (rankings for 2000 are shown in Table 3-2 and also in Table 5-2). The alphabetical listings make it easy to see at a glance which states are projected to grow well from 2000 onward and which states will show little (or no) growth. Their growth ratios can be compared to the national ratios shown in the first paragraph to identify states growing at higher or lower rates than the nation as a whole.

The ten highest growth states from 2000 through 2050 are (in order): Hawaii, California, Washington, Arizona, Oregon, New Mexico, Texas, Florida, Utah, and Nevada. Seven of these are Sunbelt states, and, as noted in Part III, Washington and Oregon can be rated as "honorary" Sunbelt states because their coastal areas, where most of their people live, meet the Sunbelt criteria. With California, Texas, and Florida in the top ten for growth, it is not surprising these three states rank first, second, and third on the population ranking list in 2050. The three states will hold 33 percent of the nation's population by 2050.

At the other end of the scale, West Virginia is the only state projected to lose population from 2000 through 2050, continuing its loss from 1950 through 2000. Pennsylvania, one of the slowest growing states from 1950 through 2000 (Table 3-3), will be the next slowest growing state from 2000 through 2050. It will not lose population, but its increase will be only 1.009, or 0.9 percent from 2000 through 2050. Ohio, Iowa, and New York will be the next slowest growing states after Pennsylvania. The population rankings for 1950, 2000, and 2050 are shown in the succeeding table.

Population Projections

Table 5-1. States Future Population Projections

State	2000 Census	2020 Census	2050 Census
Alabama	4,485,000	5,231,000	6,087,000
Alaska	699,000	866,000	1,099,000
Arizona	4,437,000	5,713,000	7,591,000
Arkansas	2,578,000	3,005,000	3,526,000
California	34,888,000	47,954,000	70,979,000
Colorado	4,059,000	4,871,000	5,774,000
Connecticut	3,271,000	3,617,000	4,011,000
Delaware	759,000	871,000	990,000
D.C.	537,000	636,000	793,000
Florida	15,313,000	19,449,000	25,407,000
Georgia	7,637,000	9,426,000	11,746,000
Hawaii	1,327,000	1,815,000	2,708,000
Idaho	1,290,000	1,600,000	1,985,000
Illinois	12,168,000	13,218,000	14,031,000
Indiana	6,045,000	6,488,000	6,641,000
Iowa	2,930,000	3,038,000	2,994,000
Kansas	2,722,000	3,130,000	3,581,000
Kentucky	3,989,000	4,313,000	4,475,000
Louisiana	4,478,000	5,193,000	6,091,000
Maine	1,240,000	1,400,000	1,594,000
Maryland	5,322,000	6,289,000	7,534,000
Mass.	5,950,000	6,363,000	6,733,000
Michigan	9,759,000	10,377,000	10,688,000
Minnesota	4,824,000	5,426,000	5,988,000
Mississippi	2,750,000	3,100,000	3,460,000
Missouri	5,437,000	6,123,000	6,847,000
Montana	920,000	1,071,000	1,240,000
Nebraska	1,704,000	1,885,000	2,039,000
Nevada	1,691,000	2,145,000	2,720,000
New Hamp.	1,165,000	1,399,000	1,700,000
New Jersey	8,135,000	9,058,000	9,984,000
New Mexico	1,823,000	2,338,000	3,082,000
New York	18,237,000	19,112,000	19,467,000
N.Carolina	7,617,000	9,014,000	10,591,000
N.Dakota	643,000	719,000	805,000
Ohio	11,453,000	11,870,000	11,661,000
Oklahoma	3,382,000	4,020,000	4,867,000
Oregon	3,404,000	4,367,000	5,814,000
Penn.	12,296,000	12,656,000	12,412,000
Rhode Island	998,000	1,090,000	1,189,000
S.Carolina	3,932,000	4,685,000	5,598,000
S.Dakota	770,000	863,000	954,000
Tennessee	5,538,000	6,434,000	7,360,000
Texas	20,038,000	25,593,000	33,472,000
Utah	2,148,000	2,749,000	3,562,000
Vermont	592,000	658,000	722,000
Virginia	7,048,000	8,388,000	9,985,000
Washington	6,070,000	7,960,000	10,780,000
W.Virginia	1,840,000	1,852,000	1,752,000
Wisconsin	5,381,000	5,846,000	6,096,000
Wyoming	522,000	658,000	824,000

State	2050 Census
1. California	70,979,000
2. Texas	33,472,000
3. Florida	25,407,000
4. New York	19,467,000
5. Illinois	14,031,000
6. Penn.	12,412,000
7. Georgia	11,746,000
8. Ohio	11,661,000
9. Washington	10,780,000
10. Michigan	10,688,000
11. N.Carolina	10,591,000
12. Virginia	9,985,000
13. New Jersey	9,984,000
14. Arizona	7,591,000
15. Maryland	7,534,000
16. Tennessee	7,360,000
17. Missouri	6,847,000
18. Mass.	6,733,000
19. Indiana	6,641,000
20. Wisconsin	6,096,000
21. Louisiana	6,091,000
22. Alabama	6,087,000
23. Minnesota	5,988,000
24. Oregon	5,814,000
25. Colorado	5,774,000
26. S.Carolina	5,598,000
27. Oklahoma	4,867,000
28. Kentucky	4,475,000
29. Connecticut	4,011,000
30. Kansas	3,581,000
31. Utah	3,562,000
32. Arkansas	3,526,000
33. Mississippi	3,460,000
34. New Mexico	3,082,000
35. Iowa	2,994,000
36. Nevada	2,720,000
37. Hawaii	2,708,000
38. Nebraska	2,039,000
39. Idaho	1,985,000
40. W.Virginia	1,752,000
41. New Hamp.	1,700,000
42. Maine	1,594,000
43. Montana	1,240,000
44. Rhode Island	1,189,000
45. Alaska	1,099,000
46. Delaware	990,000
47. S.Dakota	954,000
48. Wyoming	824,000
49. N.Dakota	805,000
50. D.C.	793,000
51. Vermont	722,000

Table 5-2 shows the states and the District of Columbia ranked by population for 1950, 2000, and 2050. The nation's population was 151.3 million in 1950, and it will be 276.2 million in 2000 and 392.0 million in 2050. Population momentum will keep eight of the top ten states in the population rankings of 1950 in the top ten in 2000. The changes result from Massachusetts and North Carolina's being pushed out of the top ten by Florida and Georgia in 2000. Only Florida will have made a dramatic change by jumping from 20th in 1950 to 4th in 2000. Georgia will have moved up from 13th in 1950 to 10th in 2000, while North Carolina will have fallen from 10th in 1950 to 11th in 2000 and Massachusetts from 9th to 15th.

The changes from 2000 to 2050 are projected to be even smaller. Nine of the top ten in 2000 will still be in the top ten in 2050. The only difference will be the exchange of places by Washington and New Jersey. Washington will go from 13th in 2000 to 9th in 2050, while New Jersey will fall from 9th in 2000 to 13th in 2050. There will be some shuffling of positions in the top ten from 2000 to 2050, but no other states will move into or fall out of the top ten. The most notable switch will be Florida's moving up to 3rd place and pushing New York down to 4th place. This will put the dynamos of Sunbelt growth, California, Texas, and Florida, together at the top of the population ranking list. They probably will stay there indefinitely.

California, Texas, and Florida will have a total population of just under 130 million in 2050. That will be 33 percent of the population of the nation in 2050. In 1950 the top three states held only 24 percent of the population of the nation, and in 2000 it will be 26 percent. The big jump from 26 percent in 2000 to 33 percent in 2050 underscores the phenomenon of the most populous states also growing the most rapidly.

California, Texas, and Florida are growing at the expense of other states in the top ten. The top ten states held 53 percent of the nation's population in 1950, and in 2000 they will hold 54 percent. In 2050 the percentage will be 56 percent. That means that the states from 4th place through 10th will have held 29 percent of the population of the nation in 1950, 28 percent in 2000, and 23 percent in 2050. Pennsylvania, New York, Illinois, and Michigan will account for most of the decline.

The three huge Sunbelt states will dominate the nation. In an iterative manner, a concentration of population produces a concentration of capital investment and jobs as well as a concentration of political power. This is shown by the succeeding table, in which the ever increasing total of electoral votes in the Sunbelt states is summarized.

Table 5-2. States Population Rankings 1950-2050

1950 Census		2000 Census		2050 Census	
1. New York	14,830,192	1. California	34,888,000	1. California	70,979,000
2. California	10,586,223	2. Texas	20,038,000	2. Texas	33,472,000
3. Penn.	10,498,012	3. New York	18,237,000	3. Florida	25,407,000
4. Illinois	8,712,176	4. Florida	15,313,000	4. New York	19,467,000
5. Ohio	7,946,627	5. Penn.	12,296,000	5. Illinois	14,031,000
6. Texas	7,711,194	6. Illinois	12,168,000	6. Penn.	12,412,000
7. Michigan	6,371,766	7. Ohio	11,453,000	7. Georgia	11,746,000
8. New Jersey	4,835,329	8. Michigan	9,295,000	8. Ohio	11,661,000
9. Mass.	4,690,514	9. New Jersey	8,135,000	9. Washington	10,780,000
10. N.Carolina	4,061,929	10. Georgia	7,637,000	10. Michigan	10,688,000
11. Missouri	3,954,653	11. N.Carolina	7,617,000	11. N.Carolina	10,591,000
12. Indiana	3,934,224	12. Virginia	7,048,000	12. Virginia	9,985,000
13. Georgia	3,444,578	13. Washington	6,070,000	13. New Jersey	9,984,000
14. Wisconsin	3,434,575	14. Indiana	6,045,000	14. Arizona	7,591,000
15. Virginia	3,318,680	15. Mass.	5,950,000	15. Maryland	7,534,000
16. Tennessee	3,291,718	16. Tennessee	5,538,000	16. Tennessee	7,360,000
17. Alabama	3,061,743	17. Missouri	5,437,000	17. Missouri	6,847,000
18. Minnesota	2,982,483	18. Wisconsin	5,381,000	18. Mass.	6,733,000
19. Kentucky	2,944,806	19. Maryland	5,322,000	19. Indiana	6,641,000
20. Florida	2,771,305	20. Minnesota	4,824,000	20. Wisconsin	6,096,000
21. Louisiana	2,683,516	21. Alabama	4,485,000	21. Louisiana	6,091,000
22. Iowa	2,621,073	22. Louisiana	4,478,000	22. Alabama	6,087,000
23. Washington	2,378,963	23. Arizona	4,437,000	23. Minnesota	5,988,000
24. Maryland	2,343,001	24. Colorado	4,059,000	24. Oregon	5,814,000
25. Oklahoma	2,233,351	25. Kentucky	3,989,000	25. Colorado	5,774,000
26. Mississippi	2,178,914	26. S.Carolina	3,932,000	26. S.Carolina	5,598,000
27. S.Carolina	2,117,027	27. Oregon	3,404,000	27. Oklahoma	4,867,000
28. Connecticut	2,007,280	28. Oklahoma	3,382,000	28. Kentucky	4,475,000
29. W.Virginia	2,005,552	29. Connecticut	3,271,000	29. Connecticut	4,011,000
30. Arkansas	1,909,511	30. Iowa	2,930,000	30. Kansas	3,581,000
31. Kansas	1,905,299	31. Mississippi	2,750,000	31. Utah	3,562,000
32. Oregon	1,521,341	32. Kansas	2,722,000	32. Arkansas	3,526,000
33. Nebraska	1,325,510	33. Arkansas	2,578,000	33. Mississippi	3,460,000
34. Colorado	1,325,089	34. Utah	2,148,000	34. New Mexico	3,082,000
35. Maine	913,774	35. W.Virginia	1,840,000	35. Iowa	2,994,000
36. D.C.	802,178	36. New Mexico	1,823,000	36. Nevada	2,720,000
37. Rhode Island	791,896	37. Nebraska	1,704,000	37. Hawaii	2,708,000
38. Arizona	749,587	38. Nevada	1,691,000	38. Nebraska	2,039,000
39. Utah	688,862	39. Hawaii	1,327,000	39. Idaho	1,985,000
40. New Mexico	681,187	40. Idaho	1,290,000	40. W.Virginia	1,752,000
41. S.Dakota	652,740	41. Maine	1,240,000	41. New Hamp.	1,700,000
42. N.Dakota	619,636	42. New Hamp.	1,165,000	42. Maine	1,594,000
43. Montana	591,024	43. Rhode Island	998,000	43. Montana	1,240,000
44. Idaho	588,637	44. Montana	920,000	44. Rhode Island	1,189,000
45. New Hamp.	533,242	45. S.Dakota	770,000	45. Alaska	1,099,000
46. Hawaii	499,794	46. Delaware	759,000	46. Delaware	990,000
47. Vermont	377,747	47. Alaska	699,000	47. S.Dakota	954,000
48. Delaware	318,085	48. N.Dakota	643,000	48. Wyoming	824,000
49. Wyoming	290,529	49. Vermont	592,000	49. N.Dakota	805,000
50. Nevada	160,083	50. D.C.	537,000	50. D.C.	793,000
51. Alaska	128,643	51. Wyoming	522,000	51. Vermont	722,000

Table 5-3 shows electoral votes for the Sunbelt states on the basis of the census in 1900, 1950, 2000, and 2050. The states are divided into those that had growth ratios greater than the nation's from 1950 through 2000 and those that did not. Electoral votes in each group are shown as a percentage of the total electoral votes in the nation for the year shown. There were 476 electoral votes in the nation on the basis of the census of 1900, although 1904 was the first election held based on that census. The 1950 census assigned 531 electoral votes for the election of 1952, and the 2000 census and the 2050 census will assign 538 electoral votes for the elections of 2004 and 2052, respectively.

The percentage of electoral votes held by the high-growth Sunbelt states will almost triple, from 14.7 percent to 39.6 percent, between 1900 and 2050. The number of votes will more than triple, from 70 to 213, but the increase in percentage is smaller because of the larger number of electoral votes in 2050. The slow-growth Sunbelt states will show a decline from 10.7 percent to 8.7 percent over the same period. This means that the total percentage for all the Sunbelt states will almost double, from 25.4 percent in 1900 to 48.3 percent in 2050.

The states are ranked by position in the population rankings in 2050. This puts California, Texas, and Florida together at the top of the list. Their total number of electoral votes will increase from 33 in 1900 to 150 in 2050, or an increase from 7 percent in 1900 to 28 percent in 2050.

If the Sunbelt states are combined with the "honorary" Sunbelt states of Oregon and Washington, the total electoral vote for the combination in 2050 would be 283 or 52.6 percent, enough to elect a president. These combined states rarely vote for the same candidate, but the overwhelming majority of the states in the combination are strong Republican states. The Republicans will thus be the main beneficiary of the concentration of electoral votes in the Sunbelt states.

This will make California the key to winning presidential elections, but not just because it has the most electoral votes. It is key because the Republicans can win a presidential election without winning California, due to their edge in the Sunbelt states and other states in the West and South. The Democrats cannot win without winning California. If California were on the East Coast, everyone could go to bed early on election night if it voted Republican. The main suspense in future elections will be centered on watching to see if the Democrats can keep the Republicans from getting to 270 electoral votes before the vote is in from California.

Political Implications

Table 5-3. Sunbelt States Electoral Vote 1900-2050

Sunbelt States with Growth Rates Greater than Average

State	1900 Census Elec. Vote	Rank	1950 Census Elec. Vote	Rank	2000 Census Elec. Vote	Rank	2050 Census Elec. Vote	Rank
California	10	21	32	2	57	1	81	1
Texas	18	6	24	6	34	2	39	2
Florida	5	33	10	20	26	4	30	3
Georgia	13	11	12	13	14	10	15	7
North Carolina	12	15	14	10	14	11	14	11
Arizona	0	48	4	38	9	23	11	14
South Carolina	9	24	8	27	8	26	8	26
New Mexico	0	44	4	40	5	36	5	34
Nevada	3	51	3	50	5	38	5	36
Hawaii	0	47	0	46	4	39	5	37

Total High-Growth States

Elec. Vote	70		111		176		213	
Percent of U.S.	14.7%		20.9%		32.7%		40.0%	

Sunbelt States with Growth Rates Less than Average

State	1900 Census Elec. Vote	Rank	1950 Census Elec. Vote	Rank	2000 Census Elec. Vote	Rank	2050 Census Elec. Vote	Rank
Tennessee	12	14	11	16	11	16	10	16
Louisiana	9	23	10	21	9	22	9	21
Alabama	11	18	11	17	9	21	9	22
Oklahoma	0	30	8	25	7	28	7	27
Arkansas	9	25	8	30	6	33	6	32
Mississippi	10	20	8	26	6	31	6	33

Total Low-Growth States

Elec. Vote	51		56		48		47	
Percent of U.S.	10.7%		10.5%		8.9%		8.7%	

Total Sunbelt States

Elec. Vote	121	167	224	260
Percent of U.S.	25.4%	31.5%	41.6%	48.3%

Note: State growth rates are compared to the national rate from 1950 through 2000 to determine whether they are greater or less than average.

About the Author

Russell O. Wright spent thirty years in the aerospace electronics industry after graduating from Drexel University at the top of his electrical engineering class. In the 1980s he took a leave of absence to write a book on management, and when it was published he left the executive suite to write. Drawing on expertise developed in doing statistical analysis with computers, he wrote two statistical histories of baseball. He then turned to a lifelong interest in politics and wrote a statistical history of presidential elections. Electoral vote pattern changes shown in that book triggered research into population shifts in the United States, and that research led to this book. Again combining a lifelong personal interest with statistical analysis, his latest book is a statistical history of life expectancy and death rates in the United States. It will be published in 1997.